Paul's Spirituality in
Galatians

Paul's Spirituality in
Galatians

A Critique of Contemporary Christian Spiritualities

P. Adam McClendon

Foreword by
Donald S. Whitney

WIPF & STOCK · Eugene, Oregon

PAUL'S SPIRITUALITY IN GALATIANS
A Critique of Contemporary Christian Spiritualities

Wipf & Stock
An Imprint of Wipf and Stock Publishers
199 W. 8th Ave., Suite 3
Eugene, OR 97401

www.wipfandstock.com

ISBN 13: 978-1-62564-923-2

Manufactured in the U.S.A.

To Adrienne,
Thank you for the love, support, and encouragement you always give.
I'm looking forward to growing old with you.

Contents

Foreword

IT'S GRATIFYING TO WATCH a student become your teacher.

I remember the first class in which I had Adam McClendon as a Master of Divinity student at The Southern Baptist Theological Seminary in Louisville, Kentucky. The class was "Personal Spiritual Disciplines," the required course at Southern on individual piety. Adam sat on the front row to my right. I'd already become acquainted with him through a staff position he held on campus and was impressed with both his maturity and people skills. The more I saw him in the classroom, however, the more he distinguished himself in terms of scholastic ability and Christian integrity. In time he graduated and enrolled in our new Ph.D. program in Biblical Spirituality, the first non-Catholic doctor of philosophy program in Christian spirituality in the United States. While engaged in full-time ministry as an associate pastor in a church across the Ohio River from Louisville, Adam maintained full speed with his academic work and became the first to graduate with a Ph.D. in Biblical Spirituality from Southern Seminary.

Adam McClendon, however, is a scholar who wants to use his gifts and education for the benefit of Christ's church. So rather than let a copy of his dissertation gather dust on a shelf in the library of his alma mater, Adam set himself to the task of revising it in a format that is useful both to those in the academy and those in the local church. The product of those labors is before you in his book, *Paul's Spirituality in Galatians*.

In a sense, it would be fair to say that a more accurate, if less marketable, title for the book would be "Paul's Spirituality in Galatians 2:20." For the lens through which the light of this book is filtered, and indeed the lens through which McClendon wants us to see the essence of the entire Bible's teaching on spirituality, is this famous text: "I have been crucified with Christ. It is no longer I who live, but Christ who lives in me. And the life I now live in the flesh I live by faith in the Son of God, who loved me and gave himself for me" (Galatians 2:20, ESV).

McClendon begins by helping us better understand what spirituality—according to the Bible—is and is not. This is especially important in a day when everyone is "spiritual." (Try to find anyone who will admit, "You know, I'm just not a very spiritual person.") From that introduction he begins to extract from Galatians 2:20 the building materials of biblical spirituality. Along the way he regularly stops to compare these divinely-engineered materials with those used to construct false spiritualities.

His examination of the spirituality taught by Galatians 2:20 starts with what he calls "Crucicentric" spirituality, that is, a spirituality animated by the centrality of the cross of Jesus Christ. Other types of spirituality typically reveal their illegitimacy at this very point. In varying ways they presume upon a person's natural ability to relate to God and to experience Him through prayer and other means. McClendon denies this possibility when he sets forth the Bible's teaching on our natural inability to know God and to be "spiritual" apart from the cross of Christ. In this book, the cross is much more than an example of spirituality, rather it is a necessary prerequisite for true spirituality since only by means of the cross has God made access to Himself possible through Jesus.

McClendon then reasons from the text that because of the necessity of the cross, Christ Himself is made central. The cross that is central to the Christian life is the cross of *Christ*. Because by faith in Jesus the believer has been "crucified with Christ" in His death, now he or she can say that by virtue of that union with Christ the resurrected Christ lives in him or her by His Spirit. Biblical spirituality is a believer's living moment-by-moment as an outward expression of the indwelling Spirit. This union with Christ, notes McClendon, is the key to understanding everything about the Christian's spiritual life. No further experience than this, contra to some sub-Christian spiritualities, is necessary for experiencing and expressing the Holy Spirit.

The reality of the indwelling presence of Christ does not, as McClendon proceeds to show, eliminate the "continued tension of the flesh." Despite the real presence of Christ in a believer and the spiritual union of a believer with Christ, a tension remains in such people because of the ongoing realities of the temptations of the world and the devil, and the continued inclination toward sin in what the New Testament calls "the flesh." Therefore any teaching on spirituality which implies that one can cease to struggle with temptation and sin on this side of Heaven is both false and dangerous.

McClendon next turns to examine what it means to "live by faith in the Son of God" and concludes that those who by faith have been crucified with Christ and are united to Christ will manifest this by living by faith in Christ, and that they will never cease to do so. True spirituality is never a temporary spirituality. Nor, says McClendon, is it a concealed spirituality. Rather, the life of Christ in a believer is irrepressible in the sense that there are "authenticating evidences of faith" for as long as the believer is on the earth. Thus to allege either that people can genuinely place their faith in Christ to make them right with God and then later can desire to remove that faith, or that they can experience the indwelling presence of Christ Himself and yet manifest no continuing evidence of His presence, is contrary to New Testament spirituality.

My student, Adam McClendon, has taught me many things from the biblical spirituality summarized in Galatians 2:20. Now, let him become your teacher too.

Donald S. Whitney

Preface

"The Bible is not the only stream from which truth can be drawn,
but it is the only pure stream against which claims to truth can be judged."[1]

ACCESS TO THE BIBLE is an enormous privilege, and yet, it seems, as access to the Bible abounds professing Christians increasingly struggle to live out a biblically-grounded faith relying ever more on religious tradition, cultural influences, and personal preference. These three aspects of modern life are all too often the plumb line by which truth is determined and acted upon. Tradition, culture, and personal preference should be placed in subjection to, rather than, on par with the Bible. The Bible is to serve as the filter through which these perspectives are brought in order to determine the proper basis for Christian belief and living. To whatever extent possible, each Christian should strive to lay aside the lenses of denominational traditions, cultural biases, and personal preferences, and evaluate all spiritual belief and living in light of the contextual truths of God's word. The Apostle Paul presents in Galatians several foundational components to the Christian life as examined within this book that when properly perceived help correct many misconceptions existing today within Christian spirituality. A hope exists that an ever-increasing commitment to the Bible as the basis for all spiritual truth will continually refine, strengthen, and unify his church.

1 Bredfeldt, *Great Leader*, 42.

Acknowledgements

GOD IS SO GRACIOUS. Looking back over this work, I'm reminded of the long nights and early mornings. I'm reminded of the hours studying, thinking, writing, and editing, but I'm also reminded of the privilege that was given to me: the privilege of studying God's word. I'm humbled by this opportunity that God provided and am reminded of the many people that God used in the process.

Immediately, I want to acknowledge my precious bride. She has labored in this task with me. She consistently pointed me to God and challenged me to be faithful to the work he placed before us. Such spouses are rare, and I'm blessed to be able to share my life with her. I can't wait to see what the future holds.

Others have also played a crucial role in this journey. While all of them cannot be mentioned here, three particular men have been extraordinarily significant. Dr. Don Whitney continually reminded me to pursue godliness in all things. His unwavering commitment to God's word as a guide for the believer's life left a lasting impression. Dr. Michael Haykin's humble, friendly, and honest guidance was remarkably instrumental. Lastly, Dr. Monte Shanks's insights and challenges proved significant time and time again. I'm indebted to these men for how God has used them in my life over the last few years.

Finally, the impact of the prayers of many who continually interceded before the throne of grace on my behalf will probably never be known in this life, but I'm humbled by the reality that many friends and family members faithfully prayed for me and my family. Emails, cards, and other expressions of encouragement helped sustain my family and I throughout this project. We are so gratefully to have so many who have loved us so deeply.

Abbreviations

AB	Anchor Bible Commentary
BJRL	*Bulletin of the John Rylands University Library of Manchester*
BSac	*Bibliotheca Sacra*
CBQ	*Catholic Biblical Quarterly*
CD	Church Dogmatics
CTQ	*Concordia Theological Quarterly*
CurrBR	*Currents in Biblical Research*
ICC	International Critical Commentary
Int	*Interpretation*
JBL	*Journal of Biblical Literature*
JETS	*Journal of the Evangelical Theological Society*
JSNT	*Journal for the Study of the New Testament*
LQ	*Lutheran Quarterly*
MNTC	The Moffat New Testament Commentary
MTP	*Metropolitan Tabernacle Pulpit*
NAC	New American Commentary
NICNT	New International Commentary on the New Testament
NIGTC	The New International Greek Testament Commentary
NovT	*Novum testamentum*
NTS	*New Testament Studies*

SJT	*Scottish Journal of Theology*
SR	*Studies in Religion*
ST	*Studia theological*
TDNT	Theological Dictionary of the New Testament
TrinJ	*Trinity Journal*
TToday	*Theology Today*
TZ	*Theologische Zeitschrift*
WBC	Word Biblical Commentary
WTJ	*Westminster Theological Journal*
WUNT	Wissenschaftliche Untersuchungen zum Neuen Testament
WW	*Word and World*
ZNW	Zeitschrift für die neutestamentliche Wissenschaft und die Kunde der älteren Kirche

Introduction

THE ORIGINS OF CHRISTIAN spirituality can be traced back to the New Testament through the use of the Greek noun πνεῦμα (spirit) and the adjective πνευματικός (spiritual).[1] As it relates to the development of Christian spirituality, the most significant meaning of πνεῦμα (spirit) is the indwelling presence of God's Spirit and the life that flows from that presence (Rom 2:29; 8:1–17, 23–27; 1 Cor 2:10–13; 3:16; 6:19–20; 12:4–11; 2 Cor 1:21–22; Gal 3:13–14; 4:6–7; 5:16–26; 6:8; Eph 3:14–19; 5:18–21; 1 Thess 4:8; 2 Tim 1:14; Titus 3:4–8; 1 Peter 2:4–5).[2] Πνευματικός (spiritual) represents that which is of the spirit in contrast with that which is of the flesh or world.[3] Thus, those who live in accordance with the Spirit of God are spiritual, and those who live in accordance with the flesh are carnal (Rom 8:6–7; 1 Cor 2:14–15; Gal 5:16–6:1). This understanding of the spiritual life that proceeds from the indwelling work of the Holy Spirit is most common in Pauline literature.

The apostle Paul demonstrated throughout his writings, as well as his life as described throughout the book of Acts, that his spirituality was grounded in a core set of beliefs. These beliefs stimulated action in his life.

---

1. The Old Testament word רוּחַ, like πνεῦμα, has a reasonably wide range of meaning. In a "spiritual" sense, to talk about this "spirit" within the Old Testament as it relates to man is to talk about the inner life of man and what drives that life (Gen 6:17; 7:22; 45:27; Judg 15:19; Ps 51:10; Ezek 11:19; etc.) (Schneiders, "Theology and Spirituality," 257–8). See also, Burton, *Spirit, Soul, Flesh*, 187; Callen, *Authentic Spirituality*, 169; McGrath, *Christian Spirituality*, 1–2.

2. This Scripture list is a sample and not exhaustive. See also Fee, "Getting the Spirit Back into Spirituality," 36–43.

3. Friberg, Friberg, and Miller, *Analytical Lexicon of the Greek New Testament*, s.v. "πνεθματικός." Rom 1:11; 7:14; 15:27; 1 Cor 2:13, 15; 3:1; 9:11; 10:3, 4; 12:1; 14:1, 37; 15:44, 46; Gal 6:1; Eph 1:3; 5:19; 6:12; Col 1:9; 3:16; 1 Pet 2:5.

Paul's expressed throughts and lifestyle are evidences of this type of Christian spirituality. Such spirituality is a life lived under the influence of the Spirit of God in conjunction with scriptural conviction. Thus, for Paul his spirituality was undergirded by a specific set of beliefs resulting in conviction expressed through living.

The term "spirituality" developed from this concept to be used in the early church in the west as descriptive of the Spirit-filled life.[4] The earliest record of the use of the word "spirituality" to date is from AD 410 where *spiritualitate* is used by an anonymous author[5] urging his audience to live in greater conformity to the Spirit.[6] Historically, this conformity to the Spirit was determined within the Christian community based on the clear teaching of Scripture.[7] This predominant meaning of "spirituality" persisted in the church into the twelfth century until the word began to lose its distinction and eventually faded into relative obscurity.

Three key influences changed the popular and theological understanding of the word. First, "spirituality" was, with increasing frequency, set against "corporality."[8] Second, the word began to be used in reference to intelligence and the rational pursuits of man.[9] It became, in a sense, what separates man from the rest of creation. Finally, in the thirteenth century, "spirituality" was understood as the authority of the church and the clergy. Thus, to be spiritual was to be part of the cleric.[10]

---

4. For a fuller history of the development of the word "spirituality," see Bouyer, *La Spiritualité du Nouveau Testament*, 1:211–537; Leclercq, "Spiritualitas," 279–96; Principe, "Toward Defining Spirituality," 44–47. Further supplemental works include Schneiders, "Theology and Spirituality," 257–60; Sheldrake, *Spirituality and History*, 34–37; idem, *Brief History of Spirituality*, 2–4. For an interesting historical look specifically as it relates to the academy, see Schneiders, "Spirituality in the Academy," 676–90.

5. Leclercq, "Spiritualitas," 280. Leclercq says that the quote was originally ascribed to Jerome and then to Faustus of Riez. He believes that both of these are incorrect and that it is actually from Pelagius.

6. "Verum, quia tibi, honorabilis et dilectissime parens, per novam gratiam omnis lacrymarum causa deters est, age, cave, curre, festina. Age, ut in spiritualitate proficias. Cave, ne quod accepisti bonum, incautus et negligens custos amittas" (Ps. Jérôme, *Epist. 7*, ed. 1865 [PL 30:118C]).

7. This statement in no way denies that there were at times conflicts and controversies; however, it does emphasize that spirituality was ultimately grounded in the Scriptures and confirmed in community.

8. Principe, "Toward Defining Spirituality," 45.

9. Sheldrake, *Brief History of Spirituality*, 3.

10. Callen, *Authentic Spirituality*, 173–4; Principe, "Toward Defining Spirituality," 45.

In the late nineteenth century, the term "spirituality" reappeared in religious contexts, but did not receive prominent theological usage until the Second Vatican council in the 1960s impacting both the Protestant and Catholic use of the word.[11] "Spirituality" by that time had already been integrated within non-Christian fields, so the broader Christian use of the term naturally became "Christian spirituality." Moreover, the general use "Spirituality" developed throughout the broader culture to be understood as the crossover of professed belief, experience, and practice as determined within a communial context.

How Society Perceives Spirituality

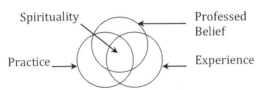

1. General Perception of Spirituality

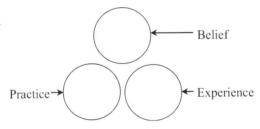

2. Completely Unspiritual Person

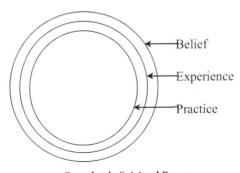

3. Completely Spiritual Person

11. Sheldrake, *Brief History of Spirituality*, 3. See also Holt, *Thirsty for God*, 7–8.

In this context, the more these three areas of professed belief, experience, and practice line up with one another, the more spiritual a person is proposed to be. The more these three areas are dissected from one another the more "unspiritual" or "hypocritical" a person is proposed to be. Hypocrisy, then, is set opposed to spirituality in this societal sense. One additional point of qualification must be made regarding the role of community in this regard. If someone's professed belief, experience, and practice are consistent and yet deemed as evil, society does not see this person as spiritual but evil. So spirituality in this cultural context has to be consistent with cultural values to some degree.

While spirituality in general developed and broadened culturally, in the wake of the Second Vatican Council, the idea of Christian spirituality continually broadened as well. As an example, mysticism has become entangled in Christian spirituality whereby one's standard for truth and action is often based on subjective self-authenticating experiences rooted primarily in "an emotive event, rather than a cognitive one."[12] Nevertheless, in contrast with the broader general use of "spirituality," the influence of the Spirit of God in Christian spirituality seems to be a relatively consistent component as is the emphasis on the way one lives in light of what one believes. Barry L. Callen explains, "Christian spirituality is particularly concerned with the conjunction of theology and practical life of faith in the church and world. The concern is not to live our way, but the Spirit's way."[13] Others, such as Sandra M. Schneiders, will also recapture a portion of the early use of the term in emphasizing community in addition to the Spirit of God and the living out of one's faith. "When the horizon of ultimate value [in spirituality] is the triune God revealed in Jesus Christ and communicated through his Holy Spirit, and the project of self-transcendence is the living of the paschal mystery within the context of the church community, the spirituality is specifically Christian and involves the person with God, others and all reality according to the understanding of these realities that is characteristic of Christian faith."[14]

While such efforts to recapture the biblical and early church's use of this term should be encouraged, direct emphasis on the necessity of grounding one's spiritual understanding and experience within the context

---

12. Johnson, *Faith Misguided*, 23. See also pp. 25–26. For a more balanced approach to mysticism, see Corduan, *Mysticism*.

13. Callen, *Authentic Spirituality*, 157.

14. Schneiders, "Christian Spirituality," 1.

of Scripture is often absent from the conversation. Therefore, the idea of Christian spirituality remains somewhat ambiguous and covers a substantial range of religious beliefs to include biblical as well as extra-biblical ideas.[15] As a result, a need has arisen within Christian spirituality to bring greater clarity concerning the authority of the Bible in determining what is and is not of the Spirit of God. The goal of this book is to model this approach in applying a particular passage of Scripture as a corrective guide governing aspects of Christian spirituality.

To demonstrate how the Scriptures can help govern limits within Christian spirituality, Galatians 2:20 will specifically be examined in this book and then various expression of faith will be evaluated in light of some of the essential elements of the spiritual life presented in this passage.[16] This passage provides a concise summary of Paul's model concerning the life a believer should live with and for God.[17] In essence, the apostle is instructing Galatian believers on the essentials of the spiritual life. As a result, it is an appropriate passage for such an endeavor.

Therefore, the concept for this book is that Galatians 2:20, when properly understood, can correct some common errors caused by the elevation of personal subjectivism and misinterpretation of the Scriptures within Christian spirituality, specifically by emphasizing the centrality of the cross, the centrality of Christ, tension between the Spirit and the flesh, and authenticating evidence in the life of the believer.

Galatians 2:20 is an appropriate passage for this approach because it frequently appears within various writings on Christian living. Within more critical works, it has long been used to promote the mysticism of Paul or, as more often than not, the verse finds itself tucked away within the huge theological discussions surrounding the context of Galatians 2:15–19.[18]

The task of emphasizing the role of Scripture in correcting some common errors within Christian spirituality through Galatians 2:20 will be

15. One contributing factor to this dilemma is the expansion of the definition of the term "Christian."

16. Gal 2:19b–20 in *Nestle-Aland Greek New Testament* 27th ed. "I have been crucified with Christ. It is no longer I who live, but Christ who lives in me. And the life I now live in the flesh I live by faith in the Son of God, who loved me and gave himself for me." All Scripture references are from the English Standard Version unless otherwise noted.

17. Pauline authorship is preferred. Additionally, the work assumes the Southern Gal Hypothesis. For more on authorship and audience, see Bruce, *Galatians*, 1–18.

18. For an example see, Reitzenstein, *Die Hellenistischen Mysterienreligionen*; Bultmann, *Theology of the New Testament*, 1:345. For a history of research regarding Gal 2:20, see "History of Research" in McClendon, "Galatians 2:20," 7–23.

accomplished by examining these four phrases in the verse: "I have been crucified with Christ"; "It is no longer I who live, but Christ who lives in me"; "And the life I now live in the flesh"; "I live by faith in the Son of God, who loved me and gave himself for me." For each phrase, at least one aspect of the verse essential to a biblically-grounded Christian spirituality will be drawn out. Then, in light of that aspect of the spiritual life, some of the current trends within Christian spirituality will be assessed. Thus, the exegetical material will be used as a guide for establishing essential concepts concerning the spiritual life and, in so doing, correct some misunderstandings of the spiritual life found in some contemporary strains of thought concerning Christian spirituality within American Protestantism since the 1960s.[19]

This book will not, nor could it, provide all of the possible implications available for the spiritual life of the believer. Such is not the point. The point is to show how the Bible is the standard to shape not just the way one understands their faith, but the way that one articulates and lives out their faith even when that goes against their denominational tradition, personal preferences, or cultural projections. Therefore, of essential importance is the theological foundation necessary for Christian spirituality.[20]

Some may question the legitimacy of such a narrow focus, using primarily Galatians 2:20, in light of the full scope of Scripture. In response, several things need to be said. First, the intent is not to show what all of Scripture says regarding the spiritual life, cruciformity, sanctification, justification, etc. Instead, the intent is to show how Christian spirituality should be rooted in God's Word that serves as the basis for living that is

---

19. The 1960's were selected because the Second Vatican Council ended in 1965 and writings regarding the spiritual life increased exponentially from that time.

20. Contra Gorman, *Cruciformity*, 4. While Gorman's book is extremely helpful, Gorman seems to create a false dichotomy between theology and spirituality within Paul's writings. He states, "The purpose of Paul's letters generally . . . is not to teach theology but to mold behavior . . . . The purpose of his letters, in other words, is pastoral or spiritual before it is theological" (ibid., 4). However, Paul sought to influence behavior, in part, by changing their thinking (Rom 12:1–2), which is a theological influence. Paul regularly used the first part of his letters to establish a theological foundation for the life principles that he promoted in the latter portions of his works. For Paul, theology seemed to serve as the bedrock upon which spiritual living is to be established. Spirituality and theology are inseparably linked. Gorman's concept appears to flow from an idea that theology can be done in abstraction from life alteration. While common in academia, such is never shown within the biblical model; rather, theology is always seen to be belief that influences life. Thus, theology is that which influences the mind first and foremost, but with the expectation that it will be demonstrated through the life. Spirituality, then, becomes the life living out belief in accordance with the influence of the Spirit of Christ.

truly spiritual (i.e., directed by the Holy Spirit) by using one short, but key, passage. Certain presuppositions underlie this attempt. For example, it is assumed true that no verse lives in isolation from the rest of the Scriptures. Each verse has a context in which it dwells without contradiction. Therefore, the context of each verse flows from a phrase, section, book, testament, and then to the entire canon of the Protestant Scriptures. Each verse, phrase, or concept rightly interpreted will be consistent with these other contexts even if these other contexts are not explicitly examined in the expressed exegetical material. Second, and similar to the first point, the idea is to do a detailed study of a New Testament passage and apply it in correcting some misunderstandings of the spiritual life found within Christian spirituality. In other words, this work is designed to show how truths from the Bible should primarily drive the way one thinks, articulates, and lives. Third, Galatians 2:20 is a verse that concisely summarizes the essence of the justified life, and therefore, to focus on it principally without expanding the scope of study is appropriate. Fourth, this book is presenting Galatians 2:20 as a concise summary of the Christian life from which some foundational principles for a Christian spirituality can be derived. It is not presenting Galatians 2:20 as a spirituality thesaurus. Several important aspects of Christian spirituality are not covered in Galatians 2:20, such as the Trinity, prayer, priesthood of believers, evangelism, etc. Fifth, this work is not intended to be a full-orbed biblical theology, but is designed to continue and deepen the discussion on the connection between Christian spirituality and the role of the Bible in relationship to spiritual living. In light of that thought, it is desired that other works would be attempted from other passages specifically to show how those passages contribute to the conversation in correcting errors that exist in Christian spirituality today.

1

The Centrality of the Cross

"I have been crucified with Christ"

Introduction

ANDREW FULLER ONCE ARGUED that "the doctrine of the cross is the central point in which all the lines of evangelical truth meet and are united. What the sun is to the system of nature, that the doctrine of the cross is to the system of the gospel; it is the life of it."[1] For Fuller, the cross was not just part of the gospel, but at the heart of it.

Some writing within Christian spirituality would argue that Fuller grossly overstates his case.[2] They argue that the cross is not central or essential to the Christian life. For them, the Christian life is to be primarily, if not exclusively, influenced by the life of Christ.

Spirituality, in general, emphasizes how one's understanding of and experience with God impacts the way that one lives their life.[3] Christian

1. Fuller, *Complete Works*, 2:182. For more concerning Fuller understanding of the centrality of the cross, see McClendon, "Crucicentrism," 311–22.

2. People who write seeking to influence one's Christian practice (life) through theology are writing in the field of Christian spirituality. Examples will be provided later in this chapter.

3. For a definition of and differitiation between spirituality, Christian spirituality,

8

spirituality is the process of general spirituality brought under the direction of and in submission to the Holy Spirit. While historically, the thought of discerning the influence of the Holy Spirit versus personal preference, etc., was grounded in Scripture, such is not necessarily the case any longer. People often speak of God telling them to do something that conflicts with the clear teaching of the Bible based on their own subjective self-authenticating experiences. Additionally, the traditional category of what is understood as Christian is often broadened to include a variety of teachings that would deny some foundational teachings of the historical church such as the deity of Jesus, the deity of the Holy Spirit, or the inspiration and truthfulness of the Bible. As a result, what one understands as the "Christian faith" becomes increasingly vague.[4] Consequently, the idea of Christian spirituality remains somewhat ambiguous and covers a substantial range of religious belief to include those who hold positions well beyond or in conflict with Scripture. Thus, due to the subjectivity that has arisen within Christian spirituality, a more qualified use of the term is necessary to ground one's understanding and experience in the normative standard of God's Word.[5]

and biblical spirituality, see McClendon, "Defining the Role of the Bible in Spirituality," 207–25. As this description relates to the last chapter, one's understand of their view of their "God" impacts each persons derived set of beliefs, which serve as a critical component of spirituality in general. This section will not address the contemporary American use of spirituality, which denotes an "other worldliness," since it is not a prevalent use of the word. "Other worldliness" means the use of the word in reference to those who denounce materialism, are "high minded," or at times strange in an unexplainable way specifically as it relates to mundane affairs.

4. Mitt Romney's 2012 run for presidency provides an interesting example of this confusion. An examination of this cultural phenomenon is too great to develop here, but the umbrella of what is "Christianity" is increasingly growing so that people are forced to distinguish between "Christianity" and "Evangelical Christianity." See Bebbington, *Evangelicalism in Modern Britain*; Haykin and Stewart, *Emergence of Evangelicalism*. Roger E. Olson argues that the term "evangelical" is insufficiently broad and needs to be prefaced by either "conservative" or "post-conservative"; however, in light of Bebbington's widely accepted work putting parameters on the term, such a move seems unnecessary (Olson, *Reformed and Always Reforming*, 37–66). A couple of online articles show the tension culturally felt concerning whether or not Mormonism (specifically Mitt Romney in this case) is "Christian" are Brown, "Is Mitt Romney a Christian?" [on- line]: accessed 2 February 2012; available from http://www.examiner.com/lds-church-in-baltimore/is-mitt-romney-a-christian; Kumar, "Pat Robertson: Mitt Romney an 'Outstanding Christian'" [on-line]: accessed 3 October 2011; available from http://www. christianpost.com/news/pat-robertson-mitt-romney-an-outstanding-christian-57017/.

5. In "Defining the Role of the Bible in Spirituality," 207–25, I argue that a new term, Biblical spirituality, is needed; however, here, I'm simply advocating that a qualification is needed on Christian spirituality necessitating that it be grounded in the normative

This view of Christian spirituality is anchored in the belief that the biblical text is foundational to the Christian life. Scripture is not to be subjected to or brought on par with one's personal subjective knowledge of or experience with God.

The Bible, in this view, should be used to shape and correct one's cultural understanding and expression of the Christian faith. As a demonstration of how the Bible can serve as such a corrective, selected contemporary views within Christian spirituality will be examined in light of Galatians 2:20. Therefore, this chapter shows how Galatians 2:20a, "I have been crucified with Christ," when contextually understood, corrects some errors related to the dismissal of the cross caused by the elevation of personal subjectivism and the misinterpretation of the Scriptures within Christian spirituality, specifically by emphasizing the centrality of the cross in the life of the believer.[6]

Galatians 2:15–19

Before focusing on the cross in Galatians 2:20a, the preceding context of the verse will be briefly examined.[7] Galatians 2:11–14 recounts Paul's confrontation with Peter and other Jews in Antioch revealing the hypocrisy of their actions and expectations in relation to their Gentile brothers in

---

standard of Scripture. See also Adam, *Hearing God's Word*; Carson, *Gagging of God*, 555–69.

6. "I have been crucified with Christ" is found in Gal 2:19b in *Nestle-Aland Greek New Testament*, 27th ed. Concerning the versification here, Longenecker states, "The versification of the KJV has accustomed Protestants to read 'I have been crucified with Christ' as the beginning of v 20, and that tradition has been followed by many modern Protestant translations (so ASV, RSV, NIV). Critical editions of the Greek text, however, are almost unanimous in placing Χριστῷ σθρεσταύρωμαι with the material of v 19. And if that be its rightful place, as we believe it is, then Paul's argument in this verse as to believers being released from the jurisdiction of the Mosaic law is fourfold: (1) that it was the law's purpose to bring about its own demise in legislating the lives of God's people; (2) that such a jurisdictional demise was necessary in order that believers in Christ might live more fully in relationship with God; (3) that freedom from the law's jurisdiction is demanded by the death of Christ on the cross; and (4) that by identification with Christ we experience the freedom from the law that he accomplished" (Longenecker, *Galatians*, 92).

7. For a more detailed examination of the context of 2:20, see "Context: Galatians 2:15–19" in the appendix. For example, how ἐὰν μή or πίστεως Ἰησοῦ Χριστοῦ should be translated are addressed there. The overall interpretation of the text is highly influenced by how these phrases are translated.

Christ. Paul then transitions back in 2:15 "resuming his polemic against the Galatians opponents."[8] Paul begins in 2:15 by using a familiar cultural expression in identifying the privileged status of the Jews as a starting point for developing his argument concerning justification.[9] The verse reads: "We

8. Scacewater, "Galatians 2:11–21," 309. Scacewater presents a convincing argument for seeing 2:11–14 as Paul's address from Antioch and a shift in 2:15 back to the Galatian opponents, contra Schreiner, *Galatians*, 150. In doing so, he provides a compelling refutation of the New Perspective on Paul's (NPP) view concerning seeing the term "works of the law" as sociological rather than soteriological. Scacewater appropriately argues that the term is soteriological in refuting the Galatians opponents. Even if, as the NPP proponents do, it is argued that 2:15–16 presents the conversation between Paul and Peter in Antioch, this conversation is presented to the Galatian opponents to refute their subversion of Paul's teaching regarding faith in Christ. Although those creating problems in Galatia apparently sought to reinstitute the law and diminish the role of Christ, such did not appear to be the intention of the Jews at Antioch. After all, the Jews in Antioch previously rejoiced and glorified God acknowledging that God had granted the Gentiles repentance that brings life (Acts 11:18). Nonetheless, their actions were wrong and Paul addresses the implications of their behavior, despite any misconceived intentions, and in doing so, corrects a false understanding of justification and the Christian life in the Galatian churches.

9. For a similar cultural expression see Matt 15:26–27 (Mark 7:27–28), where the Canaanite woman and daughter are referenced as "dogs." Justification in this Galatians context is defined as the decisive declaration of God whereby Christ's righteousness is imputed to a sinner as a gracious gift by means of faith through union with Christ, and the sinner's status is declared to be righteous (Gal 2:16–17; 3:8, 11, 24; 5:4; Col 2:13–14). See also Snider, "Sanctification and Justification," 159, and question 60 of *The Heidelberg Catechism*, 191–93. Due to the extensive range of the justification debate and the limited space available here, providing a summary of the essence of justification will be the focus in this section. One question that persists is whether this declarative act is transformative. In other words, does God simply declare his people righteous in justification or does he also make them righteous. In short, while justification and regeneration are related and to some degree interdependent (Titus 3:4–7), the issue of being declared righteous should be primarily limited to discussions of justification and the issue of being made righteous should be primarily limited to discussions of regeneration and sanctification. For further discussion on the connection between justification and sanctification, see Snider, "Sanctification and Justification," 159–78. For an alternative view that forensic justification should not be distinguished so sharply from the renewed life, see Leithart, "Justification as Verdict and Deliverance," 56–72. Leithart argues that while justification is a legal term it "is extended in a number of places to settings that are not strictly legal" (ibid., 58). For further exploration into the justification debate see Anderson, "Holy Spirit and Justification," 292–305; Bayer, "Justification," 337–42; Boer, "Paul's Use and Interpretation of a Justification Tradition in Galatians 2.15–21," 189–216; Carson et al., *Justification and Variegated Nomism*; Garlington, "Paul's 'Partisan ἐκ' and the Question of Justification in Galatians," 567–89; Husbands and Treier, *Justification*; Leiter, *Justification and Regeneration*; idem, "Justification as Verdict and Deliverance," 56–72; Piper, *The Future of Justification*; Popkes, "Two Interpretations of 'Justification,'" 129–46; Schreiner,

ourselves are Jews by birth and not Gentile sinners." Paul is not arguing that Jews are without sin; nevertheless, his statement does speak to a larger Jewish mindset regarding their perceived superiority under the law. Calling them "Jews by nature" might be a subtle reference to circumcision. The continued emphasis of the Abrahamic covenant and circumcision in Galatians would support this theory (Gen 15:4–21; 17:1–13; Gal 2:3, 7–9, 12; 3:5–9, 14–18, 29; 4:22–28; 5:2–3, 6, 11–12; 6:12–15; Eph 2:11–12). It could be further strengthened when seen in light of the thought that the false gods by nature in Galatians 4:8 could be a reference to idols made by hands, and in light of the connection between natural status (nature—"φύσις") and circumcision in Romans 2:26–27. An argument could also be made that this statement is not that involved but is a familiar way of speaking of the unique status into which the Jews were born, in which case, both circumcision and the law (as well as other elements) are probably in view, in light of Romans 3:1–2, since these elements were inherently connected to the birth status of the Jew (Rom 9:4–5). However, more than likely, Paul does have the reception of the law in view. They are "Jews" born naturally into a community over which the law had jurisdiction. The law made them unique and united them as a people. "Law" in the sense used here is the Mosaic law. Below, it will be argued that the "works of the law" refer to all that the Mosaic law demanded.

Paul then transitions in 2:16 by reminding them that, despite this privileged status, faith in Jesus Christ for the remission of sin was still required.[10] The verse reads: "yet we know that a person is not justified by

---

"Did Paul Believe in Justification by Works," 131–55; idem, "Justification," 19–34; Schrenk, "δίκαιος," in *TDNT*, 2:182–224; Seifrid, "Paul, Luther, and Justification in Gal 2:15–21," 215–30; Shanks, "Galatians 5:2–4 in Light of the Doctrine of Justification," 188–202; Slenczka, "Agreement and Disagreement about Justification," 291–316; Snider, "Sanctification and Justification," 159–78; Weinrich and Burgess, *What Is Justification About?*; Wright, *Justification*; idem, "Justification: Yesterday, Today, and Forever," 49–64; idem, *What Saint Paul Really Said*.

10. "Faith of Jesus Christ" (πίστεως Ἰσοῦ Χριστοῦ) should be understood as an objective genitive so that it is translated as "faith in Jesus Christ" (Porter and Pitts, "Πίστις with a Preposition," 33–53). Among other supports, see also Barnes, *Study on Galatians*, 111–2; Betz, *Galatians*, 117; Boles, *Galatians*, 66; Bruce, *Galatians*, 138–9; Burton, *Galatians*, 121; Carson, *Love in Hard Places*, 162; Dunn, "Once More, ΠΙΣΤΙΣ ΧΡΙΣΤΟΥ," 61–81; idem, *Galatians*, 138–9; Fung, *Galatians*, 115; George, *Galatians*, 195–6; Harrisville, "ΠΙΣΤΙΣ ΧΡΙΣΤΟΥ," 233–41; Hultgren, "*Pistis Christou* Formulation," 262–3; Hunn, "ΠΙΣΤΙΣ ΧΡΙΣΤΟΥ," 23–33; Johnson, "Paradigm of Abraham in Galatians 3:6–9," 179–99; Ladislav, "Christ in Paul," 42; Ngewa, *Galatians*, 81; Schreiner, *Galatians*, 164–66; Tarazi, *Galatians*, 84–85.

works of the law but through faith in Jesus Christ, so we also have believed in Christ Jesus, in order to be justified by faith in Christ and not by works of the law, because by works of the law no one will be justified." The remission of sin, which they received through promise, is not fulfilled through compliance to the law.[11]

Thus, the scope of the law in this passage[12] should not be limited to one aspect of the law (i.e., ceremonial)[13] or the boundary markers of the law,[14] but should be understood in the broader sense of all that the Mosaic law commands.[15] The context of Galatians itself helps clarify the issue. Galatians 3:10–14 connects the "works of the law" to everything written

"Ἐὰν μή" should be understood as adversative, and thus be translated as "but." Hunn, "Ἐὰν μή in Galatians 2:16," 288–90. See also Bruce, *Galatians*, 138; Carson, *Love in Hard Places*, 162; Dunn, *Jesus, Paul, and the Law*, 195–97; Ridderbos, *Galatia*, 99; Schreiner, *Galatians*, 163; Fung, *Galatians*, 115; Witherington III, *Grace in Galatia*, 169; Martyn, *Galatians*, 251.

11. See "Context: Galatians 2:15–19" in the appendix. Specifically, see comments under v. 16 regarding "Works of the Law."

12. "Law" appears 32 times in Gal: 2:16, 19, 21; 3:2, 5, 10–13, 17–19, 21, 23–24; 4:4–5, 21; 5:3–4, 14, 18, 23; 6:2, 13.

13. "The logic of Paul's argument [in Gal] prohibits a neat distinction of moral and ceremonial law . . ." (Moo, "'Law' in Paul," 84). See also George, *Galatians*, 195. Nor should this text be limited to the moral law (specifically the ten commands). Moo argues that there are times that Paul "singles out 'moral' commandments when discussing the demand of the law (Rom 7:7–8; 13:8–11), but this is done in order to point up the depths of the law's requirement, not to separate out these commandments as fundamentally distinct from other commandments" (Moo, "'Law' in Paul," 85). Contra Godet, *Romans*, 144.

14. Dunn, *The Theology of Paul*, 354–59; Sanders, *Paul and Palestinian Judaism*; idem, *Paul, the Law, and the Jewish People*; Wright, *Paul for Everyone*, 32; idem, *What Saint Paul Really Said*, 132. Andrew Das has an interesting article refuting Sanders showing that this "was not just a matter of ethnic exclusion but also its demand for rigorous obedience" (Das, "Beyond Covenantal Nomism," 235).

15. See also Boer, "Paul's Use and Interpretation," 197–201; Byrne, *Romans*, 120; Das, "Beyond Covenantal Nomism," 244; George, *Galatians*, 193, 195; Ladislav, "Christ in Paul," 43; Lange, *Galatians*, 48; Lightfoot, *Paul's Galatians*, 118; Moo, "'Law' in Paul," 76; Schreiner, "Justification," 27–28; idem, "Paul and Perfect Obedience," 245–78; idem, *Romans*, 173; idem, "'Works of Law,'" 221–31; Witherington, *Grace in Galatia*, 176–77; Westerholm, *Israel's Law and the Church's Faith*, 109–20. The argument that "law" in "works of the law" (ἐξ ἔργων νόμου) should be understood as a subjective genitive (Owen, "'Works of the Law,'" 553–77; Gaston, "Works of Law," 39–46) is attractive, but insufficient and unsustainable (Lindsay, "Works of Law," 80–81; Schreiner, *Galatians*, 158–59; idem, "'Works of Law,'" 231); therefore, it will not be discussed in this section.

within the book of the law.[16] Galatians 3:17–19 and 4:21–24 shows the law in relation to that which was given at Mount Sinai. Galatians 5:3 connects the ceremonial aspects of the law to the rest of the law. The point in 5:3 is the converse of that which is presented in James 2:10, which explains that whoever fails in one aspect of the law is guilty of the whole law. In the same way, if someone seeks justification through any aspect of the law, be it circumcision or otherwise, they are obligated to keep the whole law.[17]

Considering these things, "works of the law" should be understood in the broader sense of all that the law commands. As Moo highlights, these "works" are "actions performed in obedience to the law, works which are commanded by the law."[18] The emphasis is not so much on doing various aspects of the law, but fulfilling all demands of the law (Gal 5:3, 14).[19] In the end, Paul explains that no one can be justified through the law. Faith is the sole means of justification. Thus, by placing one's faith in Christ, the believer is crucified with Christ in relation to the law, whether that law was to serve as a sign of the covenant or as a means of condemnation.

Although Gentiles were viewed as sinners, both literally and as those without the God-given law, these Jews by seeking justification in Christ acknowledged that while under the law they were still sinners.[20] The law revealed their need for justification while being insufficient to provide such justification. Therefore, in order to be justified in Christ, they had to

---

16. Whether the author has in mind Deuteronomy, the Pentateuch, or something else, it is clear that the scope is broader than the ceremonial aspects of the law.

17. The text will go on to argue in Gal 6:13 that even those who have been circumcised and press that false standard upon others, themselves fall short of the law. The scope of "law" extends beyond ceremonial requirements.

18. Moo, "'Law' in Paul," 92.

19. Note the emphasis in Gal 5:3, 14 on "the whole law:" as would be argued for those who see this primarily as an indictment against Jewish legalism. Bruce, *Galatians*, 137–38; Burton, *Galatians*, 122–24, 443; Cosgrove, "Mosaic Law Preaches Faith," 155–56; Duncan, *Galatians*, 66.

20. Hunn, "Christ Versus the Law," 539–42. A critical component of the debate surrounding this verse is whether it describes the pre- or post-conversion status of the Jew. For a more detailed examination see "Context: Galatians 2:15–19" in the appendix. For some of the arguments in favor of seeing their post-conversion status, see Betz, *Galatians*, 120; Burton, *Galatians*, 125; Longenecker, *Galatians*, 89–90; McKnight, "Ego and 'I'," 277; O'Neill, *The Recovery of Paul's Letter*, 43; Witherington, *Grace in Galatia*, 185. For some of the arguments in favor of seeing their pre-conversion status, see Bruce, *Galatians*, 140–41; Hunn, "Christ Versus the Law," 540; Matera, *Galatians*, 95; Schreiner, *Galatians*, 169; Shauf, "Galatians 2:20 in Context," 89–90.

acknowledge the insufficiency of the law and their need for justification, i.e., that they were sinners before God just as the Gentiles were (Phil 3:4–11).

Galatians 2:17 continues to demonstrate the inadequacy of the law as a means of justification. Paul uses the pre-conversion status of these Jews (himself included) as a proof that justification came through faith in Christ apart from the works of the law. He writes: "But if, in our endeavor to be justified in Christ, we too were found to be sinners, is Christ then a servant of sin? Certainly not!" In so doing, Paul addresses a misconception about the implications of such justification. Though Gentiles were viewed as sinners, both literally and as those without the God-given law, these Jews in seeking justification in Christ acknowledged that while under the law, they were still sinners before God just as the Gentiles (Phil 3:4–11).[21] Does this mean that Christ promotes sin? Absolutely not! Paul continues to argue that it is the law that promotes the reality of sin (Gal 2:18). Christ redeemed them from that sin by bringing about their death in relation to the law (Gal 2:19–20a; Rom 7:1). For the law does not have jurisdiction over the dead. The condemnation brought by the law ceases at death. Therefore, Paul died through the law, to the law through union with Christ in order to live to God (Gal 2:19; Rom 7:4, 6).

Necessity of the Cross

Is the cross necessary in redemption? Is the cross a central component of Paul's spirituality? In Galatians 2:20, Paul emphasizes that he, like all believers, was crucified with Christ, writing, "I have been crucified with Christ."[22] That statement reveals the means by which one dies to the law and shows how one is then able to live to God. The cross serves as a central component in not only securing justification, but also in guiding the life of the believer. Essentially, it is through the cross that one experiences union with Christ. James Dunn highlights this thought saying that "union with Christ for Paul is *characterized* not by lofty peaks of spiritual excitement and ecstasy, experience of vision, revelation, extraordinary power or high inspiration, but more typically by self-giving love, by the cross—union with Christ is

---

21. Hunn, "Christ Versus the Law," 539–42.

22. Evidence for why "I" should be taken as inclusive of all believers and not exclusive to Paul himself will be presented below.

nothing if it is not union with Christ in his death (Rom. 6.3–6; Gal. 2:19f.; 6.14; Phil. 3.10; Col. 2.11f.)."[23]

Such a reality does not mean that every aspect of the cross is glorious. Crucifixion was a heinous act rendered through the hands of sinful men. Jesus himself despised the shame of the cross; nonetheless, he endured the hostility so that people might die to sin and live to righteousness (2 Cor 5:21; Heb 12:2–3; 1 Pet 2:24; 3:18). To glory in the cross is not to glory in the wretchedness of sinful humanity, but to glory in God leveraging the sinfulness of man and the schemes of the enemy in order to accomplish his plan of redemption.

Thus, when Paul in Galatians 2:20 proclaims that in being justified by faith alone he was crucified with Christ, he provides for all who believe in Christ an essential component in understanding and experiencing the authentic Christian life. It is through the cross that justification is secured. It is through the cross that one dies to the works of the law as a means of justification. It is through the cross that one surrenders the rights to life where the bonds of the flesh are broken and new life in Christ is birthed (2 Cor 5:17–21; Gal 5:16–17, 24).

Who "I" Am

Demonstrating that the apostle Paul uses the first person singular "I" as a reference not only to himself but as indicative of all who are justified through faith is important for seeing the contemporary relevance of the cross.[24] In verse 18, Paul makes a dramatic shift from "we" (vv. 15–17) to "I" (vv. 18–21). Why? While this change may in part be "a rhetorical feature that allows Paul to make his point in more diplomatic fashion,"[25] in the end,

23. Dunn, *Unity and Diversity*, 210.

24. What is argued here is that every believer can claim the reality of this verse with the apostle Paul; however, with the application of that truth comes the potential danger of individualism. As Peter Toon explains, "In western society it is generally assumed that I have rights, choices, preferences and views which must be taken into account by others. In fact, my rights must be honoured. We think of the individual first and society second (individuals making up society) rather than society first and the individual second (society composed of individuals). Christian spirituality says with St Paul: 'I have been crucified with Christ and I no longer live, but Christ lives in me' (Gal 2:20). . . . The pressure of individualism pushes us towards seeing spirituality as a means of self-fulfilment and self-realisation . . ." (Toon, *What Is Spirituality*, 9). Toon is not alone in his concern (Adam, *Hearing God's Word*, 26–27).

25. Longenecker, *Galatians*, 90.

Paul presents himself in this shift as an example of a truth that is applicable to all who believe in Jesus Christ.[26] In other words, this use of "I" is inclusive of all who believe in Jesus Christ.

A key criticism against seeing the shift as inclusive Pauline rhetoric indicative of all believers comes from Scot McKnight.[27] McKnight narrows the interpretive options down to three general categories.[28] The first option he discusses is the "universalistic interpretation" where Paul speaks of a personal experience that is indicative of the experience all believers have. The reasons for such a representative interpretation may be because Paul wants to emphasize his personal passion[29] or is personally addressing attacks levied against him in a manner that would reflect truth for all Christians.[30] Regardless, the apostle serves paradigmatically for all who seek justification by faith. The second option he discusses is the "autobiographical experience" where Paul speaks of his own experience in contrast with the other Jews in Antioch "to force Peter to see that Paul's experience ought to be Peter's."[31] The third option, and the one for which McKnight argues, is to see the "I" (ego) as Peter and/or Paul as Jewish Christians. This view sees the referent of the "we" of verses 15–17 as Peter and Paul and the referent of the "I" (ego) of verses 18–20 as Peter with the possible inclusion of Paul.

McKnight argues that seeing the referent as exclusively Jewish best fits the context; however, his position is problematic. Evidence exists that the Antioch conversation ends with 2:14.[32] If that transition is correct, then his entire argument fails. Even if it was determined that 2:15–21 is written from the perspective of Paul, Peter, and the Jewish community present in Antioch, his point has a flaw. The Gentiles consistently struggled between

---

26. Fung, *Galatians*, 122; Lightfoot, *Paul's Galatians*, 117; Longenecker, *Galatians*, 91–92; Martyn, *Galatians*, 249, 255, 258; Schreiner, *Galatians*, 173; Shauf, "Galatians 2:20 in Context," 91.

27. McKnight, "Ego and 'I,'" 272–80.

28. Ibid., 278–9.

29. Longenecker argues along these lines saying, "While using the gnomic 'I' and 'me' in vv 19–20, there also reverberates in Paul's words his own intense personal feeling (cf. Rom 7:7–25 for a similar gnomic treatment with intense personal identification)" (Longenecker, *Galatians*, 94).

30. Martyn argues along these lines saying, "We have already noted one of the reasons for Paul's shift to the first person singular. He is determined directly to refute a change brought against him by the Teachers" (Martyn, *Galatians*, 258).

31. McKnight, "Ego and 'I,'" 279.

32. Scacewater, "Galatians 2:11–21," 309.

concerns of whether they were to conform to the standards of Judaism or live without any standard. Even if it were determined to be correct that the initial players who need to be kept in perspective were Jewish, it should also be noted that the retelling of the conversation in Antioch (2:11–14) to the Galatian churches was for a significantly non-Jewish audience so that they would not fall into the same theological trappings. The reality that justification is not through the works of the law, but through faith in Christ alone is true of everyone. Paul's point is that any means other than faith by which someone seeks justification before God is invalid. Additionally, the law is an instrument of condemnation that highlights the righteousness of God and the sinfulness of all men (Rom 3:20–31; 4:15; 7:7–25; etc.).[33]

McKnight's argument could only works if the "works of the law" (ἐξ ἔργων νόμου) are seen as the boundary markers. However, if the "works of the law" are "all that the Mosaic law demands," as they seem to be and as previously argued, then his argument also fails. Moreover, it must be noted that Paul is not attacking the morality of the law, but the sufficiency of it.[34] Elsewhere, the apostle affirms the goodness of the law (Rom 3:31; 7:7–12; 1 Tim 1:8); however, he consistently exposes the fact that the law is insufficient if used as a means of salvation (Rom 2:12–29; 3:20–24, 27–28; 4:13–15; 8:3–4; Gal 3:10–14).[35] The law was never intended to save; rather, the law bears witness to one's need to be made righteous (Acts 16:38–39; Rom 3:21; 5:20–21; 7:5; Gal 3:19–24; 1 Tim 1:8–11).[36]

Ultimately, even McKnight cannot escape the universal implications of these verses. In trying to argue for a "sub-species" of the "ego," (I) he explains,

> However, inasmuch as Paul's attack is against anyone who contaminates the gospel by re-erecting national or ethnic boundaries, or

33. This statement is not to argue for a two or three use of the law system; rather, is simply intended to highlight at least one significant use of the law in this regard.

34. The law is primary insufficient, because of man's insufficiency to keep all that the law demands (Rom 1–3). Fung notes that "the main purpose of Paul's present statement is simply to point out the total inadequacy of the law as a means of justification" (Fung, *Galatians*, 114).

35. The law highlights one's sinfulness while demanding perfect adherence. It reveals that no one perfectly keeps the law and that everyone stands in condemnation under the law. The fact that those without the law obey the law proves the validity of the law and brings further condemnation to those who have the law.

36. Dwight Pentecost argues that there was a ten-fold purpose of the law. While Pentecost's conclusion that the law was temporary and has been completely done away may be debated, his concise summary is helpful (Pentecost, "Purpose of the Law," 176–80).

who systemically pollutes the sufficiency of Christ as ground of acceptance with God or the adequacy of the Holy Spirit as guide for Christian behavior, the gentile needs to die to that kind of law—the law that systemically pollutes the purity of that gospel with other forms of acceptance with God. The 'Ego' among gentiles that needs to die is the Ego which attempts to pollute the gospel, and surely a sub-species of this Ego is one that thinks the death of the Son of God is not good enough and, instead, needs to assert itself.[37]

Therefore, the most direct referent of "I" is Jewish, the apostle Paul; however, it is Jewish not as representative of an ethnic community, but a universal spiritual community which has sought justification by faith in Christ: for both the Jew and the Greek.

Critical to understanding the shift is seeing that Paul is not speaking of himself as distinct from other people, but speaking of his spiritual nature as one seeking justification.[38] In addition to the immediate context, one of the strongest arguments for understanding Paul's language as indicative of all believers is found in looking at other verses that teach similar truths pertaining to the role of the cross and life in Christ. Verses such as Romans 8:10, 2 Corinthians 13:5, 2 Corinthians 13:3, and Galatians 4:19 led Tichy Ladislav to conclude, "These passages confirm that Paul referred to all believers in what he expressed in Gal. 2:20a."[39]

Necessity of the Cross

In light of the "I" of Galatians 2:20, the cross becomes a key component in every aspect of the believer's spiritual life: their justification and their sanctification. The cross signifies the instrument with which believers, as disciples, are called to identify (Matt 10:38; 16:21–28; Luke 9:23; 14:27; Rom 6:6; 1 Cor 1:17–18, 23; 2:2; 2 Cor 13:4; Gal 2:20; 5:24; 6:14; Phil 3:18; Heb 12:1–2; 13:3; etc.). Their former lives are dead and their new lives are to be lived unto Christ. The cross then signifies the central location in which believers are united through faith with Christ (Acts 13:38–39; Rom 6; Gal 3:23—4:7; 5:1, 24).

37. McKnight, "Ego and 'I,'" 279–80.

38. Lightfoot reveals, "Not 'I Paul' as distinguished from other, for instance from the Gentile converts, but 'I Paul, the natural man, the slave of the old covenant.' The emphasis on ἐγώ is explained by the following verse, ζῶ δὲ οὐκέτι ἐγώ" (Lightfoot, *Paul's Galatians*, 117).

39. Ladislav, "Christ in Paul," 45.

Some writers, however, within Christian spirituality dismiss any legitimacy of the cross and focus solely on the life of Christ as the basis for Christian living.[40] The necessity of the cross as advocated in this chapter presses beyond mere non-violent atonement theories that argue for redemption through the totality of Christ's life, to include his death and resurrection.[41] Specifically opposed here are those theologies that remove any need of the cross or see the cross as altogether evil with no redemptive value. Articulating the position of many feminists,[42] Deanna Thompson explains that "feminist theologians argue that no doctrine is more problematic, and no symbol more potentially destructive to women and other marginalized persons, than the doctrine of Christology and the symbol of the cross. Exclusive focus on a male savior subjected to unjust suffering and violent death for the benefit of all human beings, feminists proclaim, all too often leads to harm for women."[43] This train of thought can be traced back to Mary Daly, who writing in the 1970s said, "The qualities that Christianity *idealizes*, especially for women, are also those of a victim: sacrificial love, passive acceptance of suffering, humility, meekness, etc. Since these are the qualities idealized in Jesus 'who died for our sins,' his functioning as a model reinforces the scapegoat syndrome for women. Given the victimized situation of the female in sexist society, these 'virtues' are hardly the qualities that women should be encouraged to have."[44]

40. Those mentioned later in this book, such as Mary Daly and Delores S. Williams, fall into the category of Christian spirituality because they explicitly promote theological ideas for the direct purpose of influencing life (Daly, *Beyond God the Father*; Williams, "Black Women's Surrogacy").

41. Weaver, *Nonviolent Atonement*, 32–33, 42–46. Yet, the "nonviolent" atonement view is problematic on several levels. Weaver elsewhere would say, "Death is not part of God's plan for Jesus . . ." (Sanders, *Atonement and Violence*, 152). See also Jersak and Hardin, *Stricken by God*; Tanner, *Jesus, Humanity and the Trinity*, 28–31.

42. "[F]eminist theology is *not* about women. It is about God. It is not a form of 'ego-logy' in which women just think about themselves. When women do it, they speak of feminist theology in order to express the fact that the experience from which they speak and the world out of which they perceive God's words and actions and join in those actions is that of women seeking human equality. Another way of expressing this is to say that the *ecology of their theology* is that of a woman living in a particular time and place" (Russell, *Human Liberation*, 53).

43. Thompson, *Crossing the Divide*, 100.

44. Daly, *Beyond God the Father*, 77.

A variety of feminist theologians followed Daly's approach to re-casting the Scriptures in light of personal or cultural experiences.[45] The Scriptures then began to be read, not in light of its original audience with appropriate application to today, but in light of personal experience based on gender, race, socio-economic status, culture or any combination of those.[46] Additionally, any possible erroneous application of the text seems to serve as a justification for re-interpreting or casting out a text.

45. Not every feminist theologian takes such a hostile approach to the cross. For a brief summary of three feminist views on atonement, see Thompson, *Crossing the Divide*, 128–31. Another example of a more balanced feminist approach to the cross can be seen here: "As a systematic theologian who is also a feminist, I am aware of the limits as well as the strengths of each of these accounts of the cross. When I consider the many ways theologians interpret the cross, I strongly reject any aspect of a theology of the cross that turns God into an intentional agent of traumatic violence; and I firmly believe that however one interprets it, the crucifixion both denounces evil and also announces the universal reality of divine love, of grace" (Jones, *Trauma and Grace*, 81). Additionally, not every feminist theologian subordinates the Scriptures to personal experience. An excellent summary of three views of the authority of the Scriptures within feminist theology can be found in Grant, *White Women's Christ*, 177.

46. This approach is particularly true of liberation feminists. "Whereas Biblical Feminists are ardent and strong biblically focused thinkers, in the sense that everything is tested against the Bible, liberation feminists, to varying degrees, employ the Bible as merely one of several sources in doing theology" (Grant, *White Women's Christ*, 115). Later, Grant would write, "For liberation feminists, it is clear that the Bible is a primary source for doing theology. However, it must be said with equal fervor that the Bible is to be viewed critically. Many questions which emerge from women's experience must be raised" (ibid., 117). Letty M. Russell, expounds further saying that "feminist theology is written out of an experience of oppression in society. It interprets the search for salvation as a journey toward freedom . . ." (Russell, *Human Liberation*, 21). Later she adds, "In the past much theology was done by deducing conclusions from first principles . . . . Today many people find it more helpful to do theology by an inductive method—drawing out the material for reflection from their life experience as it relates to the gospel message. Here stress is placed on the *situation-variable* nature of the gospel. The gospel is good news to people only when it speaks concretely to their particular need of liberation" (ibid., 53).

Furthermore, this approach is not unique to feminist theologians. It can be seen in variations within aspects of Christian spirituality. For example, explaining the hermeneutic of Black Theology, Deotis Roberts writes, "The interpretation of the black religious experience in terms of the Christian creed is the mission of Black Theology" (Roberts, *Liberation and Reconciliation*, 3–4). Gayraud Wilmore concerned that the foundation laid by James Cone and Deotis Roberts is dependent on "white theology" argues for a new hermeneutic that would promote survival and liberation for the black community centered on their experiences of oppression. He says, "If we may presuppose the critical importance of Scripture and the witness of the early church . . . it should be stressed that the first source of black theology is the black community itself. . . . Black faith as folk

Delores Williams, for example, writes as a black feminist advocating for the life of Christ, specifically in resisting oppressive authorities, as a model for Christian living.[47] Her concern for those who have been abused at the hands of falsely pious men is good and appropriate. Those who use the cross as a means for power, enslavement (physical or spiritual), abuse, or other horrific and self-serving purposes should rightly be condemned, but they should not be associated with a right understanding of the doctrine of the cross. The abuse of an image does not unravel the meaning embedded within the image itself.[48]

Nonetheless, Williams leverages a cultural sense of morality and these abusive experiences in order to re-interpret the essence of redemption and the Christian life as revealed in the Bible dismissing the necessity of the cross.

> The synoptic gospels (more than Paul's letters) provide resources for constructing a Christian understanding of redemption that speaks meaningfully to black women, given their historic experience with surrogacy. Jesus' own words in Luke 4 and his ministry of healing the human body, mind, and spirit . . . suggest that Jesus did not come to redeem humans by showing them God's love

---

religion continued to be utilized as the motivating power for revolutionary and nationalist movements in the mass-based community. . . . To the extent that these groups and others continue to draw their main strength from the masses, they will foster the rationalization of certain elements of black religion toward the pursuit of freedom and social justice. Their ideological roots, however, must go down into the soil of the folk community if they are to maintain their credibility. That is why the lower-class black community must be considered one of the primary sources for the development of a black Christian theology" (Wilmore, *Black Religion and Black Radicalism*, 234–5). A biblicaly-grounded Christian spirituality argues for the development of a theology rooted in a contextual interpretation of Scripture that is then applied to a particular community. What Wilmore in a sense is arguing for is using culture and experience alongside of Scripture to establish a black theology versus foundationally using the Scripture to examine culture and experience in deriving a biblical theological position. Additionally, Wilmore goes on to advocate the incorporation of some elements of pre-colonized African religions (ibid., 239–41). For further comments concerning the hermeneutical principles that undergird these various views, such as feminists and black liberation, see Thiselton, *New Horizons*. He gives fifteen various hermeneutical qualifications (ibid., 681).

47. Williams, "Black Women's Surrogacy," 1–14.

48. "Given its abusive history, many feminists have abandoned the cross as a theologically meaningful symbol. Indeed, use of the cross has become scandalous in ways the apostle Paul never envisioned: as supportive of oppression and destruction rather than of justification and salvation" (Thompson, *Crossing the Divide*, 101). See also Köstenberger, *Jesus and the Feminists*, 53.

'manifested' in the death of God's innocent child on a cross erected by cruel, imperialistic, patriarchal power. Rather, the spirit of God in Jesus came to show humans life—to show redemption through a perfect ministerial vision of righting relationships. . . . God's gift to humans, through Jesus, was to invite them to participate in this ministerial vision . . . of righting relations. The response to this invitation by human principalities and powers was the horrible deed that the cross represents—the evil of humankind trying to kill the ministerial vision of life in relation that Jesus brought to humanity. The resurrection does not depend upon the cross for life, *for the cross only represents historical evil trying to defeat good. . . .* Thus, to respond meaningfully to black women's historic experience of surrogacy-oppression, the theologian must show that redemption to humans can have nothing to do with any kind of surrogate role Jesus was reputed to have played in a bloody act that supposedly gained victory over sin and/or evil.[49]

Rather than getting people to rightly understanding the biblical context of the cross, due to the historic experience of surrogacy-oppression,[50] Williams seeks to re-interpret the cross in a way more meaningful for the abused.[51] Thus, Williams casts the life of Jesus as one of resistance versus one of submission.[52] Her concern that women will continually yield to violent abuse is appropriate; however, her re-working of the redemptive story is not. In an effort to encourage resistance against abusive powers in the name of Jesus, Williams continues:

The image of Jesus on the cross is the image of human sin in its most desecrated form. . . . The cross thus becomes an image of defilement, a gross manifestation of collective human sin. Jesus, then, does not conquer sin through death on the cross. Rather, Jesus conquers the sin of temptation in the wilderness (Mt 4:1–11) by resistance . . . . Jesus therefore conquered sin in life, not in death. . . . Humankind is therefore redeemed through Jesus' life and not through Jesus' death. *There is nothing of God in the blood of*

49. Williams, "Black Women's Surrogacy," 11. Emphasis added.

50. Surrogacy-oppression relates to the oppression experienced by black women who essentially were coerced to serve as substitutes for white women specifically in the areas of "nurturance, field labor, and sexuality" (ibid., 20).

51. Thompson helps in showing how this approach is not exclusive to Williams, but common among feminist theologians. "Feminist theologians reject an image of a blood-thirsty God and replaces 'him' with an image of God that functions more positively in the lives of women and men" (Thompson, *Crossing the Divide*, 128).

52. Admittedly, Jesus did at times resisted oppression (Luke 4:30; John 8:59).

the cross. . . . However, as Christians, black women cannot forget the cross. But neither can they glorify it. To do so is to make their exploitation sacred. To do so is to glorify sin.[53]

There is nothing of God in the blood of the cross? To glory in the cross is to glorify sin? How then is Paul to be understood in Galatians 6:14 or Colossians 1:19–20?[54]

Rather than seeking continuity within the canon of Scripture, Williams elevates the Gospels over and against Pauline literature.[55] Yet, even within the Gospels, this approach is problematic. How can there be nothing but evil in the blood of the cross, when it was the will of the Father that the cup not be passed from the Son (Matt 26:39, 42, 44)? How can resistance be the primary instrument within the Christian life when Jesus refused to allow Peter to resist those who came to crucify him (John 18:10–11)?

Williams has removed the cross from its central importance in God's plan of redemption. Williams is right to see that Jesus resisted evil. This fact is seen in the many instances of casting out demons, confronting the religious leaders, driving the money changers from the temple, or announcing that he would be coming back one day to judge the nations (Matt 4:24; 8:16; 21:12–14; 23:1–36; 25:31–46; Mark 3:22–27; Luke 7:21; John 2:15). But, Williams misses the reality that Jesus' life reflects both resistance and passivity at times. It is not an either or with the doctrine of the cross. The cross presents a both/and. Jesus resists the evil of the cross while submitting to the will of the Father. Jesus despises the shame of the cross while embracing the glory of redemption brought through the cross. His life reflects a degree of irony. A similar irony can be seen in the cross whereby God leverages the evil of men for his redemptive purposes; thus, both good and evil, greatness and horror, triumph and defeat, justice and grace can all be seen in the cross.[56] The veil is torn, the enemy is defeated by the very means that he

---

53. Williams, "Black Women's Surrogacy," 12. Emphasis added.

54. Gal 6:14: "But far be it from me to boast except in the cross of our Lord Jesus Christ, by which the world has been crucified to me, and I to the world." Col 1:19–20: "For in him all the fullness of God was pleased to dwell, and through him to reconcile to himself all things, whether on earth or in heaven, making peace by the blood of his cross."

55. Williams, "Black Women's Surrogacy," 11.

56. As Veli-Matti Kärkkäinen affirms, "Yes, the cross is a scandalous event, but it is also an everlasting testimony to the willingness of the triune God not only to share in the suffering of the world but also to let suffering and pain become part of the divine life" (Kärkkäinen, "'How to Speak,'" 62).

sought to establish his rule. That same irony is seen in Galatians 2:20 where true spiritual life is birth through co-crucifixion with Christ.

Alongside of Williams, other feminist dismissals of the cross exist. These dismissals are all accompanied by a rejection or re-interpreting of the cross without proper consideration of the intent of the original author and seeking to understand its essentiality in the biblical text. Experience, personal preference, and a cultural sense of morality are all used with spiritual authority equal to, or superior to, the authority of the Scriptures.[57]

One example of another feminist's dismissal can be seen in Elisabeth Schüssler Fiorenza, who argues, "For women, a theology of the cross as self-giving love is even more detrimental than that of obedience because it colludes with the cultural 'feminine' calling to self-sacrificing love for the sake of their families. Thus it renders the exploitation of all women in the name of love and self-sacrifice psychologically acceptable and religiously warranted."[58] Instead of using a right understanding of Scripture to transform the way that people view and interact with their culture, Fiorenza attempts to reconstruct biblical teachings regarding the cross in a way more palatable for women. As she readily admits, "However, if we can transform a system not by rejecting but only by reconfiguring it in a different frame of meaning, it becomes important to contextualize feminist reflections on Jesus' suffering and cross within a different politics of meaning. Only if we dislocate the doctrinal discourses of redemption and salvation from their preconstructed 'common-sense' meanings does it become possible to reconfigure and to transform them."[59]

As with Williams, the concerns of the previous abuses of the cross by men brutally perverting the doctrine of the cross for their own power and pleasure is appropriate, even noble. However, these abuses of the truth of God's Word do not justify the dismissal of God's redemptive purposes in the cross. The fact is that the New Testament shows the cross to be an

---

57. "Spiritual authority" means authority to dictate the way that one lives, since spirituality involves the idea of how one lives in light of what one believes.

58. Fiorenza, *Jesus*, 102. A more recent example of what Fiorenza is talking about here can be seen in Rebecca's story in *Proverbs of Ashes*. "I said it wouldn't be enough to write a book that criticized everything that was wrong with how Christianity spoke about Jesus' crucifixion. We were going to have to find a way to say something about what *saved life* if we were convinced, and we were, that no one was saved by the execution of Jesus" (Brock and Parker, *Proverbs of Ashes*, 211). Also, "Jesus' death was tragic, but it neither had to happen nor was part of a divine plan for salvation" (Brock, *Journeys*, 93). For a brief rebuttal of Fiorenza, see Köstenberger, *Jesus and the Feminists*, 99–101.

59. Fiorenza, *Jesus*, 107. See also Greene-McCreight, *Feminist Reconstruction*.

essential element for the life of the believer. Galatians 2:20, in a concise formula, ties the cross directly to the believer's justification in righting their standing before God and their ability to live out the Spirit-filled life.[60]

What is at stake is whether the Bible serves as the supreme foundation for Christian living or whether the Bible is set along side or even subject to one's own experience and/or one's cultural sense of morality.[61] Such minimizations of, dismissals of, or attacks against the cross are not exclusive to feminist theologians, they simply serve as one example within Christian spirituality whereby the Bible, and specifically Galatians 2:20, can and should serve as a corrective to the spirituality they are advocating.

Permanence of the Cross

The believer has been crucified in union with Christ in such a way as to die to their former self in surrender through faith. This dying, according to the apostle, is not merely an initial event that takes place at the moment of justification when one expresses faith in Christ, but has a permanent ongoing effect. This thought can be seen in part through Paul's use of the perfect tense: "I *have been crucified* with Christ" (Χριστῷ συνεσταύρωμαι).[62] While focusing on the tense of a verb to highlight a particular point can be problematic, in this case, it seems appropriate and pertinent to the discussion.[63] The use of the perfect tense in Galatians 2:20 indicates the permanent influence the cross is to have in the believer's life.[64] As Matera echoes

60. "Christ who lives in me" is a reference to Christ's living in the believer by means of his Spirit (John 14:16–20; Rom 5:5; 8:8–12, 15, 16, 23, 26; 1 Cor 6:17; 2 Cor 13:5; Gal 3:14; 4:6, 18–19 [Christ is formed in the believer through the Spirit of his Son (4:6), as emphasized later in 5:16 keeps the believer from living out the desires of the flesh, and as reiterated in Eph 3:14–19]; 5:16, 25; Eph 3:15–19; Col 1:27; 1 John 3:24; 4:15–16; 2 Pet 1:3–4).

61. Grant readily admits that the Bible is authoritatively subordinate to experience. "The point being made is that the Bible challenges us as we live and have our being, but at the same time the Bible viewed out of the context of our experiences can be challenged as well" (Grant, *White Women's Christ*, 117). The Bible is authoritative in the sense that it presents a challenging perspective, but is not seen as the normative standard which is to definitively shape Christian living.

62. Emphasis added.

63. As Wallace explains, "The perfect is used less frequently than the present, aorist, future, or imperfect; when it is used, there is usually a deliberate choice on the part of the writer" (Wallace, *Greek Grammar*, 573).

64. This perfect is best categorized as an "extensive perfect (a.k.a. consummative

in his comments on this verse, "The use of the perfect tense suggests that he [Paul] views his crucifixion with Christ as an enduring state. In Galatians 5:24, Paul exhorts his audience to crucify the flesh with its passions and desires, and in 6:14 he says that the world has been crucified to him, and he to the world."[65]

Some interpreters have overemphasized Paul's use of the perfect tense here or completely misunderstood it. For example, Dunn states, "Here particularly striking is the tense used . . . perfect (I have been nailed to the cross with Christ, and am still hanging there with him) . . . ."[66] The point of co-crucifixion via the perfect tense is not to argue that one is still "hanging there" with Christ; rather, it is to emphasize the believers union with Christ through Christ's death. Elsewhere, Witherington appears to shift the focus too far from its context in connecting the tense of the verb and its present application.

> It is important to note the tense of the verb "crucified with" at the end of vs. 19. It is in the perfect, suggesting an action which began in the past and has continuing and ongoing effects in the present. Paul is not merely talking about imitating Christ here, though that is part of the matter, nor even just that Paul suffered in Christ, when Christ died on the cross. Had the latter been the sole focus here we might have expected an aorist verb here. Paul is suggesting that he is now being conformed to the sufferings of Christ in his own person when he is persecuted for Christ's sake (cf. Gal. 6:17) and so depicts the suffering Christ in his own life and person.[67]

The context for this verse deals with justification, not persecution or association with suffering. It is about dying to the law. In this dying, there is also a dying of the flesh that begins with union and progresses through the life of the one justified. The spiritual reality of what happened when faith joined the believer to the crucified Savior has a continual and progressive transforming effect upon them. This reality requires a renewal of the way one understands their position before God and the expectations for living under the influence of the Spirit (Gal 5:16–26).

perfect)" (ibid., 577). See also Bruce, *Colossians, Philemon, Ephesians*, 144; Longenecker, *Galatians*, 92; Matera, *Galatians*, 96; Schreiner, *Galatians*, 74.

65. Matera, *Galatians*, 96.

66. Dunn, *Galatians*, 144.

67. Witherington, *Grace in Galatia*, 190. Other verses do affirm the point Witherington is making (Rom 8:17; Phil 3:10), but to make the point from Gal 2:20 is to press beyond what the context allows.

Other passages further support the permanence of the cross emphasizing the impact that the cross should have on the believer's life (2 Cor 4:10; 2 Tim 2:11). Galatians 5:16–25 brings to light that those who belong to Christ have crucified the flesh.[68] Similarly, Paul reveals in 6:24 that the cross is the object in which he boasts, because it was through that cross that he died to the world.[69] Luke 9:23 proves that the Pauline emphasis on the cross is not unique.[70] Paul affirms what Jesus already taught in his requirements of discipleship. The call to follow Jesus demands the taking up of one's cross daily in following Christ.

As evidenced in Jesus' words and various epistles, the cross serves as a picture for true discipleship and shapes the way that one understands life as a follower of Jesus. This idea is completely missed in many of the feminists previously mentioned. For example, in Williams's perspective, the cross is not only evil, but irrelevant in the Christian life. She dismisses the concept of life through death, even spiritual death, as an unintelligent misogynistic theory.

> Perhaps not many people today can believe that evil and sin were overcome by Jesus' death on the cross, that is, that Jesus took human sin upon himself and therefore saved humankind. Rather, it seems more intelligent to understand that redemption had to do with God, through Jesus, giving humankind new vision to see resources for positive, abundant relational life—a vision humankind did not have before. Hence, the kingdom of God theme in the ministerial vision of Jesus does not point to death; that is, it is not something one has to die to get to.[71]

---

68. The tense here is aorist.

69. Other evidences within Pauline literature include Rom 6:5–11, which stresses the impact in the life of one who has been crucified with Christ where one considers themselves dead to sin, but alive to God. Rom 7:1–6 repeats some of the thought of Gal 2:15–20 whereby the one who has died with Christ has forever been released from the law. Phil 3:10 speaks of being conformed to Christ's death. Col 2:11–14 speaks of a circumcision of the heart by faith and then explains that such forgiveness came through the cross. This forgiveness is a perpetual forgiveness experienced as a result of the permanent work of the cross. Gal 2:20 and 3:2–3 both show that continual reflection on the permanence of the cross should shape decisions in reference to Christian living and adherence to the law.

70. Luke 9:23: "And he said to all, 'If anyone would come after me, let him deny himself and take up his cross daily and follow me.'"

71. Williams, "Black Women's Surrogacy," 11.

For her, the cross has no real place in Christian theology. It was a temporary tool "erected by cruel, imperialistic, patriarchal power" in an attempt to stop the ministry of Christ.[72] Fiorenza, as previously shown, also misses the continuative significance of the cross.[73] From her perspective, the doctrine of the cross promotes evil, suppression, violence, abuse, etc., and is detrimental to Christian thinking and living, especially for women. This idea is not surprising since earlier it was shown that the cross serves no redemptive value in her theological scheme; thus, no need exists for the permanence of the cross in the believer's life despite the numerous passages to the contrary. For these feminist, the Scriptures supporting a doctrine of the cross for the Christian life are either dismissed altogether, subordinated to personal preference and experience, reconstructed within a modern cultural construct, or some combination of these.[74] Ultimately, in Galatians 2:20, the experience of the cross is to have an ongoing residual effect in the life of the one justified. Since, therefore, the cross serves as an essential component of a biblically-based Christian spirituality.

Significance of the Cross

The doctrine of the cross as seen in Galatians 2:20 also has significance for the Christian life. After all, "What we believe shapes the way that we behave. Behaviour is always linked to belief. What we believe about the cross (and what God was doing there) will therefore fundamentally shape our attitude to, and involvement with, wider society."[75] Therefore, this section will focus on two aspects of the cross: liberation from the law and identity.

Liberation from the Law

One significant aspect of co-crucifixion with Christ is a death through the law, to the law (Gal 2:18–19). If in Christ, one is dead to the law, then Galatians 2:20 addresses in some fashion the reality of the believer's liberty from

---

72. Ibid.

73. Fiorenza, *Jesus*, 102.

74. Ibid., 108.

75. Chalke, "Redeeming the Cross," 19.

the law; however, freedom from the law does not equal lawlessness.[76] The gospel of the cross must not result in antinomianism.[77]

Furthermore, for the believer, the law as it once stood has now been overshadowed by a new and fuller law (John 13:34; 2 Cor 3:6; Eph 2:14–16; Heb 8:7, 13; 10:1, 10; 1 John 2:7–8; 2 John 5). This new law may be called the "law of love," "the law of the Spirit," or "the law of Christ" (Gal 5:13–14, 22–23; 6:2). It is a law that brings freedom: freedom to serve God and others. Such a law summarizes the intentions of God and when followed serves in a capacity against which no other law can stand. As Timothy George explains, "[Paul] was not saying here that the law of God had lost all meaning or relevance for the Christian believer. This is the error of antinomianism, which Paul was at pains to refute both here in Galatians as well as in Romans . . . There is an ethical imperative in the Christian life that flows from

---

76. This thought brings up the issue of New Testament ethics specifically in balancing the tension of nomism and antinomism. For a good concise argument for a New Testament ethic, see Longenecker, "New Testament Social Ethics," 337–50. An antinomian approach to the spiritual life is further refuted in the context that flows out of Gal 2:20. The law was a temporary guardian (3:24–25). The slavery brought by the law is now cast aside for the promised inheritance (4:28–5:1). The freedom from the law does not equal lawlessness. A standard for living still exists. This freedom is to be used in submission to God to serve one another in love, denying the impulses of the flesh (5:13–14). Those who are led by the Spirit are not under the law (5:18) because they have crucified the flesh and live in accordance with the will of God as directed by his Spirit (5:22–25). Transgressions for the believer still exist and believers are to live in relationship to one another and the world in such a way as to fulfill the law of Christ (6:2–5).

77. The law as a means of justification is dead to the apostle. The reality is that the law was never intended to bring about justification, not because of its shortcomings, but because of the shortcomings of men. For Paul, the attempt to use the law as the means of justification is now dead, abandoned for the sake of faith in Christ. Conversely, the condemn function of the law was intended to show man his inadequacy and point him to Christ. It was an accuser. The law as a sign post to point the believer to Christ becomes nullified, in a sense, upon conversion, because its purpose has been fulfilled in Christ. See Scaer, "Third Use of Law," 237–57. This point does not mean that Paul did not acknowledge any use of the law. He read from the law and preached Christ from the law (Acts 13:13–41). Paul followed the regulations of the law when going to the temple (Acts 21:26). Paul described Ananias, the one God sent to restore Paul's sight, as a "devout man according to the law" (Acts 22:12). Paul used the principle of the law as a basis for his arguments to various church concerning supporting spiritual leaders (1 Cor 9:8–12; 1 Tim 5:18). Paul, however, did dismiss any use of the law as a means of righteousness before God. The debate concerning how many uses of the law there are extends beyond the scope of this work. For a good concise presentation of the various approaches to law and gospel, see Bahnsen, *Five Views on Law and Gospel*. See also Mattes, "Beyond Impasse," 271–91; Murray, *Law, Life, and the Living God*; Vogel, "Third Use of Law," 191–220.

a proper understanding of justification."[78] This point is important to note for the apostle continues to argue that this crucified life still lives (v. 20), and the life produced should be one that is godly; however, godliness is not measured in relation to the law, but in relation to Christ.[79] The reality that an ethical imperative still exists for those in Christ is further illustrated by the apostle in 1 Corinthians 9:21–22.[80] The apostle reveals that even when operating outside Judaic law he is not lawless per se.

Modern antinomianism within American Protestantism is generally more subtle. Rarely are professing Christians openly advocating the absence of any ethical standard or accountability in Christ. Nonetheless, various tenents of Christian spirituality display a form of functional antinomianism whereby objective ethical standards are subjugated to the perspective and preferences of the self. Gerhard Forde, addressing contemporary antinomianism, writes, "That everyone should have the right to 'do their own thing' seems virtually to be the dogma of the age. If laws and norms get in the way, they can be discredited as relics of an outmoded 'lifestyle,' and changed to fit what we call contemporary-lived experience. Antinomianism is the spiritual air we breathe."[81]

The subjective spirituality of the extreme feminist leads to functional antinomian, or at minimum an ego-nomian, approach to life as shown through the section above on the necessity of the cross. These feminists would argue that they are not antinomian, but their theology takes the objective contextual teachings of the Bible and subjugates those teachings to their own preferences making them a law unto themselves. Thus, they are functional antinomians. The apostle, however, articulates a doctrine of the law that liberates the believer from the condemnation of the law, but not from ethical norms in fulfilling the law of Christ. Self was never to be the determining factor for right or wrong. Antinomianism (or ego-nomism), in this sense, "is a theological playing with words: the attempt to get rid of, to change, to water down 'the law'—that which makes demands, attacks,

---

78. George, *Galatians*, 198.

79. Commands can reflect the intention of Christ and thus in following a command, one can be following Christ (John 14:15; 1 John 4:21; 5:2–3).

80. First Cor 9:21–22: "To those outside the law I became as one outside the law (not being outside the law of God but under the law of Christ) that I might win those outside the law. To the weak I became weak, that I might win the weak. I have become all things to all people, that by all means I might save some."

81. Forde, "Fake Theology," 246. Forde is focusing on "antinomianism from a theological rather than an ethical point of view" (ibid., 251).

accuses or threatens us—by a theological *tour-de-force*, by changing words. One tries to end the law by erasing the offensive words or finding more accommodating ones, by changing definitions and usages, or more lately by shifting or just multiplying metaphors and symbols until the matter is obscured beyond recognition."[82] According to Forde, in this context, antinomianism involves the elevation of personal preference over objective truth in shifting language, concepts, etc. in an attempt to find something more palatable. This tension is felt within various aspects of Christian spirituality and can again be seen in the Christian feminist movement.[83] Forde too sees the antinomian connection within feminist theology.

> Current discussion about the problem of 'sexist' language and the use of metaphor in theology is an example of the temptation to linguistic antinomianism. It is quite true that the language we use turns on us and attacks in unexpected and even unsuspected ways (*lex simper accusat!*). It is also true that language can be used either intentionally or unintentionally to oppress. But the idea that much of anything is *really* accomplished merely by erasing or changing the language is antinomian folly. We need, of course, to be constantly on guard against the ways in which we use language to accommodate sin and perpetuate injustice. . . . But merely changing the metaphors or the language when one has no perception of the end only makes matters worse. The law only changes its guise and becomes more devastating because it is supposed to be "gospel."[84]

Linguistic shifts and changing symbols within the contemporary feminist movement only dull the clarity of the gospel and present an antinomian approach to Christian living by relegating clear biblical teaching, specifically in reference to the cross. The Bible, in these settings, is subjected to personal experience and one's cultural sense of morality due, in many instances, to justifiable concerns relating to the abuses of certain doctrines. Despite the legitimacy of these concerns, this approach inappropriately

---

82. Forde, "Fake Theology," 246.

83. Mary Boys addresses her personal struggle for the expressed purpose of determining whether or not "Christians [should] lay aside the cross as a symbol of their life" (Boys, "Cross," 5–27). Although Boys has many Catholic ties, she is presented here as a focus within American Protestantism due to her role as a member of the faculty of Union Theological Seminary which explicitly presents itself in the Protestant Reformed tradition ("About Union").

84. Forde, "Fake Theology," 250. He continues to provide a brief example of what he is referencing using the thought of changing God as "Father" to "Mother."

turns the theological order upside down and produces teachings in direct conflict with the contextual meaning of the Scriptures.

Identity

Another significance of this co-crucifixion with Christ is a loss of one's old identity in the flesh. Christ is presented in Galatians 2:20 as the exclusive means by which one's identity and relationship in connection with God is redefined. Additionally, as the context of Galatians 2:20 affirms (vv. 15–20), personal expression of faith is the means by which one is justified, experiences co-crucifixion, and receives their new identity.[85] Klyne Snodgrass speaks of this faith-identity connection. "[F]aith confronts and seeks to exclude self-centeredness, for conversion is about ego management. Faith displaces the ego so that Christ is the primary self determinant. In other words the Christian understanding of the self is found outside oneself."[86] Such faith, as Paul describes in the context of Galatians 2:20 is intentional and specific.

This idea of the specificity of the name of the person of Jesus and the intentionality of personal allegiance to him is more than a mere "Shibboleth."[87] At stake is the reality that one is turning to God for redemption from one's sins, but not any god, rather, God as he has revealed himself through Jesus Christ and Scripture. God desires to be known and worshipped rightly.[88]

While an encounter with Christ may have been unintentional, the decision to surrender to his Lordship as one's Savior and King is not.[89] This thought is frequently challenged within Christian spirituality. One such challenge has come from Rob Bell. While Bell argues that everyone

---

85. For those arguing for the subjective genitive (Christ's faithfulness), see discussions related to ἐὰν μή and "Faith of Jesus Christ" in "Context: Galatians 2:15–19" in the appendix. In summary, ἐὰν μή should be interpreted as exceptive and πίστεως Ἰησοῦ Χριστοῦ should be interpreted as an objective genitive reading "faith in Jesus Christ." Specifically, see Hunn, "Ἐὰν μή in Galatians 2:16," 288–90; Porter and Pitts, "Πίστις with a Preposition," 33–53.

86. Snodgrass, "Hermeneutics of Identity," 6.

87. This concept is briefly addressed again under "Necessity of Personal Faith" in chapter 4.

88. As indicated by the fact that special revelation (Scripture) was given to mankind that tells specifics regarding the nature, character, and will of God.

89. For example, Paul's did not intend to encounter God on the road to Damascus (Acts 9:4–6).

is saved through the person and work of Christ, he also argues that one can be seemingly unaware of the person and work of Christ and still be saved. In other words, while holding to the exclusivity of Christ, Bell removes the intentionality of following Christ.[90] In his book *Love Wins*, Bell uses the story of God providing water through the rock in the wilderness to argue that there are rocks everywhere.[91] People may be saved by Christ without even knowing that he is the one saving them.[92] Thus, while claiming exclusivity, only through Christ, Bell argues for a form of inclusivity or universality in stating that "there is an exclusivity on the other side of inclusivity. This [view] insists that Jesus is the way, but holds tightly to the assumption that the all-embracing, saving love of this particular Jesus the Christ will of course include all sorts of unexpected people from across the cultural spectrum."[93] For Bell, these "unexpected people" include Muslims, Hindus, Buddhists, and Baptists that may or may not recognize the name Jesus, but are nonetheless saved by him since Jesus declares that "he, and he alone, is saving everybody."[94] With a little greater clarity, he adds to this thought saying that "sometimes people bump into Jesus, they trip on the mystery, they stumble past the word, they drink from the rock, without knowing what or who it was."[95]

This approach is problematic. Salvation is found specifically in Christ and not vicariously in rocks of another name (Acts 4:12). Buddha and Jesus are not the same despite similarities in certain ethical commands. The source of one's justification is the issue. Is it by faith in the saving work of Jesus or in one's own effort, or even in someone else? There was a reason the Israelites were told not to follow the false gods in the promised land. They were not merely a Yahweh by another name, they were other gods.

Galatians 2:20 speaks specifically to identity through co-crucifixion with Christ.[96] For all believers, identity is not in circumstances or by im-

90. Bell seems to be influenced in part by Brian McLaren. See McLaren, *Generous Orthodoxy*, 112–4. McLaren often writes in a style using fictional narrative to develop certain theological paradigms (McLaren, *New Kind of Christian*; idem, *Story We Find Ourselves In*; idem, *The Last Word and the Word After That*).

91. Bell, *Love Wins*, 139–61.

92. Ibid., 144.

93. Ibid., 155.

94. Ibid.

95. Ibid., 158.

96. "Dying to this idolatrous self-as-God we then discover the identity of our true self, our self-in-God. Christians believe that this process is only truly possible through

personal association, but in Christ. This new identity is embedded in Christ because believers have been united in his death and resurrection. One receives their new identity through union with Christ. Too often within Christian spirituality identity is sought by means outside of the revelation of Christ as expressed in God's Word. Authority is often given to one's experiences and cultural voices in addition to the Scriptures. Then, where the biblical text conflicts with those experiences and values, the Bible is reinterpreted in a way that gives them an identity in their own image. This tension is but one that biblically-grounded Christian spirituality seeks to relieve. Klyne Snodgrass contributes to this conversation saying, "Still the Bible gives us an identity, tells us who we are and how we fit into God's story and how that identity is to be lived out. . . . Scripture is about identity formation. In the end the whole discussion about the authority of Scripture is about identity. Do we allow Scripture to tell us who we are and who we are to be, or do we give that authority to something else?"[97] Later, he explains,

> Christ is not an accessory to our identity . . . . He takes over identity so that everything else becomes an accessory, which is precisely what "Jesus is Lord" means. It is the opposite to a cheap form of a gospel without demand and without content, as if faith were a short transaction, a prayer, a decision, to get security taken care of in order to go to heaven. A focus on identity allows us to put thinking and being back together. Christianity is not about thinking the faith. Theology is useless unless backed up by life. If we proclaim a gospel that does not lead to doing, we proclaim an alien gospel. Being does not exist without doing. We are what we do, no matter what we say. Identity cannot be shaped or exist without doing.[98]

This thought in part is why Paul immediately transitions the second half of Galatians 2:20 to speak of the life that would now flow from faith out of this crucified and now connected identity: "It is no longer I who live, but Christ who lives in me. And the life I now live in the flesh I live by faith in the Son of God, who loved me and gave himself for me." When one is dead to himself and alive to Christ, a new personal identity exists. One cannot be violated. One cannot be insulted. One cannot be humiliated. One

---

Jesus Christ in the power of the Holy Spirit" (Toon, *What Is Spirituality*, 27).

97. Snodgrass, "Hermeneutics of Identity," 4–5.

98. Ibid., 8–9. Snodgrass then talks of eight factors that shapes one's identity (ibid., 11–14).

cannot be suppressed. One cannot be taken advantage of. After all, how can a dead person experience these things? This thought does not mean that one should stand idly by while injustices take place and ungodly people corrupt the word of the cross in defense of their actions. It does mean that "self" does not become the primary catalyst for any action; rather, one's co-crucified life should be motived by the love of God brought rescue from darkness and transformation of life, as will be discussed later in the book (1 Cor 5:14–15).

Conclusion

Galatians 2:20a, "I have been crucified with Christ," contextually presents the centrality of the cross in a clear and concise way. While Paul provides a strong emphasis of the centrality of the cross, he is not alone. The apostle echoes other biblical writers and the teachings of Jesus himself. Consistently, they present the cross as a necessary component to the Christian life. Unfortunately, some within Christian spirituality miss the importance of the cross as a result of their own personal prejudices and preferences or their own misguided theological constructs. Thus, the biblical emphasis of the cross when understood helps serve as a corrective by grounding one's cultural sense of morality and personal preferences in the biblical text. The tension rests in whether self, something else, or the Bible is the foundation for faith and practice.

2

The Centrality of Christ

"It is no longer I who live, but Christ who lives in me"

Introduction

Paul argues throughout Galatians 2:15–19 for justification through faith in Jesus Christ in contrast with the works of the law. Then, in Galatians 2:20, he provides a pivotal summary of the justification found through faith in Christ with the resulting life that is to be lived. Within Paul's summary, Christ is the one with whom he is crucified, and Christ is the one who lives in him so that he may live a godly life. Christ is the one who secures salvation and commissions him showing Christ's essential role in the Christian life. Paul presents Christ at the center of the text and at the center of the justified life.

Spirit as Christ's Representative

Paul states in Galatians 2:20 that Christ now lives in and empowers the believer for Christian living.[1] But, how does Christ live in the believer?

---

1. As seen elsewhere: John 6:56; 17:22–3; 2 Cor 4:11; 13:5; Gal 4:18–9; Eph 3:17; Col 1:27; 1 John 3:24.

Christ now lives in believers by means of his Spirit. The Spirit serves to promote the life of Christ within and through the Christian.[2] Before his resurrection, Christ lived in submission to the Father under the influence of the Spirit.[3] After his resurrection, Christ sends the Spirit, which is one reason why the Spirit of God is often referred to as the Spirit of Christ (John 14:16–20; 17:22; Rom 8:8–12; Gal 4:6; Eph 3:16–17; 1 Pet 1:11).[4]

Galatians 2:20b Examined

This section of the verse buildings on the previous declaration concerning co-crucifixion with Christ (I have been crucified with Christ) highlighting a negative (It is no longer I who live) and a positive (Christ who lives in me)[5] result of that union.[6] These two results will now be discussed.

No Longer I Who Live

Paul reveals in this statement that since one has been crucified with Christ, one no longer lives unto himself. A new identity in Christ now exists free from the bondage of sin and death (Acts 13:38–39; Rom 6; Gal 3:23—4:7;

---

2. This statement simply highlights one function of the Spirit. It does not imply that this is the sole responsibility of the Spirit. Other arguments could be presented to show the role of the Spirit in sealing Christians and giving them a guarantee (2 Cor 1:22; Eph 1:13; 4:30), coming as a love gift (Rom 5:5), being the agent by whom a believer is adopted as a son and enabled to cry out to God as Father (Rom 8:15) confirming within that they are a child of God (Rom 8:16), aiding one in prayer (Rom 8:26), bringing conviction (John 16:8–11; Acts 7:51), etc.

3. Ware, *Father, Son, & Holy Spirit*, 88–94.

4. Ibid., 94–98; Dunn, *Galatians*, 145–6; Kärkkäinen, "'How to Speak,'" 60–61; Polhill, *Acts*, 64. "In a word, the one who had been *inspired by* the Spirit had now become *dispenser of* the Spirit" (Dunn, "Towards the Spirit of Christ," 13–14).

5. ζῇ δὲ ἐν ἐμοὶ Χριστός. For an interesting approach that views "Christ in you" as descriptive of "the entirety of the life of faith," see Barclay, *"Christ in You,"* 137.

6. These results are connected through the use of a continuative conjunction "δὲ," meaning it should be translated as "and." There are two "δὲ" conjunction in this section of the verse. The first one is continuative and is not reflected in the ESV ([And] it is no longer I who live). The second is adversative (but Christ who lives in me). As Longenecker explains, "The postpositive particle δὲ ('and') here is continuative (like that at the beginning of v 20), expressing a further feature of the rationale begun in v 19 and clarifying in an epexegetical manner what Paul means by 'Christ lives in me'" (Longenecker, *Galatians*, 93). So Burton, *Galatians*, 137.

5:1, 24). One has died in relation to the curse of the law (Rom 7:1, 4–6; Gal 3:13–14). For, the law no longer has condemning power over a dead man.

The spiritual life is no longer lived under the impulses of the flesh for, as Paul states, "It is no longer I who live," and "those who belong to Christ Jesus have crucified the flesh with its passions and desires" (Gal 2:20b; 5:24).[7] Paul is not arguing for a loss of personality or personal identity as such; rather, he is describing the loss of one's spiritual identity in the flesh.[8] One is no longer identified by God in the Adamic nature; rather, their identity is now found in Christ (Rom 6; Eph 4:22–24; Col 3:9–10). Thomas R. Schriener helps to clarify, writing, "We should not understand the phrase 'It is no longer I who live' to denote the suppression of Paul's personality. What Paul means is that the old 'I,' who he was in Adam, no longer lives. In other words, we have a redemptive-historical statement here. The old age of sin and death has been set aside now that Christ has died."[9]

But Christ Who Lives in Me

The believer is now to live out their newly found identity under the influential power of the one in whom this new identity is found.[10] Christ in the

---

7. This argument is developed more fully in Gal 5 to show the result of being united with Christ by faith and dying to the flesh.

8. "In Galatians 2:20 Paul is not declaring that he has lost his own distinct selfhood because he pointedly says 'I live.' But the self that he now *is* lives only because it is inseparably linked to the will and life of Christ" (Needham, *Birthright*, 165). See also Campbell, *Paul*, 163–4; Davies, *Paul and Rabbinic Judaism*, 196. Contra Weiss, *History of Primitive Christianity*, 468; Reitzenstein, *Die Hellenistischen Mysterienreligionen*. Additionally, the concept of incarnational living is not addressed in this book. Suffice to say that Paul advocates that the Christian life be lived in such a way as to promote Christ, manifest Christ, confront the world with Christ as a light placed on a hill for all to see; however, he is not arguing that Christ inhabits one to the extent that they are only a shell where Christ is present, not in influence but in form, so that all identity is lost and the person becomes Christ. Thus, the believer is to be a representative of Christ, indwelt and empowered by Christ, but never truly confused with the person of Christ. For a sample of some confusing incarnational comments that do not adequately avoid this distinction, see Brister, *Pastoral Care*, xxiii; Nelson, *Realm of Redemption*, 104; Wise, *Meaning of Pastoral Care*, 8, 24.

9. Schreiner, *Galatians*, 172.

10. The second conjunction, which begins this section of the verse, is adversative: *but* Christ who lives in me (Burton, *Galatians*, 137; Longenecker, *Galatians*, 92–93). Unlike the first conjunction ([*And*] it is no longer I who live) designed to continue the thought of co-crucifixion, this conjunction serves to contrast the negative advantage of

believer is now the source of power and strength that enables the believer to no longer live under the impulses of the flesh. He brings death to the old *ego*.[11] As Richard Longenecker explains:

> Crucifixion with Christ implies not only death to the jurisdiction of the Mosaic law (v 19), but also death to the jurisdiction of one's own ego. The "I" here is the "flesh" (σάρξ) of 5:13–24, which is antagonistic to the Spirit's jurisdiction. So in identifying with Christ's death, both the law and the human ego have ceased to be controlling factors for the direction of the Christian life. Instead Paul insists, the focus of the believer's attention is to be on the fact that "Christ lives in me."[12]

The *ego* is removed in order to focus on Christ's central role in the justified life. Christ now empowers the believer to live the spiritual life to which he is called (Phil 4:13).[13]

Considering these things, two important questions concerning how the phrase "Christ who lives in me" should be understood still need to be addressed. First, how should the phrase in me (ἐν ἐμοὶ) be interpreted? Secondly, in what way does Christ live in the believer?

First, what does Paul mean by the phrase "in me"? Most commonly, "in me" simply describes the sphere in which Christ dwells.[14] D. A. Car-

---

co-crucifixion (It is no longer I who live), by emphasizing the positive advantage, that of Christ living in the believer. Contrasting the death of their old identity, Paul next grounds the believer's identity and power for Christian living in Christ. Christ is essential in the Christian life, without whom no justification or empowered living exists. The life experienced by a believer is to be defined by the presence of Christ. As a result, any good that then flows out of this new life glorifies God. The verse 1 Cor 15:10 explains that any manifestation of goodness is only the result of God's grace working within Paul. See also Ps 16:2; 2 Cor 1:20; Eph 1:12; Phil 1:11, 20, 26; Heb 13:20–21; 1 Pet 4:10–11; 2 Pet 3:18; Jude 24–25.

11. The "ego" here is used to represent the greek word ἐγώ meaning "I" as described in the last chapter of this book where Paul declared "I have been crucified with Christ." It is not to be confused with the psychological use of "ego" (Colman, *Dictionary of Psychology*, s.v. "ego"; Loevinger, "Ego Development," 1:418–20; Padel, "Freudianism," 270–4; Reber, *Penguin Dictionary of Psychology*, s.v. "ego").

12. Longenecker, *Galatians*, 92.

13. The next phrase in Gal 2:20 (the life I now live in the flesh, I live by faith) emphasizes the life that should now flow out of one who has been united with Christ; thus, this passage is showing how Jesus provides power for Christian living as is expressed more strongly in Gal 5.

14. Locative dative, as demonstrated in numerous modern day translations (i.e., ESV, NASB, NET, NIV, NKJV, etc.).

son, however, argues against this understanding stating, "In the context, the point is not that Christ by his Spirit takes up residence in Paul . . . but that just as Christ's death is Paul's death, so Christ's life is Paul's life. In both cases the idea is forensic, substitutionary, judicial."[15] Thus, Carson believes the dative is a dative of respect and should be understood to say that "Christ lives *in relation to me* or *with respect to me* or *in my case*."[16] This approach is certainly grammatically possible; nevertheless, it seems unlikely in this case.[17] Carson's argument builds upon the idea that "ἐν + the dative of any personal pronoun is frequently not locative."[18] In response, while ἐν + the dative of a personal pronoun may frequently not be locative, it is also not uncommon (Rom 7:8, 17–18, 20; 8:9–11, 1 Cor 3:16; 6:19; 2 Cor 11:10; 13:5; Gal 4:19; Eph 3:17; 4:18; Phil 1:6; Col 1:27; 3:16; 1 Thess 2:13; 2 Tim 1:5–6), nor is the idea of Christ in the believer unique in Paul's writings (Rom 8:10; 2 Cor 13:5; Gal 4:19; Eph 3:17; Col 1:27). Carson also uses Galatians 1:24 as an illustration to show how Paul is using the dative in Galatians 2:20, but Paul's use of the dative of respect in Galatians 1:24 does not necessitate the same use in Galatians 2:20. The context and emphasis are considerably different.[19]

Additionally, Paul's point is not solely focused on justification in Galatians 2:20, but on the life that flows out of the one who has been justified. The rest of the verse will provide a glimpse of this idea (and the life I live in the flesh . . .) and that thought will be developed more thoroughly in Galatians chapter 5. Carson is correct to note that a forensic overtone to the phrase exists, but it is not merely a forensic declaration. Paul is connecting the justified life to the process of sanctification; whereby, the believer now lives out of a new center of life. Their fleshly *ego* no longer has the driver's seat; rather, their life now belongs to, is controlled by, and under the influence of another allowing them the opportunity and ability to live truly spiritual lives.[20] In consideration of this evidence, the common translation, "Christ who lives *in me*," is preferred.

Secondly, in what way does Christ live in the believer? Paul's emphasis on the central role of Christ in the redeemed life needs to be established

15. Carson, *Love in Hard Places*, 166.

16. Ibid.

17. See also Schreiner, *Galatians*, 172.

18. Carson, *Love in Hard Places*, 165.

19. Ibid., 166. Gal 1:24: "And they glorified God *because of me*." Emphasis added.

20. George, *Galatians*, 199.

before more directly answering this question. For Paul, the emphasis in the believer's life is clearly on Christ. This emphasis is not to the exclusion of the Father or the Spirit. They are both mentioned throughout the book, but time and time again, Paul places Jesus at the center of the redeemed life to serve as an essential focal point.[21] Jesus is the one who sacrificed himself in order to deliver the people of God from their sin and enable them to live in accordance with his will in the present evil age (Gal 1:1, 3–4). As a result, the apostle expresses God's grace as the grace of Christ and the gospel as the gospel of Christ keeping Jesus at the forefront (Gal 1:6–7; 6:18). While in other books, Paul refers to Christians as servants of God, in Galatians, they are servants of Christ (Gal 1:10).[22] Jesus is the one in whom those seeking justification are to trust. Justification does not exist by any means other than faith in Jesus Christ (Gal 2:15–16; 3:24–26).[23] Jesus is the one who redeemed believers from the curse of the law and enabled them to experience the promised Spirit through faith (Gal 3:13–14). The promises made to Abraham are fulfilled and experienced in Christ (Gal 3:16, 22, 29; 4:4–5).[24] As a result, the believer's identity is now found in Christ as Christ is "put on" and manifested to the world (Gal 3:25–28; 5:6). In this regard, previous social distinctions no longer contain one's identity. Moreover, Jesus is to be formed in the believer by being the controlling influence in their life in contrast to the impulses of the flesh, so that the believer now lives

---

21. God: Gal 1:1, 3–4, 10, 13, 20, 24; 2:6, 19, 21; 3:6, 8, 11, 17–18, 20–21, 26; 4:4, 6–9, 14; 5:21; 6:7, 16. Spirit: Gal 3:2–3, 5, 14; 4:6, 29; 5:5, 16–18, 21–22, 25; 6:8. Son: Gal 1:1, 3, 6–7, 10, 12, 16, 22; 2:4, 16–17, 19–21; 3:1, 13–14, 16, 22, 24, 26–29; 4:4, 6–7, 14, 19; 5:1–2, 4, 6, 24; 6:2, 12, 14, 17–18.

22. Christians are called "servants of God" in 2 Cor 6:4; 1 Thess 1:9; Titus 1:1. This thought does not imply that the idea of Christians as being servants of Christ is rare. The term is used consistently by Paul in expressing the significance of Christ (Rom 1:1; 1 Cor 7:22; 2 Cor 4:5; Eph 6:6; Phil 1:1; Col 4:12; 1 Tim 4:6). Jesus is the one who modeled service and redeemed his people as their servant King freeing them from being slaves to sin in order that they might be slaves to righteousness (Rom 6:6, 16–22; Phil 2). Christians are redeemed from slavery into slavery in one sense. The freedom that Christ brought was not a freedom to serve according to one's own will, but a freedom to serve God (Rom 6:22; Gal 5:1). Gal 5:13 will reinforce the idea that one is redeemed from being enslaved to sin so that in their freedom they would not indulge the flesh, but instead use that freedom as an opportunity to truly serve others in the name of the Lord.

23. For a defense of reading πίστεως ’Ιησοῦ Χριστοῦ as an objective versus a subjective genitive, see "Context: Galatians 2:15–19" in the appendix. The point is not the faithfulness of Christ, but the believer's expressed faith in Christ.

24. Concerning some of those "offspring" promises, see Gen 12:2–3; 15:5; 22:18; Luke 1:55; Acts 13:32; Rom 4:13, 16; Heb 6:15, 17; 7:6; 9:8; 11:9, 17.

under a new law, the law of Christ (Gal 4:19; 5:13–24; 6:2).[25] As a result of the centrality of Christ for the Christian life, Paul will conclude Galatians proclaiming that he only boasts in Christ's cross and then blesses his audience with the grace of Christ (Gal 6:14, 18). Thus, Paul presents the book of Galatians and the Christian life with a strong Christ-centered focus.[26]

Maintaining this focus on Christ, Paul presents the Spirit in certain instances as a representative of Christ.[27] Just a few verses after Galatians 2:20, in 3:2, Paul uses the same argument developed in 2:15–19 regarding justification by faith and not by the works of the law; however, this time, Paul does not reference justification, but the reception of the Spirit (Gal 3:2).[28] Paul equates the reception of the Spirit with the declaration of justification in the believer's life. That point is what Paul introduces in Galatians 2:20 when he declares that "it is no longer I who live, but Christ who lives in me." Thus, Paul speaks of the indwelling work of Christ synonymously with the indwelling presence of the Spirit, which continually reminds the

25. For some of the various views concerning what the law of Christ is, see Adeyemi, "New Covenant Law," 438–52; Barclay, *Obeying the Truth*, 125–45; Barrett, *Freedom and Obligation*, 83; Bultmann, *Theologie des Neuen Testaments*, 260–70; Charry, "Grace of God," 34–44; Davies, *Paul and Rabbinic Judaism*, 69–85; 142–46; idem, *Torah in the Messianic Age*, 84–94; Dodd, *Gospel and Law*, 64–83; Dunn, *Theology of Paul*, 632–34, 653–58, 668, 725; Furnish, *Theology and Ethics*, 59–64, 228–235; Gutbrod, "νόμος," in *TDNT*, 4:1059–78; Hays, "Christology and Ethics," 268–90; Kalusche, "'Das Gesetz als Thema biblischer Theologie,'" 194–205; Kertelge, "Gesetz und Freiheit im Galaterbrief," 382–94; Räisänen, *Paul and the Law*, 77–81; Sanders, *Paul, the Law, and the Jewish People*, 15 note 26, 97–105; Schoeps, *Paul*, 171–75; 200–03; Smiles, *Gospel and the Law*, 219–25; Stanton, "What is the Law of Christ?" 47–59; Strelan, "Burden-bearing and the Law of Christ," 266–76; Wilson, "Law of Christ," 123–44.

26. This Christ-centered focus is also known as Christocentrism.

27. This section and the thrust of the idea that in Gal 2:20 Christ lives in the believer by means of his Spirit is not to say that the Spirit and Christ are identical. The Spirit is still a distinct person and has certain distinct roles, but within the believer in this context, the Spirit serves to reveal Christ in and to the believer. The Spirit serves to empower the believer to live out the life of Christ. As Dunn writes, "Jesus did not absorb the role of the Spirit . . . *there was still a role for the Spirit not restricted to Christ*, and yet the Spirit was to be recognized now as *the Spirit of Jesus*, as the Spirit bearing and generating the character of Christ" (Dunn, "Towards the Spirit of Christ," 25). See also Kärkkäinen, "How to Speak," 61: "Considering the relationship between Christ and the Spirit mutually presupposing does not in any way deny the universal, cosmic sphere of the ministry of the Spirit." And Burton, "It is, of course, the heavenly Christ of whom he speaks, who in religious experience is not distinguishable from the Spirit of God (*cf.* chapter 5:16, 18, 25)" (Burton, *Galatians*, 137).

28. Gal 3:2: "Let me ask you only this: Did you receive the Spirit by works of the law or by hearing with faith?"

audience of the preeminent role of Christ in the spiritual life. Later in 3:14, the reception of the Spirit through faith is injected in the discussion concerning the justified life. Just as Christ lives in the believer by faith (2:20), the promised Spirit is received by faith. This connection is further clarified in Galatians 4:4–7 where believers are reminded of their redemption from under the law for the purpose of being adopted as sons.[29] The evidence, the guarantee, given to believers that they are now children of God is the indwelling presence of the Spirit of Christ.[30] When believers are justified, they are also redeemed from the law, adopted as sons, and filled with Christ by means of his Spirit. Paul is making a direct correlation between Christ and the Spirit. The Spirit serves as a representative of Jesus the Christ in the children of God. As a result, they are no longer slaves, but free to serve God as co-heirs with Christ. This more complete picture was introduced and summarized in Galatians 2:20 and then alluded to later in 4:19.[31]

Galatians 2:20 then explains that through faith Christ now lives within believers by means of his Spirit who empowers them for Christian living. That summary is expanded in greater detail in Galatians 5:16–24.[32] There, Paul, stressing the continual struggle the believer will experience against the flesh, challenges believers to live life under the controlling influence of the Spirit of Christ, crucifying the passions of the flesh.

Elsewhere, Paul presents the same thought challenging believers to live life under the influence of the Spirit, as Christ's representative, manifesting Christ's life through them to the glory of God. At salvation, the child of God is adopted, redeemed, and equipped for Christian living by the presence of his Spirit. Romans 8:8–13 challenges believers to walk in Christ's righteousness, because they have the Spirit of Christ and should no longer to live out the impulses of the flesh.[33]

29. Gal 4:4–7: "But when the fullness of time had come, God sent forth his Son, born of woman, born under the law, to redeem those who were under the law, so that we might receive adoption as sons. And because you are sons, God has sent the Spirit of his Son into our hearts, crying, 'Abba! Father!' So you are no longer a slave, but a son, and if a son, then an heir through God."

30. See also Rom 8:9.

31. Hendriksen, *Galatians*, 176. Gal 4:19: "My little children, for whom I am again in the anguish of childbirth until Christ is formed in you!"

32. As Burton explains, "It is, of course, the heavenly Christ of whom he speaks, who in religious experience is not distinguishable from the Spirit of God (*cf.* chapter 5:16, 18, 25)" (Burton, *Galatians*, 137).

33. See also 1 Cor 6:17 where the believer is said to be one spirit with the Lord and its connection to 2 Cor 3:17 where the Lord is said to be Spirit.

Nowhere, perhaps, in Pauline literature is the connection between the continual work of Christ through the work of the Spirit more evident than in Ephesians 3:14–19.[34]

> For this reason I bow my knees before the Father, from whom every family in heaven and on earth is named, that according to the riches of his glory he may grant you to be strengthened with power through his Spirit in your inner being, so that Christ may dwell in your hearts through faith—that you, being rooted and grounded in love, may have strength to comprehend with all the saints what is the breadth and length and height and depth, and to know the love of Christ that surpasses knowledge, that you may be filled with all the fullness of God.

Specifically, verses 16–17a will be examined in detail to build this connection. Having established how those who were once far away from God have been brought near to God through the priceless sacrifice of Christ Jesus, who reconciled them to God through his death (Eph 2:13), the apostle Paul prays his second prayer of the epistle.[35] After introducing the prayer, its content is provided.[36] The prayer's initial component is that God, who is the implied subject, would grant them "to be strengthened."[37] This strengthening is to be granted "according to the riches of his glory."[38] The prayer con-

---

34. Contra D. Martyn Lloyd-Jones, who adamantly denies that this text is equating the presence of Christ with that of the Spirit in the life of the believer. He proclaims, "It is Christ dwelling within the believer—not as an influence, not as a memory, not merely through His teaching, not merely through the Holy Spirit. It is Christ *Himself* dwelling within him in a mystical relationship . . . The Lord Jesus Christ is in heaven, but he is also in me" (Lloyd-Jones, *Unsearchable Riches of Christ*, 8:159–60). Lloyd-Jones mentions Gal 2:20 in connection with these comments as well. Another strong connection can be seen between Eph 5:18–20 and Col 3:16.

35. Discussions of the authorship of Eph are beyond the scope of this book; however, Pauline authorship is preferred. For a defense of Pauline authorship, see O'Brien, *Ephesians*, 4–47. Contra Lincoln, *Ephesians*, lix–xxii, who presupposes a follower of Paul to be the author. The first prayer is provided in 1:15–23.

36. ἵνα usually denotes purpose; however, in the context of praying, the purpose for the prayer is often expressed in terms of the actual content of the prayer. Therefore, in this case, ἵνα conjoins the one to whom the author prays with the content of what is actually prayed (Hoehner, *Ephesians*, 477). See Matt 24:20 as another example.

37. The implied subject "he" of δῷ is a reference to "Father" in v. 14, which is a title given to God. "To be strengthened" (κραταιωθῆναι) is a complementary divine passive infinitive. The request is that they would be strengthened by God in accordance with the riches of his glory.

38. Similar statements have been made throughout Eph: 1:7, 12, 14, 18; 2:4, 7; 3:8.

tinues to request that these saints be strengthened "with power" by means of "his Spirit." This power is God's power. It is the same power attributed to God in the middle of the epistle's first prayer in Ephesians 1:19. Now, that power, previously attributed solely to God, is requested to be bestowed upon these believers by means of the Spirit. Such a request implies the divinity of the Spirit as the One who is able to bring the power of God into the life of the believer.[39] The "inner man" where this strengthening with power by the Spirit is to take place, is best understood as the immaterial inner part of man's moral being paralleling the author's references to the "heart" of a person, which is found elsewhere throughout the epistle.[40]

The content portion of the prayer (3:16–19) is structured so that 3:16 is clarified and restated in 3:17a, while 3:18 is clarified and restated in 3:19a.[41] As a result of the pattern, "to be strengthened with power through his Spirit in the inner man" is explained as "Christ dwelling in your hearts through faith" and this is requested so that "you, being rooted and grounded in love, may be able to comprehend what is the breadth and length and height and

---

For a brief exposition on the glory of God, see Bruce, *Colossians, Philemon, Ephesians*, 326; Hodge, *Ephesians*, 181.

39. Lenski, *Ephesians*, 493. Such an implication of the divinity of the Spirit is not unique in Eph. As Lincoln explains, "Power is to be mediated to believers by the Spirit, who has been previously mentioned as the one by whom believers are sealed, as the guarantee of the full salvation of the age to come (1:13, 14), and as the means by which God is present in the church (2:22). Spirit and power of the age to come, and that association is continued here" (Lincoln, *Ephesians*, 205).

40. See 1:18; 3:17; 4:18; 5:19; 6:5, 22. Other passages demonstrate this same usage. "Inner" (ἔσω) is used eight other times in the New Testament (Matt 26:58; Mark 15:16; John 20:26; Acts 5:23; Rom 7:22; 1 Cor 5:12; 2 Cor 4:16). Of those, only Rom 7:22 and 2 Cor 4:16 are used in the same way as Eph 3:16. All other references deal with the idea of being "within" or "inside" various structures; although, all references show the inward emphasis of the word. While Rom 7:22 is a more heavily debated context (Rom 7:22 does not provide the clear grammatical links that 2 Cor does for understanding more specifically what Paul means by "inner man"), 2 Cor 4:16 proves most significant for these purposes. Within that setting, the "inner man" of 4:16 is contextually paralleled with "heart" in both 4:6 and 5:12 (O'Brien, *Ephesians*, 258). Additionally, though the words "inner man" are not used, 1 Pet 3:4 ("the hidden person of the heart" [ὁ κρυπτὸς τῆς καρδίας ἄνθρωπος]) provides an interesting parallel to Eph 3:16 supporting the view that "inner man" is to be understood as being synonymously with "heart" in this context (Lincoln, *Ephesians*, 205–6). Additionally, John 7:37–39 shows that the Spirit of Christ will reside and flow out of the hearts of believers (i.e., their inner being), and John 14:16–17 states that the Spirit will be in believers.

41. See also Witherington III for another strong argument for seeing this structure (Witherington III, *Ephesians*, 273). So also Bouttier, *L'Épître De Saint Paul Aux Éphésiens*, 153–4.

depth," which is explained as "knowing the love of Christ which surpasses knowledge." Both verses 16 and 18 begin with a content clause (ἵνα + the subjunctive) followed by two infinitives which explain one another. Thus, 3:16 is clarified by 3:17a and 3:18 is clarified by 3:19a.[42]

As a result of this pattern, the next infinitive clause (17a—"in other words, that Christ may dwell in your hearts through faith") serves to explain exactly what is meant by the request that the readers be "strengthened with power by his Spirit in the inner man."[43] Thus, the indwelling of Christ parallels the empowerment of the Spirit. The author is praying that Christ would be "at the very center of or deeply rooted in believers' lives."[44] He is praying that they would walk in faith under the abiding rule of Christ similar to Galatians 5:16, 25 where believers are encouraged to walk in the Spirit so that they will not carry out the desires of the flesh. Thus, believers need the sustaining presence of Christ. This presence of Christ is facilitated by the indwelling work of his Spirit. Therefore, to experience the Spirit is to experience the presence of Christ.[45] As Lincoln explains, "Believers do not experience Christ except as Spirit and do not experience the Spirit except as Christ. The implication, as far as this prayer is concerned, is that greater experience of the Spirit's power will mean the character of Christ increasingly becoming the hallmark of believers' lives."[46] A beautiful picture of the Trinity exists here showing how "all three persons of the Trinity are very involved in the redemption and growth of believers."[47] Moreover, this habi-

42. The second infinitive in each of these cases is taken as an "epexegetical" infinitive versus a "purpose/result" infinitive, contra Hoehner, *Ephesians*, 481.

43. So, Abbott, *Ephesians*, 96; Bruce, *Ephesians*, 326–27; Hendriksen, *Galatians*, 171; Hodge, *Ephesians*, 184; Lincoln, *Ephesians*, 206; O'Brien, *Ephesians*, 258; Westcott, *Ephesians*, 51–52.

44. Hoehner, *Ephesians*, 481.

45. Developing or elaborating upon the doctrine of the Trinity is beyond the scope of this section; however, these statements are in no way indicating that there is not distinction of person among the Trinity. While the Spirit is the Spirit of Christ, distinctions of roles among their persons still exist. For an examination of the doctrine of the Trinity, see Ware, *Father, Son, Holy Spirit*. Burton also interacts with the interchangeable use of Spirit of God and Spirit of Christ within Pauline literature arguing that "we may say that in his [Paul's] thought the Spirit of God is the personalized power of God, operative in the spirits of men, not distinguishable, in experience at least, from the heavenly Christ" (Burton, *Spirit, Soul, Flesh*, 190).

46. Lincoln, *Ephesians*, 206.

47. Hoehner, *Ephesians*, 482. Here and throughout Eph: 1:4–14, 17; 2:18, 22; 3:4–5, 14–17; 4:4–6; 5:18–20. List taken from Hoehner (ibid.).

tation of Christ in the heart of the believer is by means of faith. The same faith that was integral in procuring salvation (Eph 2:5, 8) is now described as necessary in abiding in relationship with Christ.[48] That connection is the same described in Galatians 2:20. As James D. G. Dunn elaborates in connecting the thoughts of Galatians 2:20b, Ephesians 3:17 and other similar passages,

> The idea of "Christ indwelling" the believer (Rom. viii.10; 2 Cor. xiii.5; Col. 1:27; Eph. iii.17) is much less common in Paul than its reverse, the believer "in Christ" (see on i.22 and ii.17). More typical of Paul is the thought of the Spirit indwelling or acting in the believer (Rom. v.5; viii.9, 11, 15–16, 23, 26; etc.; see on iii.2). Experientially, it comes to the same thing: the awareness of a new focus of identity expressed in different goals and new inner dynamic, with Christ as the inspiration and Christ-likeness the paradigm ('mystical' if you like, though many are suspicious of the word's connotations). Theologically, it means that for Christians the Spirit of God is also now to be recognized as the Spirit of Christ and the personal existence of the post-resurrection Christ cannot be thought of simply as having an individual bodily focus. . . . Nor should the continuity with verse 19c be forgotten: "The Christ who lives in me is the crucified Christ" (Ebeling 149).[49]

The idea that the Spirit serves as Christ's representative in the believer's life equipping them for Christian living is not unique to Paul's writings. John also makes this point. In John 14:16–20, Jesus explains that he will be in his disciples through the Spirit he will send as his representative. John makes the point that Christ abides in his followers by means of his Spirit in 1 John 3:24: "Whoever keeps his commandments abides in him, and he in them. And by this we know that he abides in us, by the Spirit whom he has given us."

Therefore, in light of the proposed evidence, Paul, maintaining a Christocentric focus concerning the Christian life, presents Christ in the

---

48. "Just as faith has played its part in believers' appropriation of the salvation (2:5, 8) and access to God (3:12) that have been accomplished for them, so also it is 'through faith' that Christ's dwelling in the heart remains a reality for them" (Lincoln, *Ephesians*, 206–7). Questions concerning what happens should someone cease to express saving faith are beyond the scope of this section; however, it will be stated that such questions are inappropriately provoked. The same faith that initiates salvation in the life of the believers is always seen as and expected to be the same faith that will sustain them in salvation. In other words, true faith never ultimately falters to the point of abandonment.

49. Dunn, *Galatians*, 145–46.

believer representatively by means of his Spirit in Galatians 2:20b. Michael J. Gorman ties these thoughts together well,

> Crucial in this text [Galatians 2:20] to Paul's overall argument in Galatians is that the Spirit is the Spirit *of the Son*. When Paul later says that believers live or walk by the Spirit (5:16, 25), he is saying that they live by the Spirit *of the Son*. In other words, they live by means of the indwelling Son of God or, as Paul puts it, "by [means of] the faith of the Son of God" (2:20). These phrases in turn cannot be disconnected from Paul's assertion that he and all believers have been crucified *with* Christ and baptized *into* Christ. The Christ in whom believers dwell and who dwells in believers is indeed equated with the Spirit, but this living Christ is also equated with the crucified Christ. Thus the Spirit is the Spirit of the Son, the Son who demonstrated *faith* (toward the Father) by giving himself in *love* (for others).[50]

No longer does the old fleshly *ego* necessitate the direction of one's life. The believer is then equipped by Christ through means of his Spirit for the life he is now to live in the flesh by faith.

If this assessment is correct, then the believer is empowered by the Spirit of Christ in conjunction with being justified and co-crucified with Christ. The life of the Spirit in the Christian is set in contrast with the reality that the *ego* no longer lives, so that Christ might be promoted.

Critique of Pentecostalism

Unfortunately, some contemporary views within Christian spirituality misunderstand the presence of the Spirit as Christ's representative equipping the believer for living in a manner reflective of Christ.[51] Those who advo-

---

50. Gorman, *Cruciformity*, 220.

51. Some also misunderstand the role of Christ. One error that will not be addressed in the flow of this book is the actual dismissal of the centrality of Christ in the Christian life. This dismissal is seen, among other places, in certain feminist theologians. Rita Nakashima Brock seeks to recast the Christian life around community versus Christ. She dismisses the idea of a heroic single savior. She explains, "In moving beyond a unilateral understanding of power, I will be developing a Christology *not centered in Jesus*, but in relationship and community as the whole-making, healing center of Christianity. In that sense, Christ is what I am calling Christa/Community [her footnote here is key. N. 2 on p. 113 correlates to this sentence. At one point she says, 'In using Christa instead of Christ, I am using a term that points away from a sole identification of Christ with Jesus. In combining it with community, I want to shift the focus of salvation away from heroic

cate that the believer is not adequately equipped for Christian ministry at conversion will be specifically discussed.[52] If at the moment the believer is declared just by faith in Christ he is also co-crucified with Christ and Christ lives in him by means of the Spirit equipping him for Christian living, then the believer is adequately equipped for Christian living at the moment of salvation. This aspect of Galatians 2:20, when heeded, corrects the misun-

---

individuals, male or female.'. Jesus participates centrally in this Christa/Community, but he neither brings erotic power into being nor controls it. He is brought into being through it and participates in the cocreation of it. Christa/Community is lived reality expressed in relational images. Hence Christa/Community is described in the images of events in which erotic power is made manifest. . . . The relational nature of erotic power is as true during Jesus' life as it is after his death. He neither reveals it nor embodies it, but he participates in its revelation and embodiment. . . . Heart—*the self* in original grace—is our guide into the territories of erotic power. . . . This feminist Christology, *in being guided by heart*, develops another way to understand Christ that will lead us away from the territories of patriarchy and into a world in which incarnation will refer to the whole of human life" (Brock, *Journeys*, 52). See also Brown and Bohn, "God so Love," 1–30; Cooey, "Redemption," 106–30. These writers are explicitly trying to change the way people live as professing Christians and change the way people understand Christianity. Due to the diminished role of Christ in some of these views, serious questions exist concerning whether or not they should fall into the category of Christianity. Joanne Brown and Rebecca Parker after redefining the redemptive role of Christ express their own questions in this regard. "This raises the key question for oppressed people seeking liberation with this tradition [Christianity]: If we throw out the atonement is Christianity left? Can we call our new creation Christianity even with an asterisk" (Brown and Bohn, "God so Love," 27)? Such views within Christianity that seek to diminish the significance of the God/man Jesus and replace his role in the Christian life with self or community are terribly misguided and conflict directly with Scripture. Matt 28:19–20 reveals that believers proclaim all that Jesus has taught them. It is his message declared. Acts 1:8 shows that believers will be Jesus's witnesses to the world. Many passages declare the central role of Jesus in the Christian life even beyond the initial act of redemption. These types of views that diminish the Christocentricism of the redeemed present a subjective approach that a biblically-grounded Christian spirituality will help correct.

52. This discussion will be limited to those, primarily within Pentecostalism, who hold to the belief that a baptism of the Spirit is needed after conversion in order to equip the believer for Christian living. What will not be addressed here, but would also be corrected by a biblically-grounded Christian spirituality as demonstrated from Gal 2:20, are those within the Campbelite tradition that either argue that one is not saved until water baptism or that one may be saved, but does not receive the Spirit until water baptism (Baxter, "Who are Churches of Christ"). As Keener appropriately critiques, "Paul is clear that one receives all of Christ's provision at conversion. Those who try to add to the finished work of Christ, whether they be circumcizers in Galatia or mystics in Colossae, undermine the gospel itself. At conversion we were 'sealed' in Christ for the day of redemption (Eph. 4:30); those who do not have the Spirit are simply not Christians (Rom. 8:9)" (Keener, *Gift & Giver*, 154).

derstanding that the believer needs to seek a second experience of grace after conversion for the baptism or filling of the Holy Spirit in order to be equipped for ministry.[53] This point does not deny that the Spirit may come upon people in unique ways for particular seasons, but dismisses the idea that believers should seek a "second experience" of the Spirit or a "baptism" of the Spirit after conversion in order to be adequately equipped to serve Christ (1 Sam 19:20–23; Ezek 3:12; 1 Pet 1:10–11; 2 Pet 1:21). The issue consistently in the New Testament is submission to the Spirit not the reception of a greater portion of that same Spirit.[54]

This error that after conversion the believer needs to seek a second experience of grace through Holy Spirit baptism in order to be equipped for ministry is prevalent in Pentecostalism.[55] Their approach in this regard should not be taken to assume that they do not see a work of the Spirit in salvation. "Responsible Pentecostals have always taught that one is indwelt by the Spirit at the time of conversion (Rom. 8:9; 1 Cor. 6:19), but that the baptism in the Spirit is an experience of the Spirit distinct from His indwelling."[56] Thus, this baptism of the Spirit in their teaching is not essential for salvation, because it is distinct from the work of the Spirit (indwelling) at salvation. For them, this approach does not diminish "the work of the Holy Spirit in the new birth," instead "it simply opens unto [believers] a whole new realm of spiritual possibilities."[57]

Part of the problem comes from the confusion that baptism into Christ is different from baptism in the Holy Spirit. Pentecostals see one's baptism into Christ in conjunction with a filling of the Spirit at conversion, while a baptism in the Spirit is a later experience.[58] They do this by arguing

53. For a more exhaustive refutation of the Pentecostal position in this regard, see Dunn, *Baptism*. For a Pentecostal critique of Dunn, see Ervin, *Conversion-Initiation*.

54. Some may argue that such a distinction is made in Acts. Below, it will be shown that the consistent New Testament witness is that the Spirit is fully received in salvation, but the believer is to grow in submission to that Spirit. Additionally, it will be argued that the Acts narrative is complementary to and not contrary to the Pauline testimony related to a filling of and baptism in the Spirit.

55. For some historical perspectives on the movement, see Blumhofer et al., *Pentecostal Currents*; Hollenweger, *Pentecostals*; idem, *Pentecostalism*; Kay, *Pentecostalism*; Robins, *Pentecostalism in America*. For a balanced and thoughtful Pentecostal approach to Baptism, see Keener, *3 Crucial Questions*; idem, *Gift & Giver*. Keener's *Gift & Giver* incorporates much of his previous work *3 Crucial Questions*.

56. Palma, *Holy Spirit*, 116.

57. Horton, "Spirit Baptism," 60.

58. "On the other hand, when Pentecostal scholars say that the Baptism is available

that there are three distinct baptisms in the New Testament: baptism into Christ, water baptism, and a baptism in the Spirit.

> The Apostle Paul, in Ephesians 4:5 says there is "one Lord, one faith, one baptism," yet it is clear that in the New Testament this 'one baptism' divides into three. In 1 Corinthians 12:13, Paul says: "In one Spirit we were all baptized into one Body . . . and were all made to drink into one Spirit." This refers to the spiritual baptism into Christ which takes place as soon as Jesus is received as Savior. This was followed by the baptism with the Holy Spirit, in which the now indwelling Holy Spirit poured forth to manifest Jesus to the world through the life of the believer.[59]

Yet, the New Testament evidence shows that to receive Christ is to receive the Spirit.[60] First Cor 12:13–31 explicitly declares that to not have Spirit baptism is to not be in the body of Christ. Additionally, Paul in his declaration assumes that every believer reading the letter has been baptized in the Spirit. The inclusion into the body of Christ and Paul's confidence that all believers have had this experience despite any new converts present indicates that this experience happened in conjunction with the new birth. Some within the Pentecostal community may try and argue that 1 Cor 12:13 does not refer to Spirit baptism, but this distinction is contextually hard to maintain.[61] The biblical distinction sought by many (especially within Pentecostalism) simply does not exist.

The Pentecostal distinction between baptism in the Spirit and baptism in Christ exists in part because many within this theological perspective see a need for the believer to be equipped for Christian living and ministry after conversion.[62] Spirit Baptism in this regard "is an initiation into power min-

---

to believers today, they are insisting upon the contemporary availability of a separable [from conversion], distinct experience that is evidenced by speaking in tongues" (Wyckoff, "Baptism," 444).

59. Bennett and Bennett, *Holy Spirit and You*, 34.

60. The New Testament evidence will be examined below.

61. The doctrinal statement for the Assemblies of God references this passage in support for the necessity of Spirit baptism ("Baptism"). See also the position paper "Baptism," yet it is surprising that attempts are still made to maintain that it happens distinct from conversion despite the text talking about it happening in conjunction with the believer's inclusion in the body of Christ. For further comments regarding Pentecostalism and 1 Cor 12:13, see Grudem, *Systematic Theology*, 766–8. Grudem has a section of his systematic theology dedicated to baptism in and filling with the Holy Spirit.

62. Spirit baptism, from their perspective, may happen in conjunction with conversion, but is an experience distinct from conversion. "This experience [Spirit baptism] is

istry distinct from salvation, regeneration, justification, sanctification or any other work we would classify as 'the Spirit within.'"[63] It is an equipping, an initiation, of power for Christian living and ministry, so that after initial baptism into Christ, a baptism in the Spirit should be sought. This baptism enables one to carry out the ministry to which that person was called. Don Basham in his *Handbook on Holy Spirit Baptism* explains, "The baptism in the Holy Spirit is a second encounter with God (the first is conversion) in which the Christian begins to receive the supernatural power of the Holy Spirit into his life. . . . This second experience of the power of God, which we call the baptism in the Holy Spirit, is given for the purpose of equipping the Christian with God's power for service."[64] He would continue to clarify part of his reasoning for such a claim. "The Lord is not satisfied with our conversion alone; He has promised us power to be His witnesses. So, a second time we are confronted with the power of God; this time in the baptism in the Holy Spirit through which the Christian is brought into a deeper relationship with Christ and the Holy Spirit for the purpose of making him—not an *object*—but an *instrument* of redemption."[65] Notice, the focus becomes the believer's equipping for ministry post-conversion, but that is not what Paul declares happens with Christ "in me." Paul declares that in conjunction with one's justification through faith in Christ, he is co-crucified with the Messiah. This co-crucifixion results in a death of one's fleshly *ego* and the indwelling presence of the Spirit of Christ within him.[66]

---

logically and theologically separate from the conversion experience, though it may take place either immediately upon conversion or some time afterward" (Palma, *Holy Spirit*, 108).

63. Long and McMurry, *Receiving the Power*, 96.

64. Basham, *Handbook*, 21.

65. Ibid., 22–23.

66. This death of one's fleshly ego, in one sense, is not an immediate and total elimination of the influence of the flesh, nor is it necessarily an immediate or total submission to the Spirit. The death is immediate and total in the sense that one is no longer defined or depicted by God in reference to their Adamic nature (identity), but in regards to the living out of this new center and no longer giving into the desires of the flesh, the process is generally progressive and not immediate. Evidence for this position can be seen with the imperative of Gal 5:16 and the admonition that follows. This idea will be developed in the next chapter of this book, but here it is sufficient to point out that a contrast should be kept between positional and progressive sanctification. The believer is made holy at salvation (positionally), and they are to grow (progressively) becoming more holy in their actions. For clarification regarding these, see Erickson, *Christian Theology*, 980–3; Grudem, *Systematic Theology*, 746–62. For an interesting look at the role of community in progressive sanctification, see Howard, *Paul*.

Most Pentecostals would agree with this point. The disagreement would come in equating this indwelling presence of the Spirit with the baptism of the Spirit that empowers one for Christian ministry. The problem with this distinction Pentecostals seek to make[67] is that the apostle in Galatians 2:20 will immediately follow the declaration that Christ now lives in the believer with the statement that the believer, as a result of the indwelling presence of Christ, now lives differently in the flesh.[68] His life is now governed by Christ through faith in a way that he is now equipped, empowered, to live differently. Paul will go on, as evidenced earlier in this book, to demonstrate the ability the believer has, as a result of Christ in him, to live in the power of that Spirit and not give in to the desires of the flesh (Gal 5:16). In other words, the believer is now, at conversion, empowered by the Spirit of Christ to carry out the life of Christ in their daily living and ministry. Dunn similarly argues:

> The life which is "Christ in me" is the same thing as the life of the Spirit in me (cf. [Gal.] 5:25).
>
> For Paul ζωή [life] is very much the result of the Spirit's operation (Gal. 3.11–14; 5.25; 6.8; Rom. 8.2, 10; II Cor. 3.3, 6; cf. 5.4f.). The thought of Gal. 2.20 is closely parallel to that of Rom. 8.10 which is an alternative way of expressing 8.9—"the Spirit of God dwells in you" . . .
>
> And for another, the crucifixion metaphor is taken up again in 5.24 as the conclusion to the exhortation: 'Walk by the Spirit and do not gratify the desires of the flesh' (5.16–24). The Spirit probably does not feature here [Gal 2.20] because Paul wishes to put his primary emphasis on Christ; but so far as Pentecostalism is concerned, it must be emphasized that the moment when Christ began to "live in me" cannot be distinguished from the reception of the Spirit who is the life of "Christ in me".
>
> As might be expected where justification is the underlying theme, faith is prominent as the means by which the individual receives this justification and lives out the life of "Christ in me."[69]

When Dunn says that the Spirit is not featured in Galatians 2:20, he is not saying that the Spirit in Galatians 2:20 is different from the empowering

---

67. Between conversion and then equipping for life and ministry.

68. Additionally, one could argue from what Paul does not say. Paul never urges believers to seek a baptism of the Spirit. The closest reference would be his command to "walk in the Spirit" (Gal 5:16) or "be filled with the Spirit" (Eph 5:18) each of which will be discussed below.

69. Dunn, *Baptism*, 107.

work as the Spirit in Galatians 5; rather, he is arguing that the Spirit is not mentioned in Galatians 2:20 because of Paul's Christological focus. The Spirit of Christ of Galatians 2:20 is the empowering Spirit of Galatians 5. They are one in the same.

At the same time, it should be noted that Pentecostals are quite right that believers cannot be effective for Christian ministry without the empowering work of the Holy Spirit. After all, Acts 1:8 clearly explains that believers will not be the witnesses they are called to be without the empowering work of the Spirit. This truth is why Jesus told the disciples to wait in Jerusalem rather than just going out on their own power. Even today, the church should seek to function under the direction and influence of the Holy Spirit for effective ministry. Nonetheless, this submission to the Spirit should not be mistaken for a baptism in the Spirit. Dunn explains this issue as well:

> The positive value of the Pentecostal's emphasis is his highlighting of the dramatic nature of the initiating Spirit-baptism: the Spirit not only renews, he also equips for service and witness. Yet, however correct Pentecostals are to point to a fresh empowering of the Spirit as the answer to the Church's sickness, they are quite wrong to call it "the baptism in the Spirit". One does not enter into the new age or the Christian life more than once, but one may be empowered by or filled with the Spirit many times (Acts 2.4; 4.8, 31; 9.17; 13.9; Eph. 5:18).[70]

This quote prompts an important question. What is this continual filling of the Spirit and is it consistent with the context of Galatians 2:20? The concept of a filling of the Spirit can be a confusing one. If not careful, this teaching can communicate that one needs a greater portion of the Spirit after conversion for Christian living. The idea that one has the Spirit as a believer, but needs to seek a continual filling of the Spirit comes primarily from Ephesians 5:18 where Paul declares to believers that they are not to "get drunk with wine, for that is debauchery, but be filled with the Spirit." Keith Warrington writes from a Pentecostal perspective and provides some helpful comments on this verse showing that it is not referring to a "Baptism of the Spirit."

> Although some have understood this verse as describing the post-conversion baptism in the Spirit, this is less the case by modern Pentecostals. Instead, they identify it as an imperative to benefit from the controlling influence of the Spirit in the lives of believers

---

70. Dunn, *Baptism*, 54. Contra Hunter, *Spirit-Baptism*, 283.

on a daily basis and distinct from the baptism in the Spirit. In this respect, it is the iterative sense of the verb 'be filled' that is often advocated though some prefer to identify it with a meaning that indicates not repeated fillings but a continued experience of the Spirit in the light of an earlier filling of the Spirit.[71]

As a result of the confusion surrounding this verse, it will be examined in greater detail. Debauchery is essentially an uninhibited living out of one's fleshly desires.[72] It is allowing one's impulses to drive them. The text contrasts the influence of alcohol and the influence of the Spirit. Paul is challenging believers. Just as when people are drunk with wine, they lose their inhibitions and allow the alcohol to influence their behavior, in the same way, believers are to yield their will to the presence of the Spirit within them in such a way as to allow him to be the controlling influence in their lives.[73] This command to "be filled" with the Spirit is in the present tense and, therefore, is taken to emphasize a continually filling that the believer needs to experience in order to live the community life to which God has called them (Eph 5:18–21).[74] The problem comes when it is argued that the believer needs a greater portion of the Spirit, or a second experience, of the Spirit post conversion.

Four imperatives concerning the Spirit in the life of believers empowering them for living out the life of Christ are given in the New Testament.[75] A glance at these four imperatives collectively helps clarify what Paul is advocating in Ephesians 5:18 and the context of Galatians 2:20. Each imperative gives a different perspective of the same command, to live in submission to the Spirit. Two are negative and two are positive.

---

71. Warrington, *Pentecostal Theology*, 115.

72. This word (ἀσωτία) appears three times in the New Testament: Eph 5:18; Titus 1:6; 1 Pet 4:4.

73. Abbott helps, stating, "The antithesis is not directly between οἶνος [wine] and πνεῦμα [Spirit], as the order of the words shows, but between the two states" (Abbott, *Ephesians*, 161). Ervin also speaks to this parallel in *Conversion-Initiation*, 101. Ryrie would comment on this verse in relationship to the spiritual life saying, "To be filled with the Spirit means to be controlled by the Spirit" (Ryrie, *Balancing the Christian Life*, 13). See also Chafer, *He that is Spiritual*, 43–44.

74. So Robertson, *Grammar*, 890. The community results of being filled with the Spirit are described as Spirit-filled praise (Eph 5:19), Spirit-filled thanks (Eph 5:20), and Spirit-filled submission (Eph 5:21, further described all the way through 6:9).

75. Gal 5:16; Eph 4:30; 5:18; 1 Thess 5:19.

The negative commands are found in Ephesians 4:30 and 1 Thessalonians 5:19.[76] Ephesians 4:22–24 stresses that Christians are no longer to live out the impulses of the flesh, but to live out the power of the new self they have in Christ. The text goes on to contrast this new life in Christ with the old life in the flesh. Paul warns believers not to grieve the Holy Spirit, by whom they are sealed for the day of redemption (Eph 4:30).[77] In this statement, Paul is explaining that the Spirit given at redemption empowers believers to live out the life to which they are called.[78] First Thessalonians 5:19 gives the second negative command. 5:16–22 lists several closing commands in a row ending with the command to abstain from every form of evil. Specifically, verse 19 tells them not to quench the Spirit, but does not elaborate contextually upon what that means. The context seems to imply that not quenching the Spirit was understood in contrast with living out evil influences and suppressing the gifts of the Spirit.[79]

The two positive commands are found in Galatians 5:16 and Ephesians 5:18. The context of Galatians 5:16 has been emphasized throughout this book. In that verse, believers are shown to be those already in possession of the Spirit. They are commanded to walk in the Spirit in order that they would not live out the desires of the flesh. The implication is that they have the Spirit, but need to live in submission to that Spirit in order

---

76. Eph 4:30: "And do not grieve the Holy Spirit of God, by whom you were sealed for the day of redemption." 1 Thess 5:19: "Do not quench the Spirit."

77. Eph 4:30 should not be taken to assume that one can lose their salvation (Abbott, *Ephesians*, 143–4; Arnold, *Ephesians*, 306–7).

78. So Arnold, "Evil speech . . . hurts the Spirit, whom God has given to his people to indwell them and empower them to live a holy life" (Arnold, *Ephesians*, 305). See also Lincoln, *Ephesians*, 306–7, who also expands this idea in regards to the eschatological redemptions believers will experience. Contra Horton, "Spirit Baptism," 68; Ervin, *Conversion-Initiation*, 124, who see the sealing of the Spirit as a post-conversion experience. In response to that perspective, Warrington states, "However, there is little evidence that would indicate that belief in Jesus is separated in time from the sealing of the Spirit" (Warrington, *Pentecostal Theology*, 114).

79. Wanamaker does not view the command in as an "ethical reorientation"; rather, views the command to specifically be given so that they would not "restrain the Spirit from manifesting itself in charismatic activities" (Wanamaker, *Thessalonians*, 202). However as Morris explains the text is not that clear and such a sharp distinction between the ethical and ecstatic manifestation of the Spirit cannot easily be made (Morris, *Thessalonians*, 175). Either way it is clear that the believer is to submit to the Spirit and not resist him. The text is not commanding the follower of Christ to seek a greater portion of the Spirit, but to allow the Spirit to lead in their lives and community.

to be effective for Christian living.[80] Galatians 5:16–23 emphasizes that contrast between living out the influence of the Spirit received at salvation (Gal 3:2–3, 5, 14; 4:6, 29) and living out the influence of the flesh whose influential power was dethroned at salvation. That is why the command of Galatians 5:16 comes to a climax in 5:24–25 when they are reminded that in their co-crucifixion with Christ the power of the flesh was done away with and the Spirit was given. Thus, spiritual life was given with the indwelling presence of the Spirit of Christ from Galatians 2:20.[81] If this life has been experienced, then believers should walk in accordance with the influence of the Spirit that now resides within them.

The second positive command is found in Ephesians 5:18. As discussed above, the command implies a continual filling of the Spirit, but this filling is not a greater portion of the Spirit. In accordance with the other four commands, it becomes evident that the filling of the Spirit is another way of challenging believers to live in continual greater submission to the Spirit received at salvation. Believers are being called to submit their wills in greater portion to the influential power of the Spirit that was bestowed upon them and resides within them at salvation. Thus, they are continually to be filled, controlled by, submitted to the Spirit of God.

Therefore, as it relates to Galatians 2:20, it becomes more apparent that those who express faith in Christ are given the empowering presence of Christ in their life by means of his Spirit for the purpose of living out a life of faith. They are, then, fully equipped for Christian living at the moment of salvation, but need to grow in awareness of and submission to the presence of the Spirit of Christ within them. That emphasis is made by Paul in Galatians 5:16 and is seen also in the other three commands given concerning the Spirit. Craig Keener helps in bringing a balanced perspective to traditional Pentecostal theology by allowing Scripture to interpret and help one understand their experiences.[82] He focuses on bridging the teaching of Spirit empowered living with the experience of Spirit empowered living. Keener acknowledges that these imperatives related to the Spirit show that all the believer needs of the Spirit is given at conversion, but continues to

---

80. Warrington reiterates this thought: "Speaking to the Christians living in the region of Galatia (Gal. 5.16–18), Paul states that the Spirit is to be their guide in life and that they should take advantage of his influence (v. 16)" (Warrington, *Pentecostal Theology*, 64).

81. Spiritual life in terms of having life with the Spirit (1 Cor 2:14–15).

82. Keener is a professor at Asbury Theological Seminary with a Pentecostal background. For more on Keener, see his personal website "About Craig Keener."

argue that some do not experience certain aspects of the Spirit's influence until after conversion. He says that "full access to God's transforming power at conversion need not imply that each of us has appropriated all that power in our daily lives. I suspect most of us will admit that in practice we may later yield more of our lives to the direction of God's Spirit."[83] Keener here helps to show that the distinction within Pentecostal theology stems more from experience than from the teachings based in the New Testament. He continues by explaining, "These passages [i.e., Eph. 5:18; Gal. 5:16–23] suggest that the whole sphere of the Spirit's work becomes available at conversion, but believers may experience some aspects of the Spirit's work only subsequent to conversion."[84] Later he would further clarify, "In other words, although all God's fullness becomes ours in Christ at the moment of our conversion, we still have to actualize that fullness in our daily lives."[85] So, while the believer receives the fullness of the Spirit at conversion, he still needs to grow in his understanding of and submission to that Spirit.

Some reading this critique of Pentecostalism and the earlier statements that the New Testament consistently presents a submission to the Spirit and not the reception of a greater portion of that same Spirit will immediately object based upon the testimony of the book of Acts. They might argue that this perspective is only taken because Acts is being read in light of Paul, while Paul should be read in light of Acts. Keener explains, "Those who emphasize the Bible's theological statements (such as Paul's comments) rather than narrative examples (such as stories in Acts) usually identify baptism in the Spirit with conversion to faith in Christ. Those who emphasize Acts over against Paul usually believe that baptism in the Spirit can occur after conversion."[86] That argument is legitimate, but if not careful, can insinuate a conflict between Acts and the Pauline epistles versus seeing them as complementary.[87] As a result, some limited comment is warranted here to show how Luke's and Paul's accounts are not in conflict, but complementary and support the thesis that the Spirit is received at salvation and the believer is to grow in greater submission to that Spirit.

---

83. Keener, *Gift & Giver*, 151.

84. Ibid.

85. Ibid., 157. Keener will continue to give a concise conclusion concerning the empowering work of the Spirit and the believers need to continue to yield in 168–9.

86. Ibid., 150.

87. As Zwiep does, "In sum, Luke's view of the Spirit differs from Paul's theology in some significant respects" (Zwiep, *Christ, Spirit Community*, 119).

Acts presents a transitional period in the life of the church through narrative, while Paul teaches more directly through letters in the second person establishing theological principles and life application. Within the Acts narrative, four specific passages give credence to a potential second-experience as advocated by some in Pentecostalism: Acts 2, 8, 10, 19.[88] Each of these passages will be briefly examined in order to show that they can and should be seen as transitional and complementary to the Pauline evidence concerning Spirit baptism at conversion.

Acts 2 is Pentecost.[89] Pentecost was a transition between the old and new covenants fulfilling the prophecy of Joel 2 and empowering the church to be Christ's witness in and throughout the world. Little doubt exists that the disciples and many others present in Jerusalem were already believers in Christ, but as Jesus proclaimed, "If I do not go away, the Helper will not come to you" (John 16:7).[90] "So Luke brings John's baptism of Jesus in the Jordan and the Spirit's baptism of assembled believers at Pentecost into a parallel in which each event is seen as the final constitutive factor for all that follows in the ministry of Jesus (cf. Luke's Gospel) and the mission of the early church (cf. Acts)."[91] As such, Acts 2 is inconclusive in attempting to provide any comprehensive doctrine concerning baptism of the Spirit; although, it should be noted that the disciples were to wait until Jesus sent the Spirit.[92] They were never to seek the Spirit on their own or as a display

---

88. Two good refutations for the Pentecostal reading of Acts are Dunn, *Baptism*, 38–102; Polhill, *Acts*, 95–122; 210–28; 249–67; 398–414. Dunn presents a particularly pointed and powerful critique. For a Pentecostal response to Dunn, see Atkinson, "Pentecostal Responses to Dunn," 87–131, and then more fully in Atkinson, *Baptism in the Spirit*; Wood, *Pentecostal Grace*, 258–72. For a Nazarene response to Dunn, see Grider, *Wesleyan-Holiness Theology*, 421–55. For a Pentecostal approach to Acts 2, 8, 10, and 19, see Palma, *Holy Spirit*, 109–60; Wierwille, *Receiving the Holy Spirit*, 65–160. Also, the progression in Acts 2, 8, and 10 tracks with Jesus command in Acts 1:8 that Christ-followers would be given power to be his witness in Jerusalem, Samarian, and beyond. These Spirit-baptism episodes help demonstrate the empowering work of the Spirit in fulfilling that pattern. For a similar idea, see also Simmons, *Biblical Anthology*, 180–82.

89. For a thoughtful Pentecostal perspective on Pentecost as it relates to Babel, see Macchia, "Babel and the Tongues," 34–51.

90. Concerning the question of whether or not the disciples were already believer in Christ, Palm rightly states that "the answer is obvious. Hardly anyone would argue otherwise" (Palma, *Holy Spirit*, 111).

91. Longenecker, *Acts*, 268.

92. As Palma admits, "The coming of the Holy Spirit upon the waiting disciples on the Day of Pentecost was unprecedented. In a very important sense, it was a unique, historic, unrepeatable event" (Palma, *Holy Spirit*, 110). Contra Keener who sees it as "a

of their devotion. The Spirit's coming was not dependent on their activity but on Jesus'.

Acts 8 reveals that some Samaritans experienced a baptism of the Holy Spirit at the hands of the apostles after having "believed" in the gospel of Jesus as preached by Philip. Pentecostalism would argue that this passage demonstrates that believers should seek an experience of Spirit baptism after conversion; however, this narrative should not be taken to teach that believers should seek Spirit baptism after conversion.[93] Dunn argues that it is possible that those in Samaria had not truly been saved before the apostles arrived.[94] From his perspective, Philip did not present a defective gospel; rather, the faith of the Samaritans seemed more keen on the potential benefits of salvation, power, than the object of salvation, Jesus. He bases this thought on the apostles's reaction to Simon the magician who was said to have believed, but is rebuked as if he is an unbeliever. However, Dunn's interpretation is not likely primarily due to the fact that Peter and John were sent to Samaria by the apostles because the Samaritans had believed and still needed to receive the Holy Spirit (Acts 8:14–15). Assuming that they were believers, this scenario seems to be presenting a special circumstance in the transition from Christian Judaism to a global Christian church as Jesus revealed would happen in Acts 1:8.[95] Rather than seeing Acts 8 as a normative two-stage process, it seems more likely that it is simply validating through the transitional leaders in the church, the apostles, to all within the Christian community that the gospel is open to all who believe whether they are circumcised or uncircumcised providing continu-

model rather than as an exception" (Keener, *Gift & Giver*, 162).

93. Contra Palma who states, "Yet the Samaritans' unusual and identifiable experience of the Spirit some time *after* their conversion and baptism is a strong argument in favor of the doctrine of subsequence" (Palma, *Holy Spirit*, 120). So Horton, "Spirit Baptism," 60.

94. This view is argued by Dunn, *Baptism*, 55–72. See also Hoekema, *Holy Spirit Baptism*, 36–37. For a thoughtful, concise, and Pentecostal refutation of Dunn on this text, see Keener, *Gift & Giver*, 164–6. See also Ervin, *Conversion-Initiation*, 25–40.

95. Contra Wierwille, *Receiving the Holy Spirit*, 103–18. While numerous Pentecostal sources could be used here, Wierwille is used because he provides specific insight to how tradition has shaped the Pentecostal reading of Acts versus allowing the contextual biblical text to shape his tradition. Concerning this passage, he states, "From just a cursory reading of Acts 8 and without the understanding of the operation of the nine manifestations of the Spirit, it would be difficult to rightly divide it. Reading verses nine through eleven, we know that devil spirits had so infiltrated the Samaritans that, of the three revelation manifestations of the Holy Spirit, discerning of spirits must have been very much in operation" (ibid., 112).

ity between the Samaritan and the Jerusalem church.[96] Anyone who truly repents and believes is restored in relationship with God and empowered to be Christ's witness. The converts in Samaria were not just the workings of some Hellenistic missionary on his own, but were consistent with and confirmed by the Jerusalem church through the apostles. It was important that the Samaritans not be identified as a different church. The unity of the one church was to be preserved: similar to the woman at the well when she speaks of the two altars and Jesus unites them in one church. As Palma, writing from a Pentecostal perspective, admits, "The endorsement of the Jerusalem leadership was indeed desirable, almost imperative, in view of the long-standing antipathy between Jews and Samaritans."[97] Longenecker further elaborates,

> But God in his providence withheld the gift of the Holy Spirit till Peter and John laid their hands on the Samaritans—Peter and John, two leading apostles who were highly thought of in the mother church at Jerusalem and who would have been accepted at the time as brothers in Christ by the new converts in Samaria. In effect, therefore, in this first advance of the gospel outside the confines of Jerusalem, God worked in ways that were conducive not only to the reception of the Good News in Samaria but also to the acceptance of these new converts by believers at Jerusalem.[98]

Within this framework, it should also be noted that unlike much of modern Pentecostalism, the Samaritans did not seek this baptism, but it does seem the apostles saw it necessary in part to ensure that the Samaritans were unified within the universal church. Additionally, this account reveals the initial reception of the Spirit and not a subsequent experience. This explanation fits the narrative of Acts and complements the theology of Paul without any necessary conflict.

But, what of Acts 10 where Cornelius and all those with him had the Spirit of God fall on them, so that they spoke in tongues? The problem with the prominent Pentecostal perspective of Acts 10 is that Cornelius and

---

96. So Green, *I Believe*, 138–9; Lampe, *Seal*, 70–77; Stott, *Baptism & Fullness*, 30, 32–34. Contra Palma whose is concerned that "a purely salvation-historical approach, however, tends to relegate charismatic reception of the Spirit solely to the Book of Acts" (Palma, *Holy Spirit*, 118).

97. Palma, *Holy Spirit*, 119.

98. Longenecker, *Acts*, 359. See also Grudem, *Systematic Theology*, 774; Polhill, *Acts*, 218.

those with him were not Christians before Peter arrived.[99] Cornelius and his household came to faith through the preaching of the gospel through Peter as confirmed by Acts 11:14 and 15:7.[100] The Spirit then was received at that time. No two stage process is present.[101] Thus, at this point, Acts 2 reveals that the Spirit is given in Jerusalem, Acts 8 reveals that he is given in Samaria, and now Acts 10 reveals that he is given to the Gentile world. This progression parallels well with the mandate that the Spirit would be given for the purpose of being Christ's witness in "Jerusalem and in all Judea and Samaria, and to the end of the earth" (Acts 1:8).

The final passage upon which the Pentecostal perspective of Spirit baptism in Acts depends is found in chapter 19 with the Ephesian converts. The common Pentecostal perspective teaches that these Ephesian "Christians" did not receive the Spirit until well after their conversion when they met Paul and were informed that they should seek such an experience.[102] The problem with this view is that it misses several important elements in the text. While these people were disciples, they were disciples of John the Baptist. No indication is given that they were followers of Christ, as a matter of fact, there is evidence to the contrary (Acts 19:4).[103] Paul in asking his series of questions reveals that something is wrong. By asking if they had

99. As Wierwille writing from a Pentecostal perspective admits, "Cornelius was a religious man, but he was not yet born again of God's Spirit" (Wierwille, *Receiving the Holy Spirit*, 128). So Keener, *Gift & Giver*, 159. Contra Ervin, *Conversion-Initiation*, 52–54; Horton, "Spirit Baptism," 63; Warrington, *Pentecostal Theology*, 110–11. For a more extensive refutation of the Pentecostal perspective as it relates to Acts 10, see Dunn, *Baptism*, 79–89.

100. Acts 11:13–14: "And he told us how he had seen the angel stand in his house and say, 'Send to Joppa and bring Simon who is called Peter; he will declare to you a message by which you will be saved, you and all your household.'" Acts 15:7: "And after there had been much debate, Peter stood up and said to them, 'Brothers, you know that in the early days God made a choice among you, that by my mouth the Gentiles should hear the word of the gospel and believe.'"

101. As admitted by many Pentecostals. So Palma, *Holy Spirit*, 122; Keener, *Gift & Giver*, 159–60; Wyckoff, "Baptism," 453. However, they will argue that this simply shows that Spirit Baptism may be experienced at conversion, but does not refute that it can be experienced post-conversion as evidenced in Acts 2 and 8.

102. So Palma, *Holy Spirit*, 129–30; Warrington, *Pentecostal Theology*, 112; Wierwille, *Receiving the Holy Spirit*, 151–6.

103. So Keener who explains that "these particular disciples had only received John's baptism and had not yet heard that the Holy Spirit had come, which suggests that they left Palestine before Pentecost and were not in fellowship with Christians. In other words, scholars who argue that these particular disciples were probably disciples of John, rather than Christians, are probably right" (Keener, *Gift & Giver*, 161).

received the Holy Spirit, Paul is connecting the reception of the Spirit with belief.[104] When they said they had not, Paul questions the foundations of their belief system and discovers that they had not heard the gospel of Jesus. This idea is further supported by the fact that after they heard, believed, and received the Spirit, he baptized them in the name of Jesus showing that Paul viewed their previous baptism as deficient. This deficiency was not in the mode, but in their failure "to recognize Jesus as the one whom John had proclaimed, as the promised Messiah."[105] Thus, again, no two stage process exists in Acts 19; rather, these Ephesians are converted and receive the Spirit all as part of the same process.[106]

Examining the proposed Pentecostal evidence from Acts reveals a further flaw in the two-fold experience proposed under their theology. Rather than viewing a normative two-fold process in Acts, the evidence seems to demonstrate that Acts 2 and 8 should be understood as theologically and historically significant unique events. The additional baptism narratives in Acts 10 and 19, then, reinforce the point that once the evidence was given that the Spirit had come and genuine conversion provided to non-Jews (Acts 2 & 8) Spirit baptism coincided with conversion making full spiritual empowerment available from that moment. Additionally, it readily becomes apparent that Paul is not presenting something in contrast with that which was established in Acts, but his theological writings complement the narrative well. The reality is that the Bible consistently presents the empowering presence of the Spirit as coinciding with conversion.

Galatians 2:20 in summary fashion, emphasizing the central role of Christ, when properly understood within the context of Galatians gives a more balanced approach to understanding the representative and equipping role of the Spirit of Christ, and in so doing, helps correct the misunderstanding that a second-experience of grace is needed post-conversion for empowered Christian living. This perspective that believers are not adequately empowered by the Spirit at conversion is inconsistent with Galatians and carries harmful implications for the church and the spiritual life.[107] It is the Spirit who empowers the believer for righteous living and

---

104. Longenecker, *Acts*, 493.

105. Polhill, *Acts*, 399.

106. For further refutation of other objections Pentecostalism might have towards this interpretation, see Dunn, *Baptism*, 83–89.

107. For a brief description of some of the dangers to believers in the church, see ibid., 226–36; Grudem, *Systematic Theology*, 775–8.

that empowerment is given at salvation. The believer should grow through the sanctification process in yielding more completely to the Spirit, but it is not a new portion of the Spirit received per se, it is greater submission to the Spirit already given. These concepts concerning the empowering work of the Spirit have implications for knowing that one has been fully endowed in salvation for victorious living. That is why Galatians 2:20 emphasizes that through faith in Christ one has died to his old *ego* and now has Christ in him by means of Christ's Spirit so that he is equipped to live out the life of faith.

Permanence of the Spirit

This new life brought by Christ through his Spirit is the result of being crucified with Christ. Therefore, the results of co-crucifixion are held in equal tension with the crucifixion itself. In other words, the role of the cross in bringing crucifixion is directly connected to the reception of Spirit of Christ in the believer. If, as previously demonstrated, being crucified with Christ is a permanent act as emphasized by the use of the perfect tense and other parallel passages, then the results of that process should also be viewed as permanent.[108]

If it is also correct that the Spirit is connected to the cross and co-crucifixion is at salvation and permanent, then the reception of the Spirit is at salvation and permanent. Basham, as a Pentecostal, connects the filling of the Spirit and co-crucifixion. "Through ineffable union now, open to every believing and obedient disciple of Jesus . . . . When Jesus hung upon the cross of shame and agony and desertion, He gave up the Holy Breath or Holy Ghost; when we are put upon the cross by the Holy Spirit we receive the Holy Breath and are filled with the Holy Ghost."[109] Basham is right to connect the reception of the Spirit to the cross; although, his understanding of the timing of that union and Spirit reception in relation to saving faith is incorrect.[110] When believers are connected to the cross in salvation, they are given the Spirit. The same permanent effect of being crucified with Christ is connected to the results of that crucifixion in the removal of the

---

108. See "Permanence of the Cross" in the last chapter for arguments concerning the permanence of crucifixion with Christ.

109. Basham, *Handbook*, 25.

110. He speaks of this union being open to the believer, missing that every believer experiences this union at salvation when they place their faith in Christ.

ego from its center of influence and the reception of the Spirit of Christ to serve as the believer's center of influence. In light of Galatians 2:20, this thought is made clear in Galatians chapter 5. Romans 8:8–10 also echoes this truth: "Those who are in the flesh cannot please God. You, however, are not in the flesh but in the Spirit, if in fact the Spirit of God dwells in you. Anyone who does not have the Spirit of Christ does not belong to him. But if Christ is in you, although the body is dead because of sin, the Spirit is life because of righteousness." Paul declares that if the believer is in the flesh, he cannot please God. Paul immediately explains that the residence of the Spirit within all believers is evidence that they are no longer in the flesh. Paul then explains that the Spirit of Christ enables believers to walk in righteousness. Condemnation has been removed because the believer has been justified in Christ through union with him in his death and resurrection, dethroning the believer's flesh and empowering him through his Spirit (Rom 6:2; 7:4, 6; 8:30).

Therefore, the reception of the Spirit is a permanent result of the believer's crucifixion with Christ. Paul's use of the perfect tense in saying that "I have been crucified with Christ" helps emphasize the permanence of this co-crucifixion. Since one's crucifixion with Christ is permanent, the results of that crucifixion are permanent.

Galatians 2:20 then declares in a concise way the permanent reception of the Spirit for all who believe, refuting any notion that the Spirit can be lost by the genuine believer. Grasping this point is important, because it specifically corrects the view within certain circles of Christian spirituality that advocate the believer's ability to lose their salvation. The Spirit is a permanent indwelling presence in the life of a true believer without whom one cannot consider themselves a child of God (Rom 8:8–10). If the indwelling presence of the Spirit can be lost, then so can salvation; at the same time, if the indwelling presence of the Spirit cannot be lost, then neither can salvation. Galatians 2:20 provides justification for the permanent presence of the Spirit that coincides with genuine saving faith and produces Spirit-evidenced works (Gal 5:16–24).

This debate concerning whether or not someone can lose their salvation is an extremely lengthy and complicated one.[111] The point here is not

---

111. Here are a few of the passages used to argue that one cannot lose their salvation: Pss 20:6; 31:23; 37:28; 55:22; 121; Is 46:3–4; Jer 32:39–40; John 5:24; 6:35–37; 10:27–9; 17:2, 12; Rom 5:9; 8:1, 35, 38–39; 9:6–8; 11:29; 1 Cor 1:6–8; 15:10; 2 Cor 5:19; Eph 1:13–14; 2:4–6; 4:30; Phil 1:6; 1 Thess 5:23–24; 2 Thess 3:3; 2 Tim 1:12; 2:13; Heb 3:14; 6:17–19; 9:12; 13:20–21; 1 Pet 1:3–5; 23; 1 John 2:19; 3:9; 5:4–5, 11–13. Here are

to provide all of the nuances of the debate; rather, it is simply to show that Galatians 2:20 in its context reveals the believer's permanent possession of the Spirit of Christ, which counters modern writers in Christian spirituality who argue that true believers can lose their salvation. This truth revealed in Galatians 2:20 does not mean that the believer will never struggle with the flesh or will not have to chose to walk in faith.[112] Real activity exists on the part of the believer in fighting against the flesh and abiding in the Spirit, and one is expected to persevere in the faith. Thus, Galatians 2:20 is simply one passage that when contextually understood adds to the evidence that the possession of the Spirit is permanent whether deemed to be the result of the preservation of God or their own perseverance.[113]

The view that a genuine believer can lose their salvation is taught within many circles of Pentecostalism to include the Assemblies of God.

---

a few of the passages used to argue that one can lose their salvation: Deut 29:18–20; 2 Chron 15:1–2; Ezek 18:20–24; Matt 5:27–30; 10:16–17, 21–22, 32–33; Luke 8:11–13; John 15:5–6; 17:12; Acts 14:21–22; Rom 8:12–13; 11:19–22; 1 Cor 3:16–17; 6:7–11; 8:9–13; 9:24–27; 10:7–8, 11–12; 15:1–2; Gal 1:6–9; 5:2–4, 16, 19–21; 6:7–10; Eph 5:3–7; Col 1:21–23; 1 Tim 1:18–19; 4:1, 13–16; 5:12, 15; Heb 2:1–4; 3:12–14; 6:4–6; 10:26–29, 36–39; Jas 1:12; 5:19–20; 2 Pet 1:8–11; 2:20–22; 3:16–17; 1 John 5:16; Jude 20–21; Rev 2:10–11; 3:2–5, 10–11; 21:7–8. Here are some of the works that provide good interaction with arguments from a variety of perspectives: Arrington, *Unconditional Eternal Security*; Bateman IV, *Four Views on the Warning Passages*; Berkhof, *Systematic Theology*, 545–54; Bing, *Lordship Salvation*; Borchert, *Assurance and Warning*; Brand, *Perspectives on Election*; Craig, "'Lest Anyone Should Fall'," 65–74; Dillow, *Reign of the Servant Kings*; Eaton, *No Condemnation*; Erickson, *Christian Theology*, 996–1008; Geisler, *Chosen but Free*; Grudem, *Systematic Theology*, 788–809; Hoekema, *Saved by Grace*; Lloyd-Jones, *Romans*; MacArthur, *Faith Works*; idem, *Gospel According to Jesus*; Marshall, *Kept by the Power of God*; Oropeza, *Paul and Apostasy*; Picirilli, *Grace, Faith, Free Will*; Pink, *Eternal Security*; idem, *Studies on Saving Faith*; Pinson, *Four Views on Eternal Security*; Ryrie, *So Great Salvation*; Schreiner and Caneday, *Race Set before Us*; Shanks, *Life in the Son*; Smith, *Living Water*; Stanley, *Eternal Security*; Volf, *Paul & Perseverance*; Walls and Dongell, *Why I'm Not a Calvinist*; Whitney, *How Can I Be Sure*; Yinger, *Paul, Judaism, and Judgment*.

112. The next chapter will argue that Gal 2:20 presents the Christian life as one lived in tension with the flesh. Addressing the distinction between justification and sanctification, Keathly states, "A person finds assurance when he trusts the justifying work of Christ alone. I also contend that the gift of faith remains (i.e., perseveres), and it inevitably manifests itself in the life of a believer. However, the level of manifestation varies from saint to saint" (Keathley, *Salvation and Sovereignty*, 165).

113. Some verses used to support preservation and/or perseverance: John 6:38–40; 10:28–29; Rom 8:28–39; Phil 1:4–6; 2:12–13; Col 1:21–23; 2 Tim 1:12; Heb 12:1; 1 John 1:5–10; 3:3–6; 2:19.

A position paper on the security of the believer produced by the General Council of the Assemblies of God states,

> In view of the Biblical teaching that the security of the believer depends on a living relationship with Christ (John 15:6), in view of the Bible's call to a life of holiness (1 Peter 1:16; Hebrews 12:14); in view of the clear teaching that a man may have his part taken out of the Book of Life (Revelation 22:19); and in view of the fact that one who believes for a while can fall away (Luke 8:13); The General Council of the Assemblies of God disapproves of the un-conditional security position which holds that it is impossible for a person once saved to be lost.[114]

Later, they declare, "God does not let anyone go easily. . . . But a believer can be lost if he disregards the continuing checks of the Holy Spirit and reaches the point where he rejects Jesus as his Saviour. It is possible to believe for a while and in time of temptation to fall away (Luke 8:13)."[115] Proponents of this view argue that the believer must not only begin their spiritual walk in faith, but continue in it by faith. This premise is built in part on present tense use of the verb believe found in a variety of biblical texts.[116] "The word 'believe' in these, and other passages (see Jn. 3:16; Jn. 6:40) is in the present tense, and means 'to believe and to continue to believe.' It is the continuous or progressive present tense and implies not only an initial act of faith, but a maintained attitude. Assurance of security, therefore, is for the believing ones. The elect 'are kept by the power of God through faith' (1 Pt. 1:5)."[117] In other words, they hold in equal tension the responsibility of God, to keep, and the responsibility of man, to believe. While God will always uphold his end, man may default to an unbelieving position, as Robert Shanks explains, "Certainly it is true that the elect (who are foreknown to God) will persevere. But that is only *half* the truth; for it is equally true that they who

114. "The Security of the Believer."

115. Ibid., 5–6.

116. πιστεύω. John 3:15–16; 3:36; 5:24; 6:35, 40, 47; 11:25, 26; 20:31; Rom 1:16; 1 Cor 1:21.

117. Duffield and Van Cleave, *Foundations of Pentecostal Theology*, 257. For more on the emphasis of the present tense "believe," see Claybrook Jr., *Once Saved, Always Saved*, 212–4; Moody, *Word of Truth*, 356. Wallace agrees. "The idea seems to be both gnomic and continual . . . This is not due to the present tense only, but to the use of the present participle of πιστεύω, especially in soteriological contexts in the NT" (Wallace, *Greek Grammar*, 621). Then in the footnote for that statement, Wallace would add, "Thus, it seems that since the aorist participle was a live option to describe a 'believer,' it is unlikely that when the present was used, it was aspectually flat" (ibid., n.22).

persevere are elect. The latter truth is presented in the Holy Scriptures, not as the inevitable outcome of some inexorable divine decree with respect to specific individuals unconditionally, but as a matter for the constant concern and holy endeavor of believers."[118]

The Pentecostal idea of persistent faith in one regard is consistent with Galatians 2:20, which declares that the true believer having been justified by faith will continued to live in that faith: "And the life I now live in the flesh I live by faith in the Son of God, who loved me and gave himself for me." The distinction comes in that Pentecostalism sees that the indwelling presence of the Spirit of Christ may be lost due to unbelieving. Galatians 2:20 does not present such a tension, but shows that the co-crucifixion with Christ results in a permanent indwelling of the Spirit of Christ which will result in a life lived out of faith. The true believer will never cease from having genuine saving faith, but will persevere and be preserved by God. Those who fall away should be viewed as those who never truly believed (1 John 2:19; 3:6).[119]

A major, and appropriate, concern for Pentecostals seems to be a prominent belief within Christian spirituality that mental assent to Christ is sufficient for saving faith resulting in eternal security.[120] Thus, the effort

118. Shanks, *Life in the Son*, 366.

119. Other passages support this view Matt 13:1–7, 18–22; Luke 8:7, 13; 1 Tim 4:1–3; 5:12; 2 Tim 4:10; Heb 3:12; 6:6. See also Berkhof, *Systematic Theology*, 545–54; Fanning, "Classical Reformed View," 172–219; Erickson, *Christian Theology*, 996–1008; Geisler, "Moderate Calvinist View," 61–134; Grudem, *Systematic Theology*, 788–809; Hoekema, *Saved by Grace*, 234–56; Horton, "Classical Calvinist View," 22–42; Schreiner and Caneday, *Race Set before Us*.

120. This view that mental assent is sufficient for saving faith resulting in eternal security is often referred to as "easy believism" and will be addressed in more detail in the next chapter. Easy believism makes a false separation between faith and works foreign to biblical texts such as Jas 2:14–7. Kendall represents this position. "*Whoever once truly believes that Jesus was raised from the dead, and confesses that Jesus is Lord, will go to heaven when he dies. But I will not stop there. Such a person will go to heaven when he dies no matter what work (or lack of work) may accompany such faith*" (*Once Saved, Always Saved*, 19). He talks about repentance on p. 30 but does not adequately show its connection to faith or works or its role in salvation. Others who teach that works or profession after the initial act of salvation (believing) have no bearing on one's future security in the faith include Hodges, *Absolutely Free*, 63, 80–94; Stanley, *Eternal Security*, 1–5, 67, 74, 80. Those who advocate for a perseverance/preservation of the saints do not argue that salvation can be lost, but that works (persistence in profession) do have a bearing on future security in the sense that they may reveal whether or not the initial profession was of genuine faith or not. In other words, works and future profession may reveal whether or not one is truly saved, but will never cause a true believer to lose salvation since a true

to balance texts that speak of one's security in Christ and the dangerous implications of one walking in sin is appropriate; however, the argument that a believer must continue in faith does not necessitate that a genuine believer would ever stop believing. Rather than setting the texts that indicate the permanence of salvation in opposition with warning passages and those showing the necessity of continued faith, a more appropriate approach is to see them as perfectly compatible arguing that such warning passages are designed to keep genuine believers from ever renouncing the faith and that once a person truly experiences grace and believes, that person will continue believing.[121] This is the perspective presented in Galatians 2:20.

Significance of Union with Christ

The topic of the indwelling presence of Christ by means of his Spirit also provokes questions concerning union with Christ. Several implications of this union exists such as the reality that as a result of the indwelling presence of Christ believers are not left alone (John 14:18–9; 15:26; 16:7, 13) and believers are now equipped to resist the desires of the flesh and walk in the Spirit (Gal 5:16, 25). Believers are not orphaned. Christ is with them in every circumstance of life. Such a perspective should bring comfort and hope in the midst of this fallen world. Additionally, by being united with Christ in the Spirit, believers are now capable of living out a life of faith pleasing to God in accordance with the will of God.

This significance of the indwelling presence of the Spirit (union with Christ) raises a question however. Is there any extent in which the idea of Christ living in the believer should be understood as the believer becoming divine? The question may seem strange at first, but is incredible pertinent to Galatians 2:20, specifically in ligh of Paul's declaration that "it is no longer I who live, but Christ who lives in me," and the fact that Galatians 2:20 is being examined in light of contemporary Christian Spirituality. As Roger Olson explains, "The search for transformation through spirituality lies at the heart of the new interest in deification."[122] This idea of becoming divine is known as the doctrine of deification (theosis).

---

believer will persist in the faith.

121.. Borchert, *Assurance and Warning*, 204–05; Schreiner and Caneday, *Race Set before Us*, 38–45.

122. Olson, "Deification in Contemporary Theology," 188.

The doctrine of deification, also known as "theosis," is developed from a variety of verses, but finds its strongest support in 2 Pet 1:4 and Ps 82:6, cited in John 10:34–35. Deification is a prominent doctrine within the Eastern Orthodox church. Definitions of deification vary but share the common idea of becoming God without detracting from his essence. "In Christian theology, theōsis refers to the transformation of believers into the likeness of God. Of course, Christian monotheism goes against any literal 'god making' of believers. Rather, the NT speaks of a transformation of mind, a metamorphosis of character, a redefinition of selfhood, and an imitation of God. Most of these passages are tantalizingly brief, and none spells out the concept in detail."[123] After listing a variety of passages, Stephen Finlan and Vladimir Kharlamov say, "Although some of these passages concern the afterlife, or events connected with the return of Christ, all of them have implications for the present life of believers, suggesting an ongoing transformation, a progressive *engodding* of the believer, to use the endearing Old English phrase."[124]

The questions previously posed still stands, does Galatians 2:20 provide any credence for the doctrine of deification (theosis)?

What briefly follows in this section is not intended to argue the merits of deification; rather, to introduce the idea and interact briefly with the concept of whether or not deification is supported by Galatians 2:20. It is only from that perspective that it will be addressed here. Due to the increased dialogue concerning deification within Pentecostalism in an American context, it is necessary to mention this topic. Although deification is more prominent in the Eastern Orthodox tradition, avenues of open dialogue have increased in recent decades whereby Protestant scholars are seeking to merge various theological distinctive of the Eastern and Western church.[125] Veli-Matti Kärkkäinen is among the voices in the conversation.

123. Finlan and Kharlamov, *Theōsis*, 1.

124. Ibid., 3. For some other brief definitions, see Chia, "Salvation as Justification and Deification," 129; Gavrilyuk, "Retrieval of Deification," 649. Some other sources addressing deification are Christensen and Wittung, *Partakers of the Divine Nature*; Gorman, *Inhabiting the Cruciform God*; Hudson, *Becoming God*; Kärkkäinen, *One with God*; Marshall, "Justification as Declaration and Deification," 3–28; O'Brien, "Partakers of the Divine Sacrifice," 68–76; Olson, "Deification in Contemporary Theology," 186–200; Wesche, "Doctrine of Deification," 169–79.

125. "The late twentieth century has witnessed a dramatic change in the attitude of Western theologians towards the concept of deification. The notion that struck most Western observers as foreign, through the joint efforts of numerous scholars of the last generation, is gradually being drawn into the fold of the Western theological tradition"

Writing from a Protestant Pentecostal perspectives, he seeks "to advance an ecumenical quest for a conciliar doctrine of deification and a pneumatological concept of grace" stating that "this is important for both the Pentecostal-Holiness tradition and their dialogue partners, the Orthodox and the Lutherans."[126] Kärkkäinen seems to see the Orthodox view of deification as compatible with (if not a culmination of) the Lutheran concepts of justification, sanctification, and union with Christ.[127]

Two obstacles must be overcome before seeing Galatians 2:20 in connection with deification.[128] First, deification is often seen as a theme and not just as a doctrine.[129] It is viewed as the goal of the Christian life. As such, it becomes difficult to talk about, because it is seen as the culmination of various other doctrines in relation to salvation. Deification for the Orthodox church has become a way of talking about the sum of the Christian life to include various other doctrines, while within the Protestant tradition, it is generally referred to in conjunction with doctrines such as justification, sanctification, and union with Christ versus the culmination of those doctrines. These two approaches make clarity and communication even more difficult. Secondly, when distinctions are made and deification is referenced in conjunction with the doctrines of justification, sanctification, and union with Christ, much disagreement exists on how these terms are theologically connected to one another and the degree to which deification is synonymous with one or all of these terms. "In some contexts deification functions as an umbrella term covering most of these notions, while in other contexts deification is placed side by side with these notions as something altogether distinct from them. Yet it is common for contemporary non-Orthodox theologians to simply collapse deification into one of these categories."[130] To

---

(Gavrilyuk, "Retrieval of Deification," 648).

126. Kärkkäinen, *Pneumatological Theology*, 149–65.

127. "First, there is an emerging consensus that the Orthodox idea of the believer's union with God, *theosis*, regardless of differing language, can be compatible with the Western notion of participation in God, an idea that is an essential part of the doctrine of justification by faith" (Kärkkäinen, *One with God*, 97; see also pp. 98, 110, 119–21).

128. These obstacles do not address the debate currently taking place within the Orthodox church concerning the distinction between God's essence and energies in connection with deification (Olson, "Deification in Contemporary Theology," 189).

129. Hallonsten, "*Theosis*," 287.

130. Gavrilyuk, "Retrieval of Deification," 652. This collapsing of deification into some of the various reformed categories of justification, sanctification, or union with Christ by Protestants is not usually well received within the Orthodox tradition. "But simply replacing theōsis with *sanctification* is an attempt to supplant Patristic theology

some extent conversation surrounding deification can become an issue of semantics resulting in a loss of distinction in general. Differing terminology from the various traditions makes it easy to talk past one another. For many Protestant theologians, union with Christ sufficiently covers the idea of deification without all the baggage.[131] Though both sides are gradually opening to further dialogue, they have a large chasm to overcome.

Therefore, until greater clarity is brought within the Protestant tradition on the meaning and significance of deification, one should proceed with caution. What should be remembered is that Galatians 2:20b, "It is no longer I who live, but Christ who lives in me," shows believers they have a new identity in Christ free from the bondage sin brought, they are not left alone, and that they have been empowered by the Spirit through whom they can live victoriously in this life. A new center of influence exists. The verse is tying the contextual conversation concerning justification with the new life that flows out of the one who has been justified. Thus, to the extent that one is seeking to emphasize some of the concepts of deification such as being united with God and empowered by God while not taking away from God's essence or denying one's personality or real humanity, it is appropriate.[132] Nevertheless, due to the many qualifications that must be made and the fact that the primary point of Galatians 2:20b is the empowerment of Christ not the deification of the believer, one should be hesitant in us-

---

with standard Reformation language" (Finlan and Kharlamov, *Theōsis*, 5). They also say, "Some Protestants try to assimilate it [theōsis] to familiar Western concepts such as 'sanctification by grace' or 'justification by faith,' trying to connect the Reformation directly to the Bible, as though the intervening centuries had no significance" (ibid., 8). Protestants who see a connection between deification and justification, sanctification, or union with Christ would argue that they are not seeking to supplant, but to clarify and help demystify the idea of deification by providing a little greater clarity to an undefined term in a culture prone to subjective mysticism.

131. Habets, "Reforming Theōsis," 147; Olson, "Deification in Contemporary Theology," 189; Grenz, *Social God and the Relational Self*, 325–8. Habets argues union with God and theosis are related but not identical. Olson uses Bloesch as an example of someone who sees deification covered in the protestant use of union with Christ. Granz uses deification, but seems to do so in a way more consistent with the protestant use of union with Christ. These examples shows some of the variances.

132. Olson seeks to emphasize these areas, but still words it in a way that would be uncomfortable to many western protestants. "Surely deification means real ontological participation in God's nature that elevates us above our humanity without infringing on God's own essence or our real humanity. Our deified humanity is still humanity just as Christ's was and is. But it is more than mere, ordinary humanity. It is humanity energized, empowered, and transformed within the divine presence" (Olson, "Deification in Contemporary Theology," 194).

ing this verse in connection with deification. In the end, further research, discussion, and consensus is needed within the Protestant community in relationship to the doctrine of deification.

A second area of significance is that believers no longer have to live in accordance to the desires of the flesh, but can, and are expected to, walk in the Spirit. Believers can now live in obedience to God as a result of the indwelling and enabling presence of the Spirit of Christ. This point has tremendous implications that will be developed in the next two chapters of this book as Paul declares that "the life I now live in the flesh I live by faith in the Son of God, who loved me and gave himself for me."

Conclusion

Teachings concerning the Spirit of God in relationship to the new birth abound in Christianity influencing the way that believers live and think in relation to God. Some of these teachings either stretch beyond the boundaries of what can be known from the Scriptures or directly conflict with the contextual teachings of Scripture. Above, it has been shown that Galatians 2:20b, when examined within its context, can serve as a corrective to some of these errors. Galatians 2:20 supports the biblical teaching that believers are indwelt by the Spirit and empowered for Christian living. They no longer have to live out the desires of the flesh. Each believer is equipped at salvation to live out the Christian life to which he has been called. This indwelling presence of the Spirit is brought about in conjunction with the believer's co-crucifixion with Christ. Just as a true believer's co-crucifixion with Christ is permanent so the results of that co-crucifixion, the dethroning of the *ego* and the indwelling of the Spirit, are permanent. As a result, Christ, as represented by the Spirit, now lives in the believer as a new center of influence empowering them to live in a manner worthy of the gospel of Jesus (Eph 4:1; Phil 1:27; Col 1:10; 2:6; 1 Thess 2:12).

3

Continued Tension of the Flesh

"And the life I now live in the flesh"

Introduction

THE SPIRITUAL LIFE IS one of tension. Although believers have been justified in and united with Christ, they still must live life in this world and in
this body: a world and a body that is wasting away and full of temptation
(1 John 2:16–17). As a result, they will still be tested, while being called to
submit to the Spirit of Christ.

Paul, in Galatians 2:20c ("And the life I now live in the flesh,"), injects
this new dynamic into his summary of the spiritual life. Paul has already
described himself, and by implication all believers, as one who has experienced co-crucifixion with Christ. As a result of this co-crucifixion, Paul
no longer lives under the impulses of the old man, but in submission to the
Spirit of Christ. While this new reality provides a new center from which
the spiritual life is lived and experienced, a tension still exists, which arises
from the reality that Paul still lives in the flesh. Paul's description reveals
that, while optimistic, the spiritual life is still one of tension.[1] Although

1. Schreiner also sees an optimistic tone in Paul's words regarding the spiritual life
while acknowledging the tension found in the present age. Commenting on Gal 5:17, he
says, "Still, Paul is fundamentally optimistic here, claiming that as one walks by the Spirit

the bondage of sin has been destroyed, the residual influences of the old identity still provide an internal tension that must be resisted.

Life of Tension

The life that has been justified and indwelt by the Spirit of Christ is still a life lived in the flesh (σάρξ). Initially, it is appears that flesh here is simply another word for the body (σῶμα).[2] Such a usage is not uncommon in the New Testament; however, a closer inspection of the context of Galatians shows that something more seems to be alluded to by the use of this word.[3] By indicating that the spiritual life is one that still must be lived out in the flesh so long as one remains living on earth, the apostle is reminding the

---

and is led by the Spirit, there is substantial, significant, and observable victory over the flesh" (Schreiner, *Galatians*, 345). Stendahl presents a similar idea in *Paul Among Jews*, 90.

2. As Bruce takes it. "The phrase ἐν σαρκί here is non-theological: as in 2 Cor. 10:3 . . . it means 'in mortal body' . . ." (Bruce, *Galatians*, 145).

3. "Flesh" (σάρξ) is often used in the New Testament to describe the material (physical) part of a person in general (Matt 16:17; 26:41; Mark 13:20; 14:38; John 1:13–14; 3:6; 6:51–52, 63; 8:15; Acts 2:26, 31; Rom 1:3; 2:28; 4:1; 6:19; 8:3; 9:3, 5, 8; 11:14; 1 Cor 1:26; 7:28; 2 Cor 1:17; 4:11; 5:16; 7:1, 5; 10:2–3; 11:18; 12:17; Gal 2:20; 3:3; 4:13–14, 23, 29; 6:12–13; Eph 2:11, 14; 5:29; 6:5; Phil 1:22, 24; 3:3–4; Col 1:22, 24; 2:1, 5; 3:22; 1 Tim 3:16; Phlm 16; Heb 5:7; 9:10, 13; 10:20; 12:9; Jas 5:3; 1 Pet 1:24; 3:18, 21; 4:1–2, 6; 1 John 4:2; 2 John 7; Jude 8; Rev 17:16; 19:18, 21). This use of "flesh" is synonymous with or similar to the primary use of "body" (σῶμα). In a similar way, "body" is used three times in Rom to describe the manifestation of sinful tendencies (Rom 6:6; 7:24 [This verse along with others, such as Rom 8:10, seems to talk about the living death of the body as a result of the curse of sin which is being redeemed. In these instances, "body" is set in contrast with "spirit" (πνεῦμα) in a fashion similar to "flesh."]; 8:13). However, as a general rule, the "flesh" is the prominent word the apostle Paul uses to describe the sinful tendencies of mankind and one of the entities against which spiritual people must battle in seeking to live out the desires of the Spirit of God (Rom 7:5, 18, 25; 8:3–9, 12–13; 13:14; 1 Cor 5:5; Gal 5:13, 16–17, 19, 24; 6:8; Eph 2:3; Col 2:11, 13, 18, 23). This use is also seen in non-Pauline epistles (2 Pet 2:10, 18; 1 John 2:16; Jude 7, 23). For a more detailed analysis of "flesh," "body," and "spirit," see Barclay, *Flesh and Spirit*; Brown, "Spirit, Holy Spirit," 1:689–709; Bultmann, *Theologie des Neuen Testaments*, 193–210, 232–38; Erickson, *Dictionary of Paul and His Letters*, s.v. "Flesh;" Johnson, "Theological Implications;" Kleinknecht et al., "πνεῦμα," in *TDNT*, 6:332–451; Motyer, "Body, Member, Limb," 1:229–42; Ridderbos, *Paul*, 57–68, 93–95, 102–3, 115–6, 548–50; Schweizer, Baumgärtel, and Meyer, "σάρξ" in *TDNT*, 7:98–151; Schweizer and Baumgärtel, "σῶμα," in *TDNT*, 7:1024–94; Thiselton, "Flesh," 1:671–82; Erickson, *Dictionary of Paul*, s.v. "Flesh."

reader that the spiritual life will be one of tension between the presence of the Spirit and the desires of the flesh.[4]

A clarification is needed before going further. What the apostle Paul is not indicating is that something is flawed with the physical form so that in order to be truly spiritual, one must be freed from their fleshly bodies in its physical form.[5] The problem is not the body as an organism per se; although, the body has been impacted by the curse of the fall (Gen 3) in such a way that it is flawed, as evidenced through all types of blemishes and medical problems. Aging also demonstrates the imperfection of the body tainted by the curse of sin. Thus, the body is not evil, but has been affected by the fall in such as way that its desires have a propensity towards sin and self. In the end, the body will not be discarded as evil, but purified from its imperfections and redeemed (1 Cor 15:42–44; Phil 3:21). This point does not begin to address questions concerning the degree to which someone's DNA gives them a particular propensity to sin. More research needs to be done in connection between the soul and someone's unique DNA makeup. The point made here is that people have been impacted by the curse of the fall in such a way that they will struggle with temptation from within themselves until the redemptive process is completed with their glorification. Thus, the problem experienced from within people are the desires that arise by the fact they live in a fleshly body, with fleshly desires, in a fallen world. Wilber T. Dayton explains that the "evil force [often] attributed to flesh is not at all a substance inherent in the human body as material. It is an attitude or mindedness. It is called *phronema sarkos*—a mindedness toward the flesh."[6] Inherent within all people, even the maturest of believers, as a result of the curse of the fall is a desire on some level to indulge fleshly desires.[7] These are desires with which one must contend. Even those who have

---

4. For a detailed analysis of the use of "Spirit" (πνεῦμα) and "flesh" (σάρξ) and the tension between them presented in Scripture, see Burton, *Galatians*, 486–95; idem, *Spirit, Soul, Flesh*; Jewett, *Paul's Anthropological Terms*, 49–200. For an analysis of these words focused particularly on Gal, see Fletcher, "Singular Argument," 264–8.

5. Burton conducts a thorough analysis of the use of these words in refuting this Gnostic concept in his work *Spirit, Soul, Flesh*. Specifically, see pp. 191–7. So also Jewett, *Paul's Anthropological Terms*, 100.

6. Dayton, "New Testament Conception of Flesh," 15.

7. It is not being argued that the believer has two natures as is assumed by some. As Neill explains, "Perhaps the gravest objection is that it rests on a false understanding of human nature, and of what sin has done to human nature. There is a tendency for preachers and others to speak of 'our sinful nature'; and this almost suggests that we have two natures, one bad and one good, that can in some way co-exist within us. Such

experienced justification by faith with Christ and have been freed from the bondage of sin through the crucifixion of the Adamic nature must still contend with the residual influences of that nature. Preaching on Galatians 2:20, William Bridge, a seventeenth-century Puritan pastor, highlights this ever lingering struggle in the spiritual life.[8]

> Though every true Beleever, be an Humble, Self-Denying person, and is made partaker of this Gospel-Self-Denial: yet know, there is something of Self, some remains of Self that still continues with the best, something still that will tast of the Cask. Though the Onion that is beaten in the morter, be taken out of the morter, yet the morter will smell of it. A godly, gracious man, is sensible of his own Pride, and Self-Advancing in spiritual things, and will cry out and say, Oh! What a Proud heart have I! A Self-Advancing heart have I! But shew me that man, that was ever so transformed, melted, changed into the mould of the Gospel; but still some savor of Self remains.[9]

The internal tension between the presence of the Spirit of Christ and the pull to indulge ungodly desires, no matter how subtle, will persist until the redemptive process is completed with one's glorification (Rom 8:29–30).[10]

---

a manner of thinking almost reproduces the dualism for which we earlier criticized the Gnostics, though in a new form" (Neill, *Christian Holiness*, 36). Rather, it is argued that the believer is torn in an age begun but not yet completed. While the believer has been justified and positionally sanctified, there is still a living out of the faith, a maturing and a growing in the faith, whereby the believer seeks to live under the influence of the Spirit of God while denying his own fleshly desires. For an interesting and helpful critique of the two-nature view, see Sanchez Jr., "Old Man Versus the New Man." The spiritual life is not one of two natures, but one spiritual nature that has to resist desires to live contrary to the leading of the Spirit.

8. For information on Bridge's life and an examination of Bridge's approach to Gal 2:20, see McClendon, "Puritan's Perspective of Galatians 2:20," 56–80.

9. Bridge, *Works of William Bridge*, 3:67.

10. So Spross, "Sanctification in the Thessalonian Epistles," 45, 209–10. Erickson speaks to this progressive nature of the sanctifying process. "Further, this divine working within the believer is a progressive matter. This is seen, for example, in Paul's assurance that God will continue to work in the lives of the Philippians: 'being confident of this, that he who began a good work in you will carry it on to completion until the day of Christ Jesus' (Phil. 1:6). Paul also notes that the cross is the power of God 'to us who are being saved' (1 Cor. 1:18). He uses a present participle here, which clearly conveys the idea of ongoing activity. That this activity is the continuation and completion of the newness of life begun in regeneration is evident not only from Philippians 1:6, but also from Colossians 3:9–10 . . ." (Erickson, *Christian Theology*, 982). Wesleyanism, which will be discussed in greater detail later, does not necessarily agree that the believer must

Galatians 2:20, then, is giving a redemptive historical summary of the Christian life providing a glimpse into the reality that although one has been justified and indwelt by Christ, and although the condemnation and penalty of the law and the Adamic nature have been removed, the Christian is still torn between the old and new age, an age begun, but not yet realized in full. D. K. Fletcher explains this tension in the Christian in this manner:

> The Christian is no longer σάρξ [flesh] but merely ἐν σαρκί [in flesh]. Galatians 2:20 is formulated in light of 2:16. . . . Paul uses the quotation in 2:16 with its idea of πᾶσα σάρξ [all flesh] as the basis for his claim that in justification the flesh is not simply justified; it cannot be justified. Instead, there is a death with Christ and the constitution of a new life in him.
>
> Thus in [Galatians] chapter two, flesh acquires a symbolic meaning. The flesh cannot be justified; rather, there is a transformation. The use of σάρξ [flesh] in chapter two sets it into an opposition. This opposition is explained in 2:20: "it is no longer I who live, but Christ lives in me." The flesh is interpreted consistently with the broader meaning of 6:13: the flesh as a source of boasting cannot be justified.[11]

As a result, the believer will still struggle in the spiritual life with the impulses and desires of the flesh.

This concept is reinforced by Paul's other uses of flesh throughout the rest of Galatians, the first of which comes only a couple of verses after 2:20 in 3:1–3 where the Spirit and flesh are set in opposition with one another. "O foolish Galatians! Who has bewitched you? It was before your eyes that Jesus Christ was publicly portrayed as crucified. Let me ask you only this: Did you receive the Spirit by works of the law or by hearing with faith? Are you so foolish? Having begun by the Spirit, are you now being perfected by

---

wait until glorification to be relieved from the internal tension of the flesh. In general, however, Wesleyanism does hold that the believer must wait until glorification to be completely free "from the effects as well as the presence of all sin" (Dieter et al., *Five Views on Sanctification*, 14).

11. Fletcher, "Singular Argument," 233. Fletcher's original quote attributes Gal 2:16 to Paul's conversation with Peter in Antioch while it seems more likely that Paul's conversation with Peter ends at the end of Gal 2:14. Fletcher also makes a statement, not presented above, concerning "Peter's problem." Such a statement could be taken to mean that Peter did not really understand justification. This language is problematic and should be avoided. If it were held that Peter's actions were being addressed in Gal 2:16, it's more appropriate to see Peter's actions being corrected by Paul, in part, because Peter did not understand the implication of his actions, not because his theology of justification was faulty.

the flesh?" "Flesh" in this context is quite possibly the pursuit of circumcision.[12] If circumcision is the act in Paul's mind, he is using it as a paradigm for all human efforts to achieve or maintain justification. The apostle appears to be using a play on words ultimately to emphasize the error of using human effort in the pursuit of perfecting that which is by nature a spiritual process.[13] That which was begun by the Spirit of God will not be perfected (completed) by human efforts; rather, as one submits to the Spirit of Christ, their activity will be transformed through the suppression of fleshly desires and the tangible manifestation of love (Gal 5:13–26). As Thomas R. Schreiner explains, "The term 'flesh' here is used in the technical Pauline sense, referring to reliance on the old Adam, the unregenerate person. The opposition between the Spirit and flesh represents the eschatological [end times] contrast between this age and the age to come (cf. 1:4) . . . ."[14]

An argument could be made that Galatians chapter 4 removes the possibility of seeing "flesh" in Galatians in this way; however, chapter 4 uses "flesh" to build to a tension towards the end of that chapter between those born of flesh and those born of promise (4:29). "The Spirit and the flesh are developed as opposing contemporary forces in 4:21 through 4:31."[15] As Jewett presents, "There are good reasons to insist that the character of 'flesh' is formally the same in both passages [Gal 4 and 5]. In both it stands in opposition to Christ and his realm. In both passages it is the flesh which takes the offensive against the spirit and in both it reduces man to slavery. Furthermore, the nature of the flesh is formally similar in both passages; it is at once a cosmic sphere and a realm of human capability or action."[16] Moreover, to be clear, what is argued in this section is that Paul in giving

12. Betz, *Galatians*, 134; Burton, *Galatians*, 148. Contra Bruce who sees it as "human nature in its unregenerate weakness, relying on such inadequate resources as were available before the coming of faith, having no access as yet to the power of the Spirit" (*Galatians*, 149).

13. So Longenecker, *Galatians*, 103, who sees that human effort is in view here. Dunn also sees a double significance here; although, he will emphasize the new perspectives view concerning ethnic identity: "The antithesis Spirit/flesh itself has a double significance: (1) between Spirit as divine power and enabling, and flesh as weak, self-centered, self-indulgent humanity . . . . (2) Jewish emphasis on ethnic identity (see on ii.20), as exemplified in the demand for circumcision (vi.13) . . ." (*Galatians*, 155). In this connection, Fletcher will argued that "flesh represents both circumcision and that which cannot be justified" (Fletcher, "Singular Argument," 234).

14. Schreiner, *Galatians*, 184.

15. Fletcher, "Singular Argument," 234.

16. Jewett, *Paul's Anthropological Terms*, 102–3.

a redemptive historical summary of the spiritual life uses "flesh" in such a way as to prepare the reader for the reality that they will still face temptation from fleshly desires as described in 5:14–26.

This redemptive historical tension presses the reader forward in anticipation to chapter 5 where this internal tension is more clearly articulated. Galatians 5:16–18 is particularly helpful: "But I say, walk by the Spirit, and you will not gratify the desires of the flesh. For the desires of the flesh are against the Spirit, and the desires of the Spirit are against the flesh, for these are opposed to each other, to keep you from doing the things you want to do. But if you are led by the Spirit, you are not under the law." Paul challenges Galatian believers. Since they are not under the law, they now have the capacity to live according to a different pattern of life; however, a temptation to follow after old patterns still exists. They are not to live their life in the same pattern as those under the law in which the passions of their flesh are aroused and satisfied.[17] The law serves to increase one's awareness of sin in part by heightening one's appetite for sin (i.e., their fleshly desires) (Rom 7:4–14).[18] Because one has been co-crucified with Christ (Gal 2:20), he is free from the bondage and condemnation of the law (5:1); however, this newly found freedom is not an opportunity to focus on himself (i.e., indulge the flesh), but an opportunity to focus on loving his neighbor (5:13–14).[19] In other words, the believer is now free from the bondage of the law in order to become a servant of love to others. Therefore, Paul explains that believers are to be on guard against themselves. Their old tendencies and desires will still seek to lure them into sin (Jas 1:14).

17. This statement does not mean that those under the law necessarily acted out all sins possible. Instead, the point being made is that where the law was sin increased (Rom 7:4–14). This same thought is seen in Paul's admonition in Rom 6 for one to submit their members as slaves of righteousness.

18. Who the "I" is in Rom 7 will not be debated here. The point to be made is the influence of the law upon man. The law aroused sinful passions within the person. Rom 7:1–14: "For while we were living in the flesh, our sinful passions, aroused by the law, were at work in our members to bear fruit for death . . . What then shall we say? That the law is sin? By no means! Yet if it had not been for the law, I would not have known sin. For I would not have known what it is to covet if the law had not said, 'You shall not covet.' But sin, seizing an opportunity through the commandment, produced in me all kinds of covetousness. For apart from the law, sin lies dead . . . For sin, seizing an opportunity through the commandment, deceived me and through it killed me . . . For we know that the law is spiritual, but I am of the flesh, sold under sin."

19. See brief excursus titled *Freedom versus Natural Desire* in Schreiner, *Galatians*, 336.

So the σάρξ [flesh] still exercises its power over the believer through enticements to sin (cf. Eph. 2:3, of unbelievers). The antidote is expressed in two ways. The one is that the believer has crucified the σάρξ, passions and all. This statement corresponds with the statement in Gal 6:14 that the believer is crucified to the world and the world to the believer. This means that believers are dead so far as the σάρξ or the world is concerned, and therefore its appeal should fall on deaf ears. The other is that believers must live and walk by the Spirit, whose power will enable them to overcome the σάρξ (5:16, 18, 25).[20]

Thus, while their internal ungodly desires will never completely vanish in this life, those desires are not to be given in to; rather, believers are to walk in the Spirit living out a life of love.

Every use of the word "flesh" in Galatians is not intended to highlight this tension (5:13), but the use in Galatians 2:20 should press the reader beyond seeing "flesh" as simply meaning the body without any further significance for the spiritual life (3:3; 4:29; 5:13–26; 6:8–15). Even Walter B. Russell III, who dismisses the internal tension view concerning the flesh and the Spirit (180), acknowledges that "flesh" in Gal 2:15–21 "create[s] a subtle foreshadowing of the σάρξ/πνεῦμα antithesis which begins in 3:1–5."[21] The reality is that Paul does present the spiritual life as one of tension to include an internal desire for sin that is to be resisted is evidenced in Galatians 5:16–26, which serves for the basis of his admonition.[22] Describing Paul's use of the flesh in this regard, F. F. Bruce explains that:

> Its surviving influences can be traced even in the regenerate: the Corinthian Christians, for example, are addressed as "men of the flesh", despite having received the Spirit, because they are still prone to jealousy and strife and judge men according to the standards of worldly wisdom (1 Corinthians 3:1–4) . . . That the "flesh" was crucified with Christ and can yet be a menace to the believer is one aspect of a paradox that recurs repeatedly in Paul's writings. Believers are said to have "put off the old man" and "put on the new man" (Colossians 3:9f), while elsewhere they are exhorted to do just that—to "put off the old man" and "put on the new man" (Ephesians 4:22, 24).

20. Marshall, "Living in the 'Flesh,'" 395. So, Ridderbos, Galatia, 203–4.

21. Russell, "Paul's Use of Sarx," 144. For an explanation and critique of Russell's view, see McClendon, "Galatians 2:20," 112–4.

22. This tension is seen elsewhere in Paul's writing Rom 8:12–17; 13:14; Col 2:23; etc.

Though "my flesh" (as Paul thus puts it) is still a reality to the believer, he is no longer "in the flesh" in this sense. To be "in the flesh" in this sense is to be unregenerate, to be still "in Adam", in a state in which one "cannot please God" (Romans 8:8). Believers were formerly "in the flesh" (Romans 7:5), but now they are "not in the flesh, but in the Spirit", if the Spirit of God really dwells within them—and if he does not, they have no title (according to Paul) to be called the people of Christ (Romans 8:9).[23]

The important point to emphasize (or remember) is that before the believer's co-crucifixion with Christ, one was powerless to resist their unregenerate nature and live rightly to God, the old man still ruled; however, because of co-crucifixion the old man has been crucified and the regenerated believer now has a new nature that by the Spirit's leading is empowered to reject the calling to give in to "fleshly" desires. This is the struggle in the spiritual life of the believer.

Significance of the Tension

This approach to the spiritual life has substantial implications regarding sanctification, specifically in that regardless of how far one progresses in holiness in this life one will always contest internally with the desires of the flesh.[24] Notice, what is not being said is that the presence of those desires necessitates submission to them, even if only occasionally.[25] While the

23. Bruce, *Paul*, 205–6.

24. For further discussion concerning the various views of sanctification, see Dieter et al., *Five Views on Sanctification*. Evangelicalism frequently takes a two or three stage position whereby the believer is sanctified, is being sanctified, and will be sanctified. So Berkhof, *Systematic Theology*, 527–44; Erickson, *Christian Theology*, 980–6; Garrett Jr., *Systematic Theology*, 2:401–2; Grudem, *Systematic Theology*, 747–50; Hodge, *Systematic Theology*, 3:213–58. Part of the issue is clouded because at times sanctification is assessed in various ways within different traditions as Dunning notes, "There seem to be four chief ways of interpreting sanctification, with the possibility of some interpenetration. These are (1) in terms of law, (2) in terms of love, (3) in terms of transformation of being, and (4) ceremonially or cultically" (Dunning, *Grace, Faith, and Holiness*, 457).

25. The primary focus of this section is to refute the notion of perfectionism as advocated within some Wesleyan circles that one can obtain a level of "entire sanctification" so that they are filled with perfect love and no longer have to deal with internal temptation. The thought that a believer has to sin is a major concern which Wesleyans rightly resist due to their understanding of the freedom from sin brought by the presence of the Spirit and the death of the old man in the new birth. Most attacks against "Christian perfection" focus on arguing that a believer cannot be sinless (i.e., they will sin

Bible does present the spiritual life as one where there is always room for improvement (2 Pet 3:17–18), the logical progression that then proceeds to argue that the believer must give in to sinful desires goes beyond and actually contradicts what Scripture advocates. Believers are fully equipped by the presence of the Spirit of Christ for the spiritual life (Rom 6; 8:1–17; Eph 2:1–10; 3:14–21; 4:1–7, 20–5:21; 6:10–18; Col 1:9–14; Heb 13:20; 1 Pet 1:13–25; 2:16, 24; 4:1–6; 1 John 3:4–10; 5:4–5; etc). They no longer have to give in to sinful temptation, although experience reveals that they often do. Moreover, whether temptation comes from within or without, Christians are guaranteed a way of escape by God so that they can resist and not give in (1 Cor 10:13).[26] Thus, to be clear, this section is not addressing the frequency of sin in the believer or even the capacity of the believer in regards to sin; rather, what is being argued in this section is that an internal tension

---

so long as they are on earth) (Berkhof, *Systematic Theology*, 537–9; Erickson, *Christian Theology*, 983–6; Geisler, *Systematic Theology*, 3:237–40; Grudem, *Systematic Theology*, 750–3; Hodge, *Systematic Theology*, 3:245–58; Wenham, "Christian Life," 80–94). For example, even Wenham who titles his work "Christian Life: A Life of Tension?" focuses primarily on the question of whether or not the Christian will continually fall into sin. "Did Paul believe that his readers could experience consistent victory in their spiritual warfare, or did he know that their Christian lives would be up and down affairs in which they would experience defeat" (Wenham, "Christian Life," 80–94)? As another example, Erickson will say, "Our conclusion is that while complete freedom from and victory over sin are the standard to be aimed at and are theoretically possible, it is doubtful whether any believer will attain this goal within this life" (Erickson, *Christian Theology*, 986). However, Wesleyans see such statements as a diminishing of the power, presence, and promises of God in salvation. For them, the argument that one will continue to sin is an assumption unsupported by Scripture and one which limits the freedom believers have from the bondage of sin. As Dieter explains, "The doctrine of entire sanctification, or Christian perfection . . . has often been attacked as a purely perfectionist ideal—an attractive one, but unrealizable in this world of imperfection and sin. Wesleyans, however, have focused on that very ideal, which they regard as the reigning vision of the Scriptures themselves, set forth throughout as the essence of the gospel. To deny the expectation of its realization in some true measure when properly presented in its biblical balance and integrity is to fail to communicate the full riches of God's grace now available to His people for life and service" (Dieter et al., *Five Views on Sanctification*, 29). This section critiques the Wesleyan doctrine of entire sanctification from a unique perspective addressing the reality of the persistence of fleshly desires after sanctification that persists throughout this life.

26. Yet, as Wenham notes, this does not diminish the intensity and reality of the attack against the believer from without as well as within. "Paul also knew the strength of the forces ranged against the believer. So as well as promising the way of escape from temptation, he warned, 'Let him who thinks he stands take heed lest he fall' (1 Cor. 10:12)" (Wenham, "Christian Life," 89).

will always exist in the life of the all believers because they live "in the flesh" (Gal 2:20).

Some major movements within Christian spirituality disagree with the idea that the spiritual life is necessarily one of continual tension.[27] They instead advocate that in the spiritual life one has the potential of progressing to a point of "entire sanctification" where one is filled with perfect love and no longer has to deal with internal temptation. This view is most commonly known as "Christian perfection,"[28] and is most commonly associated with the teachings of John Welsely.[29]

Entire sanctification is the view that the believer can reach a place of total commitment to the Lord by the indwelling power of the Holy Spirit through a second work of grace whereby they now live out of perfect love.[30] Two prominent proponents of this view within Wesleyanism are Methodists and Nazarenes.[31] The United Methodist Church in article eleven of its confession of faith describes entire sanctification.

27. This section will focus exclusively on Wesleyan theology. Keswick theology is not critiqued for the following reasons. First, Keswick theology has already been extensively critiqued in regard to its view of sanctification in Naselli, *Let Go and Let God*. Secondly, Keswick theology does not have as clear parameters as Wesleyanism does with its denominational boundaries so it is not as clearly identifiable. Third, it is unclear how extensive Keswick theology is within contemporary American Protestantism, while Wesleyanism is evident and prominent. Fourth, Keswick theology rejects Wesleyanism and does not hold to a life without tension; rather, promotes moment-by-moment victory through faith (ibid., 185, 190, 198); thus, it does not fit within the critique provided here.

28. "Christian perfection" is not to be confused with "perfectionism" (i.e., sinlessness). This distinction will be address later in this section. "Christian perfection" is known by a variety of names within Wesleyanism: "entire sanctification," "perfect love," "the second blessing," "the second work of grace," "Christian holiness," "Canaan," "the second rest," "baptism with the Holy Spirit," "heart purity," "the fullness of the blessing" (Grider, *Wesleyan-Holiness Theology*, 367–75). See also "Preamble and Articles of Faith." "Christian perfection" is not necessarily to be equated with the New Testament use of perfect or complete τέλειος. For a thorough analysis of τέλειος see Du Plessis, ΤΕΛΕΙΟΣ; Delling, "τέλος," in *TDNT*, 8:49–87.

29. Wesley's critical work that serves as the fundamental basis for this view is *Plain Account of Christian Perfection*.

30. Concerns regarding a second work of grace or the baptism of the Holy Spirit subsequent to conversion were addressed in the previous chapter and will not be reiterated here. For an introduction into the debate concerning whether entire sanctification is gradual or instantaneous, see Grider, *Wesleyan-Holiness Theology*, 393–404.

31. For a picture of a Wesleyan approach to Scripture, see Green, *Reading Scripture as Wesleyans*. Wesleyans have a high view of Scripture. In their case, the issue becomes one of tradition; whereby, their tradition overly influences the reading of various texts in relationship to sanctification. The issue is not one of a dismissal of God's Word, but a

Entire sanctification is a state of perfect love, righteousness and true holiness which every regenerate believer may obtain by being delivered from the power of sin, by loving God with all the heart, soul, mind and strength, and by loving one's neighbor as one's self. Through faith in Jesus Christ this gracious gift may be received in this life both gradually and instantaneously, and should be sought earnestly by every child of God.

We believe this experience does not deliver us from the infirmities, ignorance, and mistakes common to man, nor from the possibilities of further sin. The Christian must continue on guard against spiritual pride and seek to gain victory over every temptation to sin. He must respond wholly to the will of God so that sin will lose its power over him; and the world, the flesh, and the devil are put under his feet. Thus he rules over these enemies with watchfulness through the power of the Holy Spirit.[32]

The Church of the Nazarene in article ten in its articles of faith describes entire sanctification.

We believe that entire sanctification is that act of God, subsequent to regeneration, by which believers are made free from original sin, or depravity, and brought into a state of entire devotement to God, and the holy obedience of love made perfect.

It is wrought by the baptism with *or infilling of* the Holy Spirit, and comprehends in one experience the cleansing of the heart from sin and the abiding, indwelling presence of the Holy Spirit, empowering the believer for life and service.

Entire sanctification is provided by the blood of Jesus, is wrought instantaneously by *grace through* faith, preceded by entire consecration; and to this work and state of grace the Holy Spirit bears witness. . . .

We believe that there is a marked distinction between a pure heart and a mature character. The former is obtained in an instant, the result of entire sanctification; the latter is the result of growth in grace.

We believe that the grace of entire sanctification includes the divine impulse to grow in grace as a Christlike disciple. However, this impulse must be consciously nurtured, and careful attention given to the requisites and processes of spiritual development and improvement in Christlikeness of character and personality.

---

misunderstanding of it as a result of tradition.

32. "The Confessions of Faith."

Without such purposeful endeavor, one's witness may be impaired and the grace itself frustrated and ultimately lost.[33]

Although, as evidenced above, some variance exists within Wesleyanism in explaining entire sanctification, general unanimity exists regarding what is and what is not being said. Below are five key unifying beliefs regarding entire sanctification that can generally be seen within contemporary Wesleyanism. Only the last of these five points will be extensively critiqued.

1. Entire sanctification does not equal sinlessness (i.e., perfectionism), but as a result of one's consecration to God, one lives life out of an impulse of perfect love resulting in moment-by-moment obedience.

This point is an important one within mainstream contemporary Wesleyanism. As a result, Wesleyan authors repeatedly address it in trying to create greater clarity concerning the doctrine. Consequently, several of them will be presented here, and throughout this section, to show this unifying principle within their belief while highlighting some of the unique nuances within their individual perspectives.

Mildred Bangs Wynkoop, for example, seeks to dispel some of the confusion that exists in equating entire sanctification with sinlessness (perfectionism) explaining:

> It is customary to class all theological positions which stress the subjective aspect of grace as "perfectionism." But there is a very real and important theological and practical difference between perfection which can be called Christian and that which we may term perfectionism. This difference may not be indicated in the dictionary definitions, but the inherent connotations can be utilized "by an arbitrary decree" to serve to distinguish two very different ways of approaching Christian teaching on the subject. The major problems arising out of any theological or religious use of the term perfection occur because this distinction is not recognized and taken into account.[34]

Melvin E. Deiter also seeks to clarify the confusion and correct the mistake some have made in equating entire sanctification (Christian perfection) with perfectionism.

---

33. "Articles of Faith." The italics reflect changes in the word of the *Manual of the Church of the Nazarene*, 29–30.

34. Wynkoop, *Theology of Love*, 273. Wynkoop has been very influential in shaping modern day Wesleyanism (Quanstrom, *Century of Holiness Theology*, 137–70).

He [Wesley] never allowed that entirely sanctified Christians could become sinless in the sense that they could not fall again into sin through disobedience. He did teach that so long as men and women were the creatures of free will, they were able to respond obediently or disobediently to the grace of God. They would never be free from the *possibility* of deliberate, willful sinning in this life. They could, however, be delivered from the *necessity* of voluntary transgressions by living in moment-by-moment obedience to God's will. Whatever difficulty might arise in defining the theology, content, or means of attaining such a loving relationship with God, it could mean no less than freedom from the dominion of sin in this life. It did not, however, mean freedom from all the effects of sin in the deranged worldly order in which we experience even the most perfect of our present relationships under grace. Total freedom from the effects as well as the presence of all sin had to await the glory to come.[35]

Lastly, J. Kenneth Grider's comments sufficiently and succinctly summarize the issue. "Conduct springing from purified human nature may still be incongruent with God's highest will for us. We are not made errorless or faultless. . . . While 'perfection,' then, is appropriate, being often used in Scripture, it is inappropriate because it suggests to outsiders a life perfect in the fullest possible sense."[36]

Although such great strides are taken to avoid the accusation that entire sanctification equals sinless, the implication is nonetheless subtlety there as Robin Maas rightly concedes.[37]

35. Dieter et al., *Five Views on Sanctification*, 13–14.

36. Grider, *Wesleyan-Holiness Theology*, 368.

37. This point that entire sanctification by default implies sinlessness continues to be a source of contention within Wesleyanism. Quanstrom talks of some of the contention it has created within the Nazarene church. "Thoughtful persons within the Church of the Nazarene have indeed pondered the impact of the 'rediscovery of the deep sinfulness of man' on the distinctive doctrine that promised nothing less than the entire eradication of sin. The doctrine has been changed. In short, by the end of the century [20th], entire sanctification would not be taught so much as an instantaneous change in the heart of the believer appropriated by consecration and faith, but rather more as an unremarkable event in a process of growth, if taught at all. The 'eradication of the sinful nature' would be terminology that many Nazarenes would eschew, even though the words would remain in the Articles of Faith throughout the century" (Quanstrom, *Century of Holiness Theology*, 23). He continues to explain, "The high expectations concerning the positive consequences of entire sanctification would diminish drastically. While the Article of Faith would remain for the most part unchanged, many in the Church of the Nazarene would understand the doctrine in a way that most early Holiness leaders of the

At the same time, the church assumed that when the individual reached the point where this kind of total, self-giving love was possible, then a certain (i.e., a *qualified*) type of sinlessness was also possible. The heart captured by God would not be tempted by lesser loves, the mind filled with the thought of God would not be distracted with the inessential, with the banality of evil. The perfect, or 'complete,' love of God necessarily excludes everything contrary to the goodness God intends for the created order.[38]

Thus, while it is conceded that some "accidental" sins may occur, willful defiant sin against God becomes something of an impossibility because no source exists for such defiance as seen later in Maas's work.

The working of the Spirit within the individual believer was not simply a revivification but a purgation, a cleansing tongue of fire that destroyed, first, the grossest effects of original sin . . . . Perfection, like sin, resided in the will. Love, like sin, was not a feeling but a *decision*. Thus the person who had committed herself—heart, soul, mind, and body—to God could be counted on not to commit serious (or deadly) sins as well as deliberate, not deadly but still debilitating sins. Hidden, subconscious sins, personal quirks and imperfections, or mistakes based on ignorance were not considered obstacles to perfection as the church understood it. . . . Perfection in love . . . means *loving to full capacity*—however small or great that capacity may be. . . . We are perfected when we are filled to the brim with a yearning for God. And we cannot be filled to the brim with desire for God until we are emptied of all lesser loves.[39]

Keith Drury also points to this idea that while sin is potential, willful sin will never be actualized in the entirely sanctified person. "The difference for the Spirit-baptized or completely sanctified person is that *the will is set*—there is total commitment to obedience, and there is power from God to resist. Being baptized with the Holy Spirit won't deliver you from temptation. But

---

movement would have lamented" (ibid., 24). Yet, despite the openness within Wesleyanism to be generally unified around the idea that entire sanctification is not sinlessness, they still insist on a singleness of intention motivated by pure love that dissolves and removes the internal tension of the flesh within the believer. Thus, while they have made strides in seeking to correct and clarify some of the implications of the doctrine, such corrective measures have not gone far enough. See also ibid., 27–52.

38. Maas, *Crucified Love*, 28.

39. Ibid., 29–30.

it can deliver you from yielding to it."[40] H. Ray Dunning poses the question of potential sin even more directly.

> But there is an instantaneous moment in the process that may be called perfect love, or entire sanctification, perfect only in the sense of being unmixed. Wesley's own description verifies John Peters' claim that the most appropriate term for Wesley's understanding of entire sanctification is "expulsion," or love expelling sin: "It is love excluding sin; love filling the heart, taking up the whole capacity of the soul. . . . For as long as love takes up the whole heart, what room is there for sin therein?"[41]

Therefore, even though it is argued that they are not sinless, by default, that is the implication especially since within Wesleyanism sin is narrowly defined as a "voluntary transgression of a known law of God."[42] If is there is no room for lesser loves, then intentional sin can never exist because one can never be persuaded intentionally to follow after something contrary to God. Nevertheless, a unifying principle within Wesleyanism regarding entire sanctification is that it does not equal sinlessness.

This point continues to present problems for Wesleyans and is inherently confusing due to the seemingly contradictory flow of logic. To say that one can be entirely sanctified (set apart for God), but still sin, does not make sense when it is also argued that those who are entirely sanctified cannot be tempted from within, they will not willful choose to sin, and sin is redefined as a willful versus ignorant violation of God's standard. Thus, logically, advocates of entire sanctification seem to be advocating a form of sinlessness by default; although, it is repeatedly denied.

2. Entire sanctification does not remove the humanness of the person (i.e., personality; preference; personal identity; etc.), but it does mean that in their humanness and limitations they will be fully motivated by pure love.

Those who promote "entire sanctification" also recognize that a person remains human. Just as when Paul said, "It is no longer I who live," (Gal 2:20b) he is describing the loss of his spiritual identity in Adam and not his personal identity as such, so entire sanctification is not advocating a loss of personality or personal identity. Grider touches on this point. "As

---

40. Drury, *Holiness for Ordinary People*, 23.

41. Dunning, *Grace, Faith, and Holiness*, 465.

42. Richards, *A Practical Theology of Spirituality*, 40. So Greathouse and Lyons, *Romans 1–8*, 1:255.

significant as cleansing from carnality is, it does not remove what is essentially human, such as temperament, the sex drive, and the deficiencies that we come by during this life (for example, prejudices)."[43]

3. Entire sanctification does not equal Christian maturity, but it does mean that a person will continue to mature as a Christian.

Operating out of perfect love does not "imply maturity as a Christian person. Instead [it] speaks of 'a heart cleansed from sin and filled with the Holy Spirit' so that 'the love of God has been poured out within our hearts through the Holy Spirit who was given to us' (Rom. 5:5)."[44] 2 Peter 3:18a still applies to the one entirely sanctified: "But grow in the grace and knowledge of our Lord and Savior Jesus Christ." Spiritual growth does not stagnate with entire sanctification. For example, Christians may be completely committed to Christ and still grow in their understanding of vocabulary, grammar, human behavior, culture, etc. As they grow in their understanding of these things, they will grow in their understanding of the Bible and be better able to discern God's will and follow it. They will better understand how to love within the environment in which God has placed them. Thus, their complete commitment motivated by love does not equal perfect maturity in the faith. Room to grow still exists.

4. Entire sanctification does not remove the possibility that one could lose their salvation, but it does mean that someone is not likely to ever lose their salvation.[45]

Even though someone has experienced entire sanctification, they could "fall from God's redeeming grace through willful sin"; although, it is readily admitted that entire sanctification makes it very unlikely.[46] This point stems in part from the theological position within Wesleyanism that due to free will, people are just as free to walk away from grace as they were to choose grace in the first place. This point also becomes problematic for Wesleyans and creates a great deal of confusion. Stating that it is possible for those who are entirely sanctified to fall away still does not adequately

---

43. Grider, *Wesleyan-Holiness Theology*, 412.

44. Richards, *A Practical Theology of Spirituality*, 40.

45. The view that a genuine believer can lose their salvation has already been refuted in this book. It will not be readdressed here except to say that it stands in direct conflict with other passages of Scripture such as John 10:27–30 and Rom 11:29.

46. Grider, *Wesleyan-Holiness Theology*, 410. So Drury, *Holiness for Ordinary People*, 23.

explain the apparent paradox that exists. If those who are entirely sanctified are fully motivated internally by love, cannot be tempted from within, and will not willfully violate God's standard, then what possible avenue exists whereby they could walk away from the faith, especially since walking away from the faith becomes a willful rejection of the gospel?

5. Entire sanctification does not mean that the person will never be tempted, but it does mean that they will not be tempted *from within* because they now have a singleness of intention with which to serve God and others out of pure love.

Entire sanctification is a total consecration of the person. A person completely consecrated to God internally can only be tempted by outside influences. This point is the one with which this chapter takes the greatest objection. Dieter in seeking to explain and defend a Wesleyan view of sanctification speaks to the idea that entire sanctification results in an internal singleness of intention. "Negatively, entire sanctification is a cleansing of the heart, which brings healing of the remaining systemic hurts and bruises from Adam's sin. Positively, it is a freedom, a turning of the whole person toward God in love to seek and to know His will, which becomes the soul's delight."[47] By "whole person," Deiter is saying that all internal influences of the old man and flesh are eradicated, as he has more clearly stated elsewhere,

> There was a remedy for the sickness of systemic sinfulness, namely, entire sanctification—a personal, definitive work of God's sanctifying grace by which *the war within oneself might cease* and the *heart be fully released from rebellion into wholeheated love for God and others.* This relationship of perfect love could be accomplished, not by excellence of any moral achievements, but by the same faith in the merits of Christ's sacrifice for sin that initially had brought justification and the new life in Christ. It was a "total death to sin and an *entire renewal in the image of God.*"[48]

In this quote, the confusion and blending of the end of time redemptive work of God in the believer with the present world ethical mandates for the believer becomes blurred as will be address fully later in the chapter. What should be noted at this point from this quote is that entire sanctification argues that one is sets inwardly in complete devotion to God so that no

47. Dieter et al., *Five Views on Sanctification*, 18.
48. Ibid., 17. Emphasis added.

divergence or tension of allegiance is present. As explained in unifying point three above, this thought does not mean that the Christian is made completely mature, but their growth in maturity is uninhibited by any internal conflict. Grider explains, "They [others who misunderstand entire sanctification] seem to think that it means that our expressions of love to God and others are perfect [i.e., mature or complete]—whereas we only mean that such love is not mixed with carnal motivations, is not self-seeking [pure or single in intention]."[49] "Not mixed with carnal motivations" means that there is not internal tension or struggle. Entirely-sanctified believers have a singleness of intention, which means they do not struggle with fleshly desires that arise from within. Others within Wesleyanism address entire sanctification from a different perspective. Wynkoop, who approaches this subject from a relational versus ethical perspective, explains, "It is a single-hearted, unalloyed love for God,"[50] while Keith Drury, explains the experience of entire sanctification in the spiritual life of the believer as:

> Perhaps you might recall how as a growing believer you struggled with two conflicting desires—sometimes wanting to please God, sometimes wanting to sin, often wanting *both*. But now you discover something new: a single desire dominates your heart—a powerful single-minded desire to be Christlike. Your consuming passion is to obey Christ. This is what you want with all your heart. . . . Sure you will still face temptation—Jesus faced temptation.[51] Yet, like Christ, your will is already set. You are now personally committed and Spirit-enabled to live in obedience.
>
> While your performance may still be less than perfect, your heart is totally perfected in love. Your commitment is complete. Your heart is magnetized toward Jesus Christ. Rebellion is gone. Your battle of conflicting desires has ended. Only one desire fills your heart and mind. You are now a fully devoted follower of Jesus Christ.[52]

---

49. Grider, *Wesleyan-Holiness Theology*, 368. So also Dunning, *Grace, Faith, and Holiness*, 479.

50. Wynkoop, *Theology of Love*, 338. Wynkoop's approach is similar to the use of "perfection" that Du Plessis describes in point 1 on p. 242 of ΤΕΛΕΙΟΣ.

51. Notice that Drury uses Jesus as an example of how an entirely sanctified person is tempted. His point is that temptation will arise, but the temptation comes from without and never from within.

52. Drury, *Holiness for Ordinary People*, 20–21.

The problem is that this perspective is not consistent with the picture of the spiritual life presented throughout the New Testament, and for the sake of argument here, the picture presented in Galatians 2:20 or the admonitions that Paul gives in 5:13–26. Paul's warning, in 5:13–26, for believers against indulging in fleshly desires indicates that fleshly desires are still present in believers's spiritual experiences, even if only sporadically. The understanding presented by Paul in Galatians is that by the continual yielding of the will to the Spirit of Christ one will resist these fleshly desires and continue to live out a life of love to God and to others. These points from Galatians 2:20 and 5:13–26 were discussed earlier in this chapter; therefore, only two additional aspects will be addressed to show how the biblical text should serve as a corrective to the Wesleyan picture of entire sanctification by reinforcing the reality that the believer will experience the internal tension of fleshly desires in this life.

First, the Wesleyan view of entire sanctification misunderstands the "anthropological eschatological" now/not yet tension presented in Scripture regarding the spiritual life.[53] Their system demonstrates an inherent failure to understand the redemptive historical imagery presented by the apostle Paul; whereby, the redeemed struggle in their experience between two ages. Paul introduces that tension in Galatians 2:20 by reminding his audience that although Christ lives within him, he still must live his life in the flesh by continual faith in the Son of God. This revelation of Paul's struggle[54] foreshadows the reality presented throughout chapters 3 through 6 concerning the flesh/Spirit tension. James D. G. Dunn, focusing on the tension Christians will continually experience on some level as a result of this now/not yet reality, argues that:

> The eschatological [end times] tension comes to its sharpest existential expression for Paul in the believer's recognition that he is *a divided man*, a man of split loyalties. He lives in the overlap of

53. Schreiner speaks of this tension in the heart of the believer, "A great battle wages in the hearts of believers. Believers are indwelt by the Holy Spirit, and hence the promised gift of the age to come is now theirs. And yet the present evil age has not passed away (1:4)" (Schreiner, *Galatians*, 343). A few of the other helpful works that emphasize the now/not yet tension the believer will experience are Beker, *Paul the Apostle*, 149, 287–9; Bruce, *Paul*, 197–8; Dunn, *Jesus and the Spirit*, 308; Cullmann, *Christ and Time*, 212; Jewett, *Paul's Anthropological Terms*, 116; Ladd, *Presence of the Future*; Longenecker, *Paul*, 110.

54. As previously stated, Paul is writing in the first person of truths indicative of every believer. It is not just Paul's experience in view, but everyone who places their faith in Jesus Christ (Gal 2:16).

the ages and belongs to both of them *at the same time*. So long as this age lasts he has a foot in both camps—both sinner and justified *at the same time*. As a "living soul" he is of the stock of "the first Adam", but as one who experiences the "life-giving Spirit" he belongs *also* to "the last Adam" (1 Cor. 15:45). As a Christian he has the Spirit, is "in Christ" (Rom. 8.9); but *at the same time* he is . . . still living in some sense at least "in the flesh" (II Cor. 10.3; Gal. 2.20; Phil. 1.22).[55]

Jewett, similarly acknowledges the continual internal conflict between flesh and Spirit.

Thus it is that the conflict between flesh and spirit takes place in the anthropological sphere, within man himself, as well as in the wider course of history.

The effect of this struggle upon man is that he is no self-sufficient individual capable of moral neutrality. . . . He cannot remain neutral, for, led by the flesh, he enters into enmity against the new aeon and thus opposes God. Only when he affirms the crucifixion of his flesh and its empty promises and allows himself to be led by the spirit does he come to freedom and find life. He gains thereby the self-control of those in the spirit who daily leave the flesh's lures powerless behind them. Yet his life is characterized until its end by the struggle between the leading of the spirit and the luring of the flesh.[56]

David Wenham repeats this theme:

The explanation of Paul's two-sided view lies . . . in Paul's eschatology: he believes that the new age has broken into history in Christ, the new Adam, especially in his resurrection and in the pouring out of the Spirit. He believes that by being united to Christ in faith and baptism the believer enters into that new age, receives a new relationship with God and experiences the power of the new age in this life. But he is not taken out of the old age (cf. Rom. 12:1–2; 13:11–14); he is still part of Adam's humanity. . . . The final victory over the old self and the old age will not be experienced until the end, and in the meantime the Christian should be a continual

---

55. Dunn, *Jesus and the Spirit*, 312. Eschatology is the study of last things or end times concerning what happens at the end of one's life or the end of the age when Jesus comes back again.

56. Jewett, *Paul's Anthropological Terms*, 116.

process of purification and growth through the Spirit that has
been given to us.[57]

This now/not yet reality is in part why the apostle Paul constantly challenges his audiences to walk in accordance with the Spirit (Gal 5:16; Eph 4:30; 5:18; 1 Thess 5:19). "Christian experience is one of conflict between flesh and Spirit, a conflict, that is, between the believer's desires as a man of this age (particularly his self-indulgence and self-sufficiency) and the compulsion of the Spirit—a real conflict . . . so that the believer has constantly to be exhorted to follow the direction of the Spirit."[58] Thus, Paul regularly calls believers to rely on the direction and power of the Holy Spirit rather than their own abilities.

What the various authors above are all picking up on is the consistent eschatological theme that man is caught between an age begun and not yet consummated, and an age ending but not yet fully passed. As a result, believers will continue to experience temptation from without as well as from within regardless of the degree of sanctification accomplished in this life. The result will be an ongoing tension, at least on some level, between the leading of the Spirit and the desires of the flesh; nevertheless, the believer is commanded and expected to submit their will to the Spirit. Such a tension does not justify sin, but reveals the reality of the now/not yet tension presented in Scripture.

Secondly, the Wesley view of entire sanctification misunderstands various passages that demonstrate the believer's lifelong need to resist fleshly desires. Romans 8:12–17 is one such passage. It reads:

> So then, brothers, we are debtors, not to the flesh, to live according to the flesh. For if you live according to the flesh you will die, but if by the Spirit you put to death the deeds of the body, you will live. For all who are led by the Spirit of God are sons of God. For you did not receive the spirit of slavery to fall back into fear, but you have received the Spirit of adoption as sons, by whom we cry, "Abba! Father!" The Spirit himself bears witness with our spirit that we are children of God, and if children, then heirs—heirs of God and fellow heirs with Christ, provided we suffer with him in order that we may also be glorified with him.

Paul affirms that "the deeds of the body," that is living according to the flesh, are to be put to death. The emphasis on the "body" is just one key that

57. Wenham, "Christian Life," 90.
58. Dunn, *Jesus and the Spirit*, 313.

Paul uses to allude to the continual struggles children of God will experience so long as they live in this world.[59] The believer will be tempted to live according to the flesh, not only from external sources, but from within their own body. Greathouse, writing from a Wesleyan perspective, hints at the point made here concerning this text.[60] Concerning Romans 8:13, He comments,

> Paul knew the challenges presented by the necessity of *ongoing life in this present age*, despite *our participation in the age to come* . . . The Spirit empowers us to refuse to allow Sin to rule our desires (6:12) . . . Death is the inevitable result of either self-gratification or self-reliance—gratifying the flesh (6:23) or trying to live by fleshly resources (7:7–25). Even though we are not in the Flesh but in the Spirit (8:9a), we are still in the body (sōma) . . . We *can exercise bodily self-control* in the power of the Spirit (Gal 5:22–23). The deeds of the body we must put to death involve psychological and physical impulses—tendencies of the psyche (to rationalize, overcompensate, etc.) and the *instinctual desires and drives of our common humanity.*[61]

However, in an attempt to preserve the traditional understand of entire sanctification, in the next sentence he attempts to push these natural desires to the subconscious, thus, they cannot be intentional (in his view) and therefore fall out of the Wesleyan definition of sin. He states, "Since such impulses reside beneath the level of consciousness, they may be considered morally neutral."[62] Then he continues supporting the claim of this chapter that the believer will also live a life of tension and never one of unhindered desire,

> However, they may lead to sin, thus, they must be controlled and subjugated by the power of the Spirit. If we *repress* or deny their existence, we only deceive ourselves, but if by the Spirit we acknowledge and surrender them to God, he will give us victory over them. The inward stirring of such subconscious impulses are

---

59. Schreiner, *Romans*, 421. While MacArthur is not necessarily perceived as a critical academic New Testament scholar, his pastoral perspective on this point is helpful. "Although there will always be some lingering influences of the flesh until we meet the Lord, we have no excuse for sin to continue to corrupt our lives" (MacArthur, *Romans 1–8*, 422–3).

60. For another Wesleyan perspective of Rom 8:12–17, see Bence, *Romans*, 143–8.

61. Greathouse, *Romans 1–8*, 1:247–8. Emphasis added.

62. Ibid., 1:248.

very real forms of temptation but need not lead to sin (Sangster 1954, 235–6).[63]

A few pages later, Greathouse will have an excurses from the passages discussing entire sanctification. In explaining Wesley's view of entire sanctification, he will argue for a singleness of intention despite the thoughts previously made to the contrary. "Wesley's standard definition of Christian perfection is salvation from *known* sin—from its *power* in the new birth and its *root*—affections contrary to love (1979, 6:489; sermon 'On Patience') . . . ."[64]

Returning to Romans, Paul makes this tension even clearer later in Romans 13:14: "But put on the Lord Jesus Christ, and make no provision for the flesh, to gratify its desires."[65] Paul is writing to all Christians in all stages of their spiritual maturity. Those who have been born again are not to make provision for the flesh. The implication is that there will be a tension, a desire for things of the flesh, but the believer is to submit to the Lordship of Christ instead.[66] Robert H. Mounce comments on this verse, "While the appetites of sin remain until the glorious day of our complete transformation into the likeness of Christ (1 John 3:2; Phil 3:21), we are to deny them any opportunity of expression."[67] The desires of the flesh will persist so long as one lives in this now/not yet reality. Brendan S. J. Byrne echoes the points previously made. "So long as believers remain in the 'overlap' of the ages, their bodies not yet sharing the risen life of their Lord, they necessarily remain 'in the flesh' and feel the pull of its orientation towards sin (cf. Rom. 8:5–8)."[68]

63. Ibid.

64. Ibid., 1:255. Interestingly, in this section Greathouse also connects Rom 8:13 with 1 Cor 9:21, which is addressed below.

65. This verse, in conjunction with Gal 3:27 and Col 3:9, reinforces the previous point regarding the redemptive historical view concerning the now/not yet tension within man. Gal 3:27: "For as many of you as were baptized into Christ have put on Christ." Col 3:9: "Do not lie to one another, seeing that you have put off the old self with its practices." Paul could at the same time speak of something as having been done (the old self is put off), while speaking of it as needing to be done (put off the old self). See Schreiner, *Romans*, 700–01, for more interaction with this concept within the context of Rom 13:14.

66. Greathouse is again helpful here. "In fact, Paul refers to the entire Christian life from justification to glorification, the process of sanctification, as progressive conformity to the image of Christ (8:29; see 2 Cor 3:18)" (Greathouse, *Romans 9–16*, 2:199).

67. Mounce, *Romans*, 249.

68. Byrne, *Romans*, 401.

Commenting on his own spiritual life, Paul states in 1 Corinthians 9:27: "But I discipline my body and keep it under control, lest after preaching to others I myself should be disqualified." Why does Paul discipline the body? It seems in part to exert self-control, so that he will not give in to temptation and thus be disqualified. While it could be argued that Paul only experienced external temptation, such does not seem to be the case. Paul tells the church in Colossians 2:23: "These have indeed an appearance of wisdom in promoting self-made religion and asceticism and severity to the body, but they are of no value in stopping the indulgence of the flesh." The way to stop the indulgence of the flesh is submission to the Spirit; however, the temptation to indulge the flesh will still be there. Later in Colossians 3:5, he reiterates the internal temptations they will face saying: "Put to death therefore what is earthly in you: sexual immorality, impurity, passion, evil desire, and covetousness, which is idolatry." By put to death, Paul is challenging them to reckon themselves as dead to sin. Because of the believer's co-crucifixion with Christ, fleshly desires are not to be considered as options, even though one will still be tempted by them.

Titus 2:11–14 supports this claim linking the need to suppress and resist such desires with the second coming of Jesus.[69] "For the grace of God has appeared, bringing salvation for all people, training us to renounce ungodliness and worldly passions, and to live self-controlled, upright, and godly lives in the present age, waiting for our blessed hope, the appearing of the glory of our great God and Savior Jesus Christ, who gave himself for us to redeem us from all lawlessness and to purify for himself a people for his own possession who are zealous for good works." This key passage highlights the lifelong tension in anticipation of redemption fulfilled at the return of the Lord. Believers must continually denounce the ungodly desires they experience throughout their spiritual life. These passions confront people from within as well as from outside, and are passions that must faithfully and regularly be denied.

Yet, some Wesleyans may point to Matthew 22:37–39[70] and 1 Thessalonians 5:23 in an effort to support the doctrine of entire sanctification. Matthew 22:37–39 reads: "And he said to him, 'You shall love the Lord your God with all your heart and with all your soul and with all your mind. This

---

69. So Phil 1:6: "And I am sure of this, that he who began a good work in you will bring it to completion at the day of Jesus Christ."

70. Also found in Mark 12:30–31 and Luke 10:27. The Wesleyan Bible Commentary has little to say in regard to these verses (Earle et al., *Acts*, 98, 177, 268).

is the great and first commandment. And a second is like it: You shall love your neighbor as yourself.'" Love for God is manifested by obedience as Jesus affirmed in John 14:15: "If you love me, you will keep my commandments." Thus, "Matthew saw the love-commandment as giving meaning and direction to the whole Torah. . . . He understood the commandment(s) to love God and neighbor as providing a coherent perspective for observing the Torah."[71] To love God with all your being does not mean that you do not experience internal fleshly desires, but with your "heart, soul, and mind" you choose God above those things as your highest intention and good. "To love God in the way defined by the great commandment is to seek God for his own sake, to have pleasure in him and to strive impulsively after him."[72] And yet, some may suggest that it is very questionable whether one will ever truly fulfill this command at any given moment in this life.[73] Either way, the command itself provides context for the Torah and living a life to God, but in no way necessitates the removal of the tension that a life lived in the flesh creates.

First Thessalonians 5:23 reads: "Now may the God of peace himself sanctify you completely, and may your whole spirit and soul and body be kept blameless at the coming of our Lord Jesus Christ."[74] Writing in the *Wesleyan Bible Commentary*, W. O. Klopfenstein proclaims,

> He [Paul] prays that this sanctifying experience, begun in a crisis, may continue in process until the *whole man* is fully purged and set apart for God's glory. Who can deny, then, that God wants His children to be wholly cleansed from *all* sin, and in every sense of the word set apart for His own glory? To omit this great truth is to proclaim a partial and emasculated gospel!
>
> The thoroughness of sanctification is clearly indicated. The sanctifying act is designed to penetrate and permeate not only the conscious nature of the believer but also the subconscious strata of his personality. We affirm that the mysterious province of the

---

71. Harrington, *Matthew*, 316.

72. Lane, *Mark*, 432. Lane is commenting on the parallel statements made in Mark 12:30.

73. Berkhof, *Systematic Theology*, 537–9; Erickson, *Christian Theology*, 983–6; Geisler, *Systematic Theology*, 3:237–40; Grudem, *Systematic Theology*, 750–53; Hodge, *Systematic Theology*, 3:245–58. These theologians argue against entire sanctification based on this idea that one will never be sinless in this life.

74. For a comprehensive look at sanctification throughout both Thessalonian epistles, see Spross, "Sanctification in the Thessalonian Epistles."

subconscious must also be transformed by the redemptive process before God's work of grace is complete![75]

Klopfenstein is again supporting the idea that the entirely sanctified person serves God with a singleness of intention from a heart of pure love grounded in faith. His comments focus too much on the components and role of man, but that is not Paul's point. First, Paul is not making detailed distinctions here regarding the components of man, but using this three-fold approach to speak of the entire person.[76] Secondly, Paul's prayer is directed to God seeking a work from him. His emphasis is on the redemptive work of God in their lives. This thought does not remove the reality of the ethical imperatives noted throughout the book that are expected to be followed. The request of 5:23 is not that one should surrender himself to God, but that God would sanctify the person. The idea is that as people who have been redeemed, they are to walking in holiness, so that God might present them perfectly holy at the day of Christ.[77] Thus, the emphasis in 5:23 is eschatological in nature. Jon A. Weatherly's comments are helpful in clarifying the thought of the passage in light of the Wesleyan doctrine of entire sanctification.

> Holiness is, of course, already an attribute of the readers, as they have been made God's people through Christ (3:13). It is also their ongoing responsibility to live in holiness (4:3–4, 7). Here, then, is the final assurance that God will indeed bring to completion the work which he began at their conversion and continues as they live their lives as Christians. . . .
>
> A controversial theological issue hinges on the interpretation of this statement, namely the idea of "entire sanctification," that God gives to some a second act of grace by which they are made

75. Klopfenstein, *1 & 2 Thessalonians*, 543. This directly contradicts what Greathouse in his Wesleyan commentary wrote as noted above in the footnote regarding Rom 8:12–17 and the entire sanctification of the believer. See *Romans 1–8*, 1:247–48.

76. So Green, *Thessalonians*, 269; Martin, *1, 2 Thessalonians*, 189; Morris, *Thessalonians*, 180–1; Plummer, *Thessalonians*, 103–4; Richard, *First and Second Thessalonians*, 286; Wanamaker, *Thessalonians*, 206–7; Weatherly, *1 & 2 Thessalonians*, 190–91; Witherington III, *1 and 2 Thessalonians*, 173.

77. First Thess 5:9–10 is key to this eschatological perspective. "For God has not destined us for wrath, but to obtain salvation through our Lord Jesus Christ, who died for us so that whether we are awake or asleep we might live with him." Salvation is not just something future (as sanctification), but something believers have now; nevertheless, the now/not yet tension is seen whereby salvation will be completed at the day of Jesus Christ.

incapable of sinning. Exegetically this conclusion is drawn from the use of the aorist tense [in the Greek text] here, which, it is argued, indicates a single, momentary action. Even if this were the case, Paul could be referring to the moment of the Lord's return, as the end of the verse shows. However, it is simply not true that the aorist tense alone indicates a one-time action, as many counter-examples demonstrate. The aorist tense leaves the specific manner of action to the context; Paul elsewhere envisages an ongoing process of God's work in the believer's life, climaxing at the return of Jesus (e.g., Phil 1:6; 9–11).[78]

Charles A. Wanamaker agrees, writing that "we must interpret the aorist optative ἁγιάσαι [sanctify] as embracing the whole process. Aorists used in this way are common in prayers (see BDF §337.4). The living of sanctified or holy lives is directed toward the coming of Christ and the day of God's judgment when believers will stand before God (3:13)."[79] In other words, the use of the aorist "to sanctify" does not necessatitate or mean a one time actions. The verb to sanctify is a reference to a process that is brought to fruition at the return of Jesus Christ. The divine work and the end times focus of the passage should not be missed. For this reason, the command should not be seen as merely ethical but soteriological. The ethical is only part of it[80] (1 Thess 4:3) as the outworking of the eschatological hope, but the scope of the passage is soteriological.[81] Richard elaborates further, adding,

> Its [Sanctification's] usage here [5:23] conforms to Paul's other verbal uses; it indicates, in relation to the adjective modifier, the completion or perfection at the parousia of the soteriological activity which God brought about through Christ Jesus. Believers were sanctified by God (or by the Holy Spirit: Rom 15:16) at the

---

78. Weatherly, *1 & 2 Thessalonians*, 189–90.

79. Wanamaker, *Thessalonians*, 206.

80. As appropriately stressed by Wanamaker, though, he does not tend to comment or include the soteriological eschatological focus (Wanamaker, *Thessalonians*, 206). Green, *Thessalonians*, 267–8; Martin, *1, 2 Thessalonians*, 188 also stress the ethical imperative associated with the sanctification process here.

81. Morris speaks to both elements in his comments on 1 Thess 3:13. "There is in Paul's complex thought for them a pronounce ethical and spiritual element. This comes out in the succeeding expressions. He prays for them to be 'unblamable' ... But the thought is not simply ethical. The Apostle goes on to bring in the notion of holiness, in which the basic idea is that of being set apart for God. The word that Paul uses signifies the state rather than the process" (Morris, *Thessalonians*, 113).

time of conversion and so are placed in a state of holiness, a state for which Paul employs the term *hagiasmos* [sanctify] and which requires appropriate behavior (see 4:3–8). Paul is not speaking of the latter in 5:23 but the former; in other words, the prayer is not ethical but eschatological in focus. Such a conclusion is further confirmed by the use of the aorist rather than the present optative. The activity is not that of bringing the believer's moral behavior to a perfect conclusion but of establishing the believer in the sphere of holiness (3:13 and its use of *hagiōsynē*).[82]

Regardless of one's understanding of First Thessalonians 5:23, the reality of the internal tension of the spiritual life is revealed from within the body of First Thessalonians. First Thessalonians 4:3–4 reads, "For this is the will of God, your sanctification: that you abstain from sexual immorality; that each one of you know how to control his own body in holiness and honor." Here, within the context of sanctification, believers are told to control their own body in holiness. Even in the sphere of holiness before the believer's glorification, one will need to control desires contrary to the Spirit and submit one's self in obedience to the Lord.

Conclusion

The Wesleyan tradition has demonstrated a great passion for holiness, because of their rightful conviction that the believer has been called and enabled to live a holy life. God has delivered the believer from the condemnation and power of sin. However, in the passion for promoting holiness, some have overstated the potential of the believer's spiritual life before glorification. This overstatement comes from the argument that believers can achieve a place of entire sanctification whereby they will no longer be tempted from within themselves. Allegiance will be so totally set towards God and they will be so filled with the love of God that no room for temptation from within exists, because the entirely sanctified Christian has a single intention. Not only is this a false understanding of what "filled with the Spirit" means, as discussed in the previous chapter of this book,[83] but also removes the reality presented in Scripture,

82. Richard, *First and Second Thessalonians*, 288–9. Similarly this eschatological focus is discussed on 166–7; 176–7; 194–7; 285. Beale, *1–2 Thessalonians*, 176; Witherington, *1 and 2 Thessalonians*, 173 also emphasize the eschatological component of the text.

83. Being filled with the Spirit is not a command to seek a greater portion of the Spirit, but to live in greater submission to the Spirit.

that the believer must always battle against and resist the desires of the flesh. These are temptations that believers experience both from within and without. Nevertheless, they are not to give in to these temptations; instead, believers are to live under the controlling influence of the Spirit. Again, it is important to emphasize that this critique is not arguing that the believer must sin; rather, it is simply acknowledging that Scripture presents the spiritual life as one involving tension. The Christian lives the spiritual life torn between two ages and as a result experiences the influences of both ages. Believers are to live holy lives and resist fleshly desires. This is evident because the Scriptures reveal that fleshly desires are to some degree a present reality in the believer's spiritual life.

4

Authenticating Evidence of Faith

"I live by faith in the Son of God, who loved me and gave himself for me."

Introduction

AT THIS POINT IN Galatians 2:20, Paul shifts the emphasis of the verse to show that faith is not just a moment at the beginning of one's spiritual life, but is a governing factor throughout one's spiritual life. Such faith is also shown to be intentional and specific. It is intentionally exercised, not an accidental by-product. Moreover, it is specific in its focus. Paul's faith is not generically exercised, but rests specifically on Jesus the Son, who demonstrated his love through his sacrifice on the cross.

Thus, at this juncture in Galatians 2:20, Paul declares that his life has been revolutionized by faith in Jesus Christ. His life is now different. The trajectory of his life has changed from being that of the "chief of sinners" to one committed to serving the Lord Jesus (1 Tim 1:15; Rom 1:1; 12:11). His life is now lived by faith in the Son of God, who loved him and gave himself for him.

This statement regarding living by faith in Jesus at this place in the verse provides two key insights into the spiritual life. First, it reveals the role of continued faith in the life of the believer. Second, it shows how the personal sacrificial love of Christ serves as a motivation for one's life of faith.

Faith-Infused Living

In this section of Galatians 2:20, Paul reveals that the exercise of saving faith is not just a single act at the beginning of one's spiritual life, but it is a continued element that undergirds one's spiritual life. He writes, "And the life I now live in the flesh *I live by faith* in the Son of God, who loved me and gave himself for me."[1] Paul's spiritual life not only began by a personal expression of faith in Jesus Christ (Rom 3:23–26; 5:1–2; Gal 2:16; 3:14, 22–26; Phil 3:8–11; 1 Tim 1:13–4), but continued to be lived out by that same faith (1 Cor 16:13; 2 Cor 1:24; 5:7; Gal 3:11; 5:5; Eph 3:11–2; 1 Thess 5:8; 2 Tim 3:10; 4:7). That same faith that brought Paul to Christ is the same faith that then sets the course of his life. Paul previously explained that he personally believed in Jesus Christ in order to be justified by faith in Galatians 2:16. Now in 2:20, he reveals that this faith that saved him, also sustains and directs him.[2] Consequently, personal faith is a necessary part of the spiritual life.

Necessity of personal faith

This topic concerning the necessity of personal faith goes beyond the emphasis of personal responsibility to place faith in Christ. In other words, it is more than saying that each person is uniquely responsible for their acceptance or rejection of Jesus Christ. That issue was addressed under "Identity" in chapter 1. As a point of reiteration, attacks against the necessity of personal faith and confusion concerning the role of faith are not uncommon as demonstrated in the distorted view presented by Spencer Burke and Barry Taylor: "For most of my Christian life, I have heard people say that it is not enough to do good works or care for the world. There has to be faith in Jesus—which usually means assent to a set of propositions. But actually, the Apostle Paul said it is good works without love—not good works without a belief system—that are empty and worthless."[3] Later in their work, this confusion of the role of faith and God's use of means is made even clearer:

---

1. Emphasis added.

2. As Ernest De Witt Burton explains, "Having in the expression ἐν πίστει [by faith] described faith qualitatively as the sphere of his new life, the apostle now hastens to identify that faith by the addition of the article τῇ and a genitive expressing the object of the faith [the Son of God]" (Burton, *Galatians*, 138–9).

3. Burke and Taylor, *Heretic's Guide to Eternity*, 131–2.

An exclusivist theology is based on a clear line between the insiders and everyone else. People are easily labeled and categorized, based on where they fit in the particular theological view. The theology advances by converting outsiders into insiders. It's an opt-in version of religion that turns faith into a necessary requirement in order to receive grace. *Faith becomes a work, and grace is the carrot held out in front of the person's face.*

Faith is many things, but it is not a requirement. It is faithfulness, the giving of oneself, trust in God, and belief that something greater than the material world exists for all of us.[4]

Paul, however, does present the requirement of the personal expression of faith in the specific object of the Lord Jesus Christ (Gal 2:16–20).[5]

In this section, the point is made that the personal expression of faith in Jesus the Son is not merely a one-time act in the life of the believer. Faith is to be a continued element in the life of the believer that brings them, keeps them, and guides their actions in the spiritual life. That seems in part why Paul addresses faith in relationship to the life that flows out of one who has died in relation to the law through co-crucifixion with Christ. Faith does not end with justification.

Conversely, some leaders within the Free Grace theological system do not see faith as a necessary component of the spiritual life.[6] They see faith as necessary for the initial reception of salvation and the Spirit; however, faith does not have to continue. Saving faith is viewed as a singular act through which one experiences the justifying grace of God distinct from and with no correlation to sanctification. Once justification has been received, a believer has no further obligation to believe.

Two such leaders that represent this view are Charles F. Stanley and Zane Hodges. Stanley, writing on the issue of assurance, addresses the limited necessity of faith. "Faith *was* the agent whereby God was able to apply His grace to the life of the sinner."[7] In his perspective, once grace has been permanently applied, belief is no longer necessary. He explains the independence of faith and salvation this way, "Salvation or justification or adoption—whatever you wish to call it—stands independently of faith. Consequently, God does not require a *constant attitude* of faith in order to be saved—only an *act* of faith . . . Forgiveness/salvation is applied at the

---

4. Ibid., 184.

5. Paul is not alone requiring faith (John 6:28–29).

6. Free Grace theology is a position prevalent within the Lordship salvation debate.

7. Stanley, *Eternal Security*, 78.

moment of faith. It is not the same thing as faith. And its permanence is not contingent upon the permanence of one's faith."[8] Paradoxically, Stanley also believes that faith is expected and should continue. His contention is with the idea that faith must continue. He proceeds to explain that "in all probability, a Christian who has expressed faith in Christ and experienced forgiveness of sin will always believe that forgiveness is found through Christ. But even if he does not, the fact remains that he is forgiven!"[9] His conclusion is based on a faulty view that if faith and salvation are intricately connected then one cannot be sure that they are saved, since one can never be sure that they will persevere in faith. Since he is convinced from Scripture that salvation cannot be lost and that the believer should have assurance of their salvation, he reduces the necessary role of faith to a momentary act.[10] Faith is presented as an essential singular act necessary to procure the benefits of the cross (i.e., co-crucifixion).[11] Once those benefits are applied, the means of salvation (by faith) is no longer necessary.

Zane Hodges echoes this view. "Of course, our [believers's] faith in Christ *should* continue. But the claim that it absolutely must, or necessarily does, has no support at all in the Bible . . . For now, however, it is sufficient to observe that the Bible predicates salvation on an *act* of faith, not on the

8. Ibid., 80. Stanley is right that faith and salvation are not the same thing, but fails to see the permanent connection between faith and salvation. He also describes the act of faith this way, "*Our faith, however, is the thing that bridges the gap between our need and God's provision;* specifically, it is a point in time at which the expression of faith in Christ brings God's provision together with our need . . . Once we believe, we are saved" (Ibid., 79).

9. Ibid., 80. Elsewhere, he would reaffirm this idea stating, "Even if a believer for all practical purposes becomes an unbeliever, his salvation is not in jeopardy. Christ will remain faithful" (Ibid., 93).

10. This same approach is taken by Hodges when stressing why true faith does not necessitate good works. He argues, "Even if they [good works] are only the inevitable outcome of true saving faith, they still become indispensable to assurance. That is, only the presence of good works in the life can verify the genuineness of one's faith" (Hodges, *Gospel Under Siege*, 9). The point he stresses is that if one cannot have assurance without good works, then there is something wrong with the gospel in which they have believed, because the true believer has assurance regardless of the presence of any subsequent faith or correlated actions. Another problem exists with Free Grace logic concerning assurance in that assurance is not based on future faith, but on the fact that faith has already endured in the past in one's life coupled with the evidences of God's presence and power in, through, and around one's life in the past.

11. "Again, saving faith is not necessarily a sustained attitude of gratefulness of God's gift. It is a singular moment in time wherein we take what God has offered" (Stanley, *Eternal Security*, 81).

continuity of faith."[12] He further elaborates that "the biblical portrait of saving faith is an act of appropriation. This appropriation is the means by which both regeneration and justification become permanent realities for the believer."[13]

As evidenced in both Stanley and Zane's writings, each is seeking to be consistent and true to the picture of assurance and security as revealed in the Scriptures, yet in doing so, they go too far in missing the biblical evidence related to the durative nature of authentic saving faith. They are right that the Bible teaches that salvation is secure at conversion, but wrong to disconnect faith from the process of a transforming life united with Christ or assume that genuine faith can ever cease.[14] Moreover, Paul presents the reality that faith should, must, and does continue for those who are truly born again.[15]

12. Hodges, *Absolutely Free*, 63.

13. Ibid., 106–7.

14. Several New Testament passages emphasize the permanence of salvation including John 5:24; 6:51; Rom 8:29–30; 1 Cor 1:7–9; 2 Cor 1:21–22; Eph 1:13–4; 4:30; Phil 1:6; 2 Tim 4:18; Heb 7:24–25; 1 Pet 1:3–5. Three particularly strong passages come from the gospel of John. John 4:14 speaks to the transforming permanence of salvation: "but whoever drinks of the water that I will give him *will never be thirsty again*. The water that I will give him will become in him a spring of water welling up to eternal life" (emphasis added). "Will never be thirsty again" is οὐ μὴ διψήσει εἰς τὸν αἰῶνα, which uses οὐ μὴ plus the future indicative to create an emphatic negation denying the potentiality of ever becoming thirsty again (Wallace, *Greek Grammar*, 468). It is not possible for one truly born again to become thirsty again. Another example of the durative nature of saving faith is found in John 6:37–39, which also utilizing the emphatic negation, but this time using οὐ μὴ plus the aorist subjunctive, which is the more common structure: "All that the Father gives me will come to me, and whoever comes to me *I will never cast out* [οὐ μὴ ἐκβάλω ἔξω]. For I have come down from heaven, not to do my own will but the will of him who sent me. And this is the will of him who sent me, that I should lose nothing of all that he has given me, but raise it up on the last day" (emphasis added, Wallace, *Greek Grammar*, 468). A third example is found in John 10:27–28, which also utilizes οὐ μὴ plus the aorist subjunctive creating an emphatic negation: "My sheep hear my voice, and I know them, and they follow me. I give them eternal life, and they *will never perish* [οὐ μὴ ἀπόλωνται], and no one will snatch them out of my hand" (emphasis added).

15. As Hoekema declares, "For, as the Bible teaches, those who have true faith will persevere, not in their own strength, but through the power of God" (Hoekema, *Saved by Grace*, 248). While Grider will go too far in believing that faith can be lost by a genuine believer, his understanding of the call of Scripture for sustained faith is certainly accurate. He explains, "The way in which 'faith' is used in Scripture, in scores of passages, also suggests that it has duration. Jesus exhorted people to 'have faith in God' (Mark 11:22), which would have been continuous faith, because 'have' is in the Greek present tense. Faith could 'increase' (Luke 17:5). Stephen was 'full of faith' (Acts 6:5). There is

First, those who argue that saving faith is not durative or a necessary element in the Christian life fail to realize that Paul in Galatians 2:20 is presenting the normative position for the Christian's spiritual life. He is not merely providing a personal model, but presenting the soteriological truth to be experienced by every authentic believer. Additionally, nowhere does Paul present a bifurcated spiritual life where one type of faith is necessary for justification and another type for sanctification. Thus, the spiritual life is a life *lived by faith* in the Son of God.

Second, in support of the necessity of personal faith as presented in Galatians 2:20, the use of "to believe" (πιστεύω) in the present participle and indicative in the Greek text elsewhere in the Scriptures consistently demonstrates the durative intention of genuine faith (some key examples are Matt 9:28; 18:6; Mark 1:15; 5:36; 9:23–24; John 1:12; 3:15–16, 18, 36; 4:42; 5:24, 38; 6:29, 35, 40, 47; 7:38; 9:35–38; 11:25–6; 12:44, 46; 14:1, 11–12; 20:31; Acts 2:44; 5:14; 10:43; 13:39; 15:11; 22:19; Rom 1:16; 3:22; 4:5, 11, 24; 6:8; 9:33; 10:4, 10–1; 15:13; 1 Cor 1:21; Gal 3:22; Eph 1:19; Phil 1:29; 1 Thess 1:7; 2:10, 13; 4:14; 1 Pet 1:8; 2:6–7; 1 John 5:1, 5, 10, 13). The use of the present tense is one reason why those who have been born again are called "believers." The word itself is an affirmation of the biblical testimony that Christians continue in belief (1 Cor 14:22). The reality of continued (or permanent) faith does not remove the reality of degrees or depths of faith, nor does it necessarily remove any element of doubt, discouragement or struggle as demonstrated in Mark 9:23–24 (see also Rom 14; 2 Cor 10:15).[16]

---

an 'obedience that comes from faith' (Rom. 1:5). We can 'walk in the footsteps of faith' (4:12). It is something that can 'remain' (*menei*, present tense), in a sustained way (1 Cor. 13:13)" (Grider, *Wesleyan-Holiness Theology*, 408). For more on faith's essential role in salvation, see Bates, *Saved Forever*, 25–31; MacArthur, *Faith Works*, 49–54; Reisinger, *Lord and Christ*, 41–42.

16. This point is missed by Hodges, who commenting on John the Baptist's struggles in Luke 7:18–20, argues, "But let this be said clearly. At the point in his life which Luke describes for us, John the Baptist is *not* believing. On the contrary, he is doubting. And the truth he doubts is nothing less than the saving truth proclaimed by the fourth evangelist: 'But these are written that you may believe that Jesus is the Christ, the Son of God, and that believing you may have life in His name' (Jn 20:31). To put it plainly, at this critical juncture in time, John the Baptist *does not believe* that Jesus is the Christ, the Son of God. Instead, he questions this truth. Does he then have eternal life? Of course" (Hodges, *Absolutely Free*, 106). Hodges interpretation of John is questionable, but his conclusion is clear (For a more balanced interpretation of this text, see Bock, *Luke*, 1:656–67; Morris, *Luke*, 155–6). Hodges fails to see John's question as a verifying question and instead concludes that one can be saved and have *no* faith. He misses that Scripture consistently presents two categories of people. Those who believe and are uncondemned and those

John 11:25–26 is one example that demonstrates the durative nature of faith for the believer from the use of the Greek text: "Jesus said to her [Martha], 'I am the resurrection and the life. Whoever believes [ὁ πιστεύων] in me, though he die, yet shall he live, and everyone who lives and believes [ὁ πιστεύων] in me shall never die. Do you believe this?'" In reference to John 11:25, among other verses, Daniel B. Wallace addresses the continuative aspect of belief in the New Testament based on the present participle ὁ πιστεύων [the one who believes]. "Thus, it seems that since the aorist participle was a live option to describe a 'believer,' it is unlikely that when the present was used, it was aspectually flat. The present was the tense of choice most likely because the NT writers by and large saw *continual* belief as a necessary condition of salvation. Along these lines, it seems significant that the *promise* of salvation is almost always given to ὁ πιστεύων . . . almost never to ὁ πιστεύσας . . . ."[17] The fact that "to believe" (πιστεύω) is used in the present tense to demonstrate the continuative nature of saving faith is significant. It shows that genuine belief in Jesus as the Son of God is persistent.[18] Highlighting this connection between sustained faith and eternal life from this text, Anthony A. Hoekema writes:

---

who do not believe and stand condemned (John 3:18, see also John 3:36; 5:38; 1 Pet 2:6–7; 1 John 5:5). One cannot be unbelieving and uncondemned. Additionally, Luke 8:13 distinguishes between durative genuine belief and false, temporary belief: "they believe for a while, and in a time of testing fall away." Furthermore, Hodges fails to acknowledge the various degrees of maturity (or information) connected with one's faith. In this connection to faith, Randall explains, "Unfortunately, believers often do rebel. Initial faith is always less than perfect. However, God does not leave it there. He uses the process of discipline (Heb. 12:4–13) and trials (1 Pet. 1:6–7) throughout the believer's life to bring his faith to maturity" (Randall, "Lordship Salvation," 60). In contrast with temporary faith, genuine faith persists. Reisinger develops this point, "Temporary faith soon falters. Its dubious nature becomes evident by its lacking the following characteristics of saving faith: 1. Continuance in trusting Christ, and in devotion to Him and His service. 2. Desire to be useful in the work of Christ. 3. Attendance to Christian duty. 4. Love of prayer, the Word of God, and worship with His people. 5. Devoted love of the children of God. 6. Progress in knowledge of self and sin and of Christ as Savior. 7. Progressing in loving holiness and hating sin, with increased conviction of and humility concerning sinfulness" (Reisinger, *Lord and Christ*, 41–42).

17. Wallace, *Greek Grammar*, 621, footnote 22. Robertson also speaks of the "timeless and durative" role of the present participle and explains that with the article it "has often the iterative (cf. pres. Ind.) sense" (Robertson, *Grammar*, 891–2, see also p. 1111). He would later write about the present participle, "As the aorist participle is timeless and punctiliar, so the present participle is timeless and durative" (ibid., 1115).

18. In response to the claim that the use of the present tense proves the durative nature of faith, Stanley argues, "The normal use of the present tense does not denote continuous,

Those who listen to my word and *keep on believing him* who sent me, Jesus here teaches, will not be condemned for their sins, but have been permanently transferred from death to life. The verb rendered "crossed over" is *metabebēken*, from *metabainō*, meaning 'to go or pass over.' The verb is in the perfect tense . . . . The action pictured is final and irrevocable, like that of a person who has burned his bridges behind him. The possibility that a true believer could cross back again from life into death is contrary to the finality of the passage.[19]

Additionally, as previously stated, Jesus never presents a bifurcated experience where salvation exists apart from faith or where one type of faith is necessary for salvation and another for sanctification; rather, authentic believers are marked with sustained evident faith (John 5:37; 6:27, 56; 8:31; 12:44–50; 14:12; 15:1–11, 16). In conjunction with this thought, Craig S. Keener comments regarding the necessity of continued faith from John 3:15–16.

In the context of the whole Fourth Gospel, however, it becomes clear that mere "signs-faith" can prove inadequate (e.g., 2:23–25); though sometimes starting with signs-faith, one must develop the sort of faith that perseveres to the end (8:31–32, 59), that ultimately trusts God's gift of eternal life so fully that it is prepared to relinquish the present life (12:25; cf. 12:9–11). Modern readers of 3:15–16 who assume that it rewards passive faith with eternal

uninterrupted action. Certainly it can, but it does not have to" (Stanley, *Eternal Security*, 85). The question is not the potential of the present tense, but what the present tense does in certain contexts. While the durative sense does not monopolize the present tense, it is often used that way showing the expected continuative nature of an action, as Jesus proclaims in John 11:25. As A. T. Robertson notes in his grammar that "the durative sense does not monopolize the 'present' tense, though it more frequently denotes linear action. The verb and the context must decide" (Robertson, *Grammar*, 879). Later, Stanley adds, "There is another problem with the present tense argument. Not every reference to saving faith is in the present tense" (Stanley, *Eternal Security*, 88. See also p. 93). No one is disputing that faith had a beginning as communicated in those contexts. Although the initial act of salvation is sometimes demonstrated in these passages, it, nonetheless, does not discount the durative nature of saving faith as evidenced in other passages such as John 11:25. The fact that faith had a beginning does not mean that faith does not continue. Despite these attempts by Stanley, the biblical evidence sufficiently shows the reality that genuine saving faith continues. Jesus in John 5:24, for example, connects the durative nature of saving faith with the reality of secure eternal life. "Truly, truly, I say to you, whoever hears my word and believes him who sent me has eternal life. He does not come into judgment, but has passed from death to life."

19. Hoekema, *Saved by Grace*, 237. Emphasis added.

life, apart from perseverance, read these verses in accordance with a very modern theological understanding that is utterly foreign to their Johannine context.[20]

Finally, other passages reiterate this point by showing the necessity of durative faith as a mark of genuine believers (Matt 10:22; John 8:31–32; 15:5; Rom 9:30–34; 1 Cor 16:13; Gal 3:13–14, 22, 26; 5:5–6; Col 1:21–23; 2:5; Heb 3:14; 1 Pet 1:3–5; Rev 2:10; 3:11). Paul writes in Galatians 5:5–6, "For through the Spirit, *by faith*, we ourselves eagerly wait for the hope of righteousness. For in Christ Jesus neither circumcision nor uncircumcision counts for anything, but only *faith working through love*."[21] The spiritual life is lived in anticipation of "the hope of righteousness" through the Spirit by faith. It is faith continually working in the believer's life through love.[22] First Peter 1:3–5 further supports this truth, "Blessed be the God and Father of our Lord Jesus Christ! According to his great mercy, he has caused us *to be born again* to a living hope through the resurrection of Jesus Christ from the dead, *to an inheritance that is imperishable*, undefiled, and unfading, kept in heaven for you, *who by God's power are being guarded through faith for a salvation ready to be revealed* in the last time."[23] Biblical faith expressed by genuine believers in salvation is rooted in God's preserving power. Paul J. Achtemeier explains from 1 Peter 1:5 that "Christians are being guarded by God's power . . . . That divine guarding is now visibly appropriated by the Christians' trust (διὰ πίστεως) [faith], which becomes the instrument whereby the divine protection becomes reality. Such Christian

---

20. Keener, *John*, 1:569–70.

21. Emphasis added.

22. This passage helps show the close connection between faith and love. Stanley attempts to create a false tension between the believer's faith and God's love saying, "The Bible clearly teaches that God's love for His people is of such magnitude that even those who walk away from the faith have not the slightest chance of slipping from His hand. . . . *Faith* is not the reason God saves men. *Love* is the reason" (Stanley, *Eternal Security*, 74. See also pp. 86–87, 92). The reason God saves men (i.e., love) does not deny the means by which God chooses to apply his love (faith). Additionally, it is probable that the connection between Gal 5:4 (falling away) and Gal 5:5 (continual faith) demonstrates that "true believers will not be cut off from Christ nor will they defect from grace" (Schreiner, *Galatians*, 315). While at the same time, "Those who do not manifest love or who do not keep God's commands show that they do not have genuine faith and that they are not part of the new creation" (ibid., 318). See Shanks, "Galatians 5:2–4," 188–202 for further support that those who "fall away" are not genuine believers.

23. Emphasis added.

faith is therefore the visible evidence of unseen reality evoking that trust."[24] The biblical evidence reveals no tension between the truths that the believer is secured by God, while at the same time required to persevere in faith. Again, faith is a necessary continual element in the spiritual life. The idea that a genuine believer would ever cease to exercise authentic faith is to miss the nature of saving faith and the power of God throughout one's spiritual life.[25] God secures the eternal destiny of the believer and sustains their faith.[26]

Despite such biblical evidence for the reality of sustained faith, Stanley and others continually reference 2 Timothy 2:13 in support of their position: "if we are faithless, he remains faithful—for he cannot deny himself."[27] Commenting on 2 Timothy 2:13, Stanley argues, "Christ will not deny an unbelieving Christian his or her salvation because to do so would be to deny Himself,"[28] yet in doing so, he misses the context of this incredible anthem. Verse 13 is not an admission of apostasy. Verse 12 provides the critical context for understanding verse 13. Verse 12 proclaims that "if we endure, we will also reign with him; if we deny him, he also will deny us." One will only reign, if they endure, while if they deny him, he will deny them (Matt 10:33).[29] Thus, verse 13 proclaims the faithfulness of God to

24. Achtemeier, 1 Peter, 97.

25. As Hoekema communicates, "Believers persevere only because God in his unchangeable love enables them to persevere" (Hoekema, Saved by Grace, 235).

26. One of the ways in which God keeps the believer is through means as revealed in John 16:1: "I have said all these things to you to keep you from falling away." As Hoekema supports, "God keeps his people from falling away through means, and these means include warnings against apostasy. By giving heed to warnings of this sort believers persevere" (Hoekema, Saved by Grace, 247). This thought brings to question the passages that speak of people falling away (Matt 13:21; Mark 4:17; Luke 8:13; Gal 5:4; 1 Tim 1:18–20; 4:1; 6:20–21; Heb 2:1–4; 3:12; 6:4–6; 10:26–31; 12:15; 2 Pet 2:20–22; 3:17; etc.) and the passages that teach that only those who endure to the end will be saved (Matt 10:22; 24:12–13; Mark 13:13; John 8:31–32; 15:5–8; Col 1:21–23; 1 John 2:19; Rev 2:10; 3:11). This issue was adequately addressed under "Permanence of the Spirit" in chapter 2. For more on how passages concerning apostasy should be understood in light of the position proposed above see Hoekema, Saved by Grace, 247–53. Hoekema aptly states that "those who have true faith can lose that faith neither totally nor finally" (ibid., 234).

27. Stanley, Eternal Security, 92–100. See also Bing, Lordship Salvation; Hodges, Absolutely Free, 112, 220; Lightner, Sin, Savior, Salvation, 238–44; Ryrie, So Great Salvation, 140–41.

28. Stanley, Eternal Security, 94.

29. "The verb 'endure' is in the present tense of continuous action (hypomenomen). It is only as we keep on enduring to the end that we will be saved in time of persecution

himself despite the faithlessness of man.[30] Specifically, it is God's covenantal faithfulness despite the shortcomings of believers. As Philip H. Towner explains that

> ("if we are faithless") means either to "to be unfaithful" or "to be disbelieving." . . . In this parenetic context, where we should assume a continuous development of thought applicable to Timothy, "unbelief" as such does not really fit. More likely the verb refers here to lapses in loyalty to Christ . . . The two thoughts of disavowal and faithlessness converge in this letter, and the insertion of the line referring to "faith*lessness*" may be intended rhetorically to set up the contrast with Christ's "faith*fulness*." Here the rhythm of the faithful saying departs from the "act-consequence" pattern, as the apodosis underlines the certainty of Christ's continuing "faithfulness" in contrast to the reality of human faithlessness. The language of faithfulness is used to describe God and Christ in reference to keeping promises related to the covenant, especially in the context of the trials that make human faithfulness so difficult to maintain.[31]

Thus, the "faithlessness" described is a "lapse in loyalty" not a disregard of all belief (i.e., a denial of Jesus as described in v. 12). Towner's point is helpful in showing that this passage is to serve as encouragement to believers when they fail, but "unbelief," "disbelief," or "apostasy" are not in view as evidenced from verse 12.[32] Therefore, in no way does 2 Timothy 2:13 allow

---

(Matt 10:22; cf. context)" (Earle, 2 *Timothy*, 401). Towner's comments are also helpful, "The second line (v. 12) returns specifically to the parenetic purpose of the passage as it proceeds to explore the theology and promise of the first line from the perspective of human responsibility. . . . Finally, the present tense is probably intentional, suggesting the endurance in affliction is to be a normal way of life for the believer ('if we keep on enduring') . . ." (Towner, *Timothy and Titus*, 510).

30. The meaning of 2 Tim 2:13 is not exactly the same as Rom 3:3, "What if some were unfaithful? Does their faithlessness nullify the faithfulness of God?" In Rom 3:3, the unbelieving Jew is in view while in 2 Tim 2:13 Paul is speaking to encourage believers, yet at the same time the principle of God's covenant faithfulness is in view.

31. Towner, *Timothy and Titus*, 512–3. See also Knight III, *Pastoral Epistles*, 407. For reasons why v. 13 should be taken as a promise and not a warning, see Mounce, *Pastoral Epistles*, 517–8.

32. Mounce explains that "most see line 4 as a promise of assurance to believers who have failed to endure (line 2) but not to the point of apostasy (line 3). Peter's denial of Christ (Matt 26:69–75; Mark 14:66–72; Luke 22:54–62; John 18:15–17, 25–27) and his repentance and forgiveness (John 21:15–19) are often used as an illustration" (Mounce, *Pastoral Epistles*, 518).

for the dismissal of all faith and the guarantee of salvation at the same time. Faith is still an integral part of the spiritual equation.

Activity of faith

Paul, in presenting the persistence of genuine faith, also emphasizes the reality that such faith is lived and sets the course of his life. He writes, "And the life I now live in the flesh *I live by faith* in the Son of God, who loved me and gave himself for me."[33] His Spirit-filled life is *lived by faith*. The result of co-crucifixion with Christ is faith-infused living centered in Christ. His faith is a lived faith. Thus, faith sets the course of his spiritual life, resulting in increased conformity to Christ, by increased submission to the indwelling presence of Christ by means of his Spirit.

He makes this point even more evident in Galatians 5:16–25.

> But I say, walk by the Spirit, and you will not gratify the desires of the flesh. For the desires of the flesh are against the Spirit, and the desires of the Spirit are against the flesh, for these are opposed to each other, to keep you from doing the things you want to do. But if you are led by the Spirit, you are not under the law. Now the works of the flesh are evident: sexual immorality, impurity, sensuality, idolatry, sorcery, enmity, strife, jealousy, fits of anger, rivalries, dissensions, divisions, envy, drunkenness, orgies, and things like these. I warn you, as I warned you before, that those who do such things will not inherit the kingdom of God. But the fruit of the Spirit is love, joy, peace, patience, kindness, goodness, faithfulness, gentleness, self-control; against such things there is no law. And those who belong to Christ Jesus have crucified the flesh with its passions and desires. If we live by the Spirit, let us also walk by the Spirit.

Faith now begins to define the direction of his life, as by faith, he submits his will to that of the Spirit. "Real faith inevitably produces a changed life (2 Cor. 5:17). Salvation includes a transformation of the inner person (Gal. 2:20). The nature of the Christian is different and perpetually new (Rom. 6:6). The unbroken pattern of sin and enmity with God will not continue

---

33. Gal 2:20c. Emphasis added.

when a person is born again (1 John 3:9–10)."[34] In summary, true faith is made visible in the way one lives.[35]

Galatians 2:20 is not alone in showing that this continual faith in the believer's life results in a changed pattern of life directed by faith. Paul expresses this point elsewhere (Rom 1:17; 15:18–19; 16:26; 2 Cor 5:6–10; 13:4–5; Gal 5:5–6, 13–26; Eph 2:8–10; 5:7–11; 1 Tim 1:5; 5:8; Titus 1:16; 2:9–14; 3:8; etc.).[36] One such reference is Galatians 5:5, where Paul writes,

---

34. MacArthur, *Faith Works*, 24.

35. See Ibid., 139–56. This thought in no way diminishes the various degrees of faith one may have or the various degrees of maturity that may be found from believer to believer (Rom 14), nor does this point in any way imply that the believer will live perfectly, only that true faith will be made visible in their action.

36. This point related to the connection between faith and action can be seen throughout the New Testament (Matt 3:8; 7:21–23; John 8:36–47; 15:4–10; Acts 6:7; 26:19–20; Heb 5:9–10; 10:24–39; 11; Jas 1:12; 1:21–27; 2:14–26; 3:9–12; 2 Pet 1:3–10; 1 John 3:23–24; Rev 14:12). The book of James stresses the point particularly well, as Warfield highlights in his comments, "When read from his own historical standpoint, James' teachings are free from any disaccord with those of Paul, who as strongly as James denies all value to a faith which does not work by love (Gal. v. 6, I Cor. Xiii. 2, I Thess. i.3). In short, James is not depreciating faith: with him, too, it is faith that is reckoned unto righteousness (ii. 23), though only such a faith as shows itself in works can be so reckoned, because a faith which does not come to fruitage in works is dead, non-existent. He is rather deepening the idea of faith, and insisting that it includes in its very conception something more than an otiose intellectual assent" (Warfield, *Biblical Doctrines*, 495–6). Nevertheless, despite the weight of the biblical evidence from other passages in conjunction with James, Hodges and others, out of a fear that the connection between works and faith will remove the believer's assurance and create a false system based on works, argue that James 2:14–26 is not referencing a genuine versus false faith (Bing, *Lordship Salvation*, 33; Hodges, *Absolutely Free*, 138; idem, "Dead Faith"; idem, *Gospel Under Seige*, 21–38; Kendall, *Once Saved, Always Saved*, 171–2, 207–17). Yet, even some who hold to Free Grace theology cannot escape the contextual message of James that genuine faith reveals itself in a changed life. As Ryrie affirms when commenting on James 2, "Justification before the bar of God is demonstrated by changes in our lives here on earth before the bar of men. . . . *Unproductive faith is spurious faith*; therefore, what we are in Christ will be seen in what we are before men" (Ryrie, *So Great Salvation*, 132. Emphasis added). Lightner, also a supporter of Free Grace theology, sees this connection in James 2 as well, stating that "true faith really will express itself in good works. They may not always be seen by others at all times, but life cannot be hidden forever" (Lightner, *Sin, Savior, Salvation*, 208). Lastly, this point related to the connection between faith and works is further strengthened when understood that throughout the New Testament works are continually revealed as a basis for judgment (Matt 3:10; 7:24–27; 10:14–15, 40–42; 12:33–37, 49–50; Luke 12:41–48; John 5:28–29, 36; 8:31; 14:23; 15:4, 10; Rom 2:6–11, 13, 25–26; 6:23; 1 Cor 7:19; 2 Cor 5:9–10; Titus 1:16; Heb 5:9; 10:24–39; 1 Pet 1:22–23; 3:5–6; 1 John 2:3–6, 9–11, 17, 29; 3 John 11; Rev 20:13; 21:7–8; 22:15; etc.). The way that one lives reveals to some degree the authenticity of their faith. While works is

"For through the Spirit, by faith, we ourselves eagerly wait for the hope of righteousness." It is by faith that the apostle, along with other believers, wait in anticipation for this eschatological hope.[37] Their faith sustains them, and that is the nature of saving faith. In Romans, Paul bookends the epistle with the idea that faith shapes the Christian's behavior. Romans 1:17 reveals, "For in it the righteousness of God is revealed from faith for faith, as it is written, 'The righteous shall *live by faith,'*[38] and then later in 16:26, the book closes with a reference to the mystery that has now been revealed stating that it "has now been disclosed and through the prophetic writings has been made known to all nations, according to the command of the eternal God, *to bring about the obedience of faith.*"[39] Regarding Romans 16:26, Schreiner argues,

> The words "for the obedience of faith to all nations" . . . recall the words of the introduction (1:5). This phrase designates God's purpose or goal (εἰς) in making known the gospel (so Cranfield 1979:

the basis of judgment, the primary work by which everyone will be judged is what they did or did not do with Jesus as the Messiah; however, other activities reveal to what extent one has truly believed in this declaration.

37. "The hope believers await *is* the final verdict of righteousness. Such a reading does not contradict the truth that believers are righteous now, nor should it be read as implying that justification is a process of renewal. Rather, the eschatological verdict differs from what God pronounces in history in that on the last day God's verdict is announced before the whole world. Believers are already righteous before God by virtue of their union with Christ Jesus. Still, their righteousness is hidden from the world and will only be unveiled on the last day. Indeed, the righteousness of believers is hidden to some extent even to them since they grasp it now by faith." (Schreiner, *Galatians*, 316).

38. Emphasis added. The interpretation of this verse is highly debated; however, in reference to the discussion as to whether it is God's faithfulness or human faith in view, the position that it is human faith seems most likely and is taken here. As Schreiner explains regarding the righteous living by faith, "It is likely, then, that ἐκ πίστεως εἰς πίστστιν is emphatic in nature, highlighting the centrality of faith (Schalatter 1995: 24–25; Cranfield 1975: 100; Ziesler 1989: 71; Moo 1991: 71; Byrne 1996: 54). This interpretation accords with v. 16, where salvation is for the one who believers (τῷ πιστεύοντι), and with the citation of Hab. 2:4 in v. 17, where faith is necessary for one to be right before God. The use of the participle πιστεύοντι in v. 16 demonstrates that *human* faith is in view. Since v. 17 is joined to v. 16 logically (γάρ, *gar*, for), πίστις in v. 17 refers not to the faithfulness of God or Christ but to human faith. . . . The simplest interpretation discerns human faith as the subject throughout . . . in the phrase εἰς πίστιν (v. 17) demonstrates that human faith should not be eliminated from the orbit of God's eschatological saving activity. . . . Rather, God's eschatological work is so powerful because it creates a new anthropological reality—faith. . . . 'To be righteous by faith' and 'to live by faith' are alternate ways of communicating the same reality" (Schreiner, *Romans*, 72–74).

39. Emphasis added.

812). Gentiles participate in the Abrahamic blessing through the obedience that flows from faith. Paul never conceived of salvation taking root among the nations without a change of behavior. The gospel that takes hold of human beings changes them so that they become servants of righteousness. Such new behavior, however, has its roots in faith, in trusting God for the strength and power to live a new life.[40]

Ephesians 2:8–10 is another example, "For by grace you have been saved through faith. And this is not your own doing; it is the gift of God, not a result of works, so that no one may boast. For we are his workmanship, created in Christ Jesus for good works, which God prepared beforehand, that we should walk in them."[41] While salvation is not the result of works, salvation by faith inevitably results in a degree of work described as that which Christ Jesus prepared beforehand for believers to walk in.

These verses do not mean that faith and works are synonymous, but that genuine faith produces a measure of good works as a necessary by-product. Kim Riddlebarger elaborates, "That is, one who has exercised faith in Christ, and is united to Christ by that faith, will repent and will struggle to obey and yield. But these things are not conditions for nor component parts of faith itself. They are fruits of saving faith. They are the inevitable activity of the new nature. They are 'effect'—signs that there has been an exercise of saving faith. They are not constituent parts of faith itself."[42] Thus, while still being distinct by definition, faith and works are certainly connected in reference to operation, so that, one's faith is made evident to some degree in works.

This biblical reality exposes a false bifurcation made by some proponents of Free Grace theology who see no direct correlation between faith

---

40. Schreiner, *Romans*, 815.

41. Hodges argues against the use of this verse to support the connection between saving faith and good works. "Good works are not seen as the *evidence* that we are God's workmanship, but rather as the expected *result* of that workmanship. Whether this result will be achieved is not stated" (Hodges, *Gospel Under Siege*, 16). In other words, he does concede that good works should be a byproduct of saving faith, but denounces the idea that they are inevitably. However, Reisinger refutes this approach saying, "The power of God's grace to bring salvation through faith (Eph. 2:8) is the same power that produces good works through faith. That is because good works or sanctification is part of salvation, not something opposed to it. It is a serious mistake to think of salvation as stage one of the Christian life and sanctification as stage two" (Reisinger, *Lord and Christ*, 147–8).

42. Riddlebarger, "What is Faith," 104.

and works.[43] R. T. Kendall represents this false distinction saying, "*Whoever once truly believes that Jesus was raised from the dead, and confesses that Jesus is Lord, will go to heaven when he dies. But I will not stop there. Such a person will go to heaven when he dies no matter what work (or lack of work) may accompany such faith.*"[44] Kendall is right to emphasize that permanent saving grace is received by faith alone; however, to imply that such faith provides no imperative for works or could exist without any manifestation of works is a faulty conclusion (Jas 2:14–26).[45] As Ernest C. Reisinger warns, "We should never think of works as something unattached to saving faith as though the one could exist for long without the other. Obedience to Christ is the necessary result of true faith."[46] Conversely, it is equally wrong to say that because genuine faith facilitates a degree of changed behavior, that such

---

43. A faulty understanding of repentance adds to the confusion within the Free Grace system. Some proponents of Free Grace theology portray repentance simply as a change in understanding (change of mind) regarding who Christ is, with no indication that it involves a change of mind that produces a change in action. Ryrie, for example, writes, "The content of repentance which brings eternal life, and that which Peter preached on the day of Pentecost, is a change of mind about Jesus Christ" (Ryrie, *Balancing*, 176). However, he fails to see that this repentance is a change in mind concerning who Jesus is that must produce a changed response in light of that revelation. In other words, seeing that Jesus is who he is necessitates a different order of life. See also Blauvelt Jr. who sees salvation as synonymous with faith (Blauvelt, "Bible Teach Lordship Salvation," 41–42). Unfortunately, these advocates within Free Grace theology miss that the Jewish perspective of repentance included a change of actions as John the Baptist demonstrates in Luke 1:7–14. Even when Free Grace theologians reference repentance in connection to life, it is shown as something distinct from salvation rather than something that takes place in salvation and then proceeds from salvation. Stanley makes this mistake. "The word *repent* means to have a change of mind. The Holy Spirit dwelling within a person will cause a person to want to have a change of mind, and therefore, a subsequent change of behavior. Repentance comes in the wake of salvation" (Stanley, *Understanding Eternal Security*, 16). However, such a separation between salvation and repentance is biblically unsupported and unwarranted. "First, this saving belief is revealed and applied by the Holy Spirit in regeneration (John 3:3). Second, this belief is expressed by the sinner in his response to the Savior. Third, this belief is made apparent in its fruit—repentance toward God and faith toward our Lord Jesus Christ (Acts 20:20, 21)" (Reisinger, *Lord and Christ*, 40).

44. Kendall, *Once Saved, Always Saved*, 19. Quoted again on pp. 49, 53, 56.

45. Boice explains that the distinction between faith and works within Free Grace theology is a "defective theology." "There are several reasons that the situation I have described is common in today's church. The first is a *defective theology* that has crept over us like a deadening fog. This theology separates faith from discipleship and grace from obedience" (Boice, *Christ's Call*, 14).

46. Reisinger, *Lord and Christ*, 149.

a salvation is based on works. No, such a salvation based on grace by faith produces works. Kendall confuses this issue of a salvation that produces works with a works-based salvation as he argues, "It is not faith *plus* works, it is faith *without* works. . . . The righteousness that is required is answered by faith. . . . Such righteousness is in fact the righteousness of *God* (Romans 1:17) and it is too powerful to be rivaled by any subsequent work, good or bad."[47] Unfortunately, Kendall argues for a bifurcated faith by concluding that saving faith is a single act that then has no necessary connection to a fruitful Christian life. Joel B. Green helps to provide a corrective to this erroneous distinction between genuine saving faith and Christian living.

> Let me turn now to . . . the false distinction between "faith" and "life" with regard to human response to the gift of salvation. Here I refer to a variety of dualisms by which we have learned to make sense of our lives: my inner self versus my outer self, my "being" versus my "doing," right faith versus right actions, and the like. It is imperative that we recognize the degree to which this way of constructing our lives has been culturally determined, and the degree to which it runs counter to the witness of scripture. As we noted in chapter 1 . . . personal identity has come to be shaped by such assumptions such as these: Human dignity lies in self-sufficiency and self-determination; identity is grasped in self-referential terms: I am who I am; persons have an inner self, which is the authentic self; and basic to authentic personhood are self-autonomy and self-legislation. Biblical anthropology, on the other hand, places a premium on the construction of the self as deeply embedded in social relationships, a premium on the integrity of the community and thus the contribution of the individuals to that integrity, and a premium on the assumption that a person *is* one's behavior—that is, that one's dispositions are on display in one's practices. To take seriously the implications of this change in perspective for our present interests, this would mean that transformation in the arena of one's essential beliefs, commitments, and allegiances is unavoidably on display in one's behavior and practices in the world. Conversion, then, is the transformation of our imaginations, which is necessarily rooted and manifest in faith and life. Put simply, the call to salvation is the call to live according to another world order; faith is entrusting ourselves to God's view of things . . . and this faith is on display in faithfulness.[48]

47. Kendall, *Once Saved, Always Saved*, 25.

48. Green, *Salvation*, 115–6. Someone may try to argue that Paul himself downplayed the role works in the Christian life, emphasizing grace alone, when he stated that he

Thus, Paul writing in Galatians 2:20 emphasizes what is reiterated consistently throughout the New Testament: the spiritual life is a life of faith. As such, genuine faith is durative and produces a changed life. Therefore, one needs to be cautious in dismissing one theological reality (the connection between faith and works) in an effort to preserve and uphold another (assurance of the believer and preservation of the saints).

Fuel of Faith-Infused Living

Paul now reveals, in Galatians 2:20, the object of this continued faith that motivates him in his Christian living: "the Son of God." Yet, it is his description of the Son that becomes most telling. He explains that he lives "by faith in the Son of God, *who loved me and gave himself for me.*" This thought concerning the particular sacrificial love of God serves as sufficient motivation for the apostle's life of faith.

This thought is not new to the epistle. Earlier, in Galatians 1:3–5, Paul builds upon this same foundation as a motivation for all believers to be faithful in their spiritual lives. "Grace to you and peace from God our Father and the Lord Jesus Christ, who gave himself for our sins to deliver us from the present evil age, according to the will of our God and Father, to whom be the glory forever and ever. Amen." Similarly, the redemptive work of Christ is the focus in Galatians 3:13–14[49] and 4:4–5[50] and serves as a foundation for living by faith. Thus, for Paul, the sacrificial love of Christ in redemption is fuel that sustains and motivates his faith.[51]

---

was the chief of sinners (1 Tim 1:15); however, Paul is referencing God's saving work in salvation in that verse not life that flows out of one who has been saved. Paul is explaining that he was as undeserving of salvation as anyone could be. He is not explaining how he currently sees his Christian life. Consistently, Paul expresses that the believer is expected to live a life of continual conformity to Christ in holiness (Rom 12:1–2; 2 Cor 7:1; Eph 4:20–24; 1 Thess 3:13).

49. "Christ redeemed us from the curse of the law by becoming a curse for us—for it is written, 'Cursed is everyone who is hanged on a tree'—so that in Christ Jesus the blessing of Abraham might come to the Gentiles, so that we might receive the promised Spirit through faith."

50. "But when the fullness of time had come, God sent forth his Son, born of woman, born under the law, to redeem those who were under the law, so that we might receive adoption as sons."

51. Again, this point is not unique in Paul's writings, he consistently views the love of Christ as a motivation for righteous living by faith (Rom 4:25; 8:37–39; Eph 3:14–20; 5:2, 25; Phil 2:1–13; 2 Thess 2:16–17; 1 Tim 2:3–6; Titus 2:11–14). Nor is this point

The essential point is that the motivation for Paul's faithful living is who Christ is and what he has done, not the physical benefits following Christ might bring. Ironically, Paul often expresses how following Christ is a detriment to his physical being (2 Cor 11:23–28) and has cost him financially to the point that he is regularly dependent upon others (Phil 4:10–19). Moreover, nowhere in all of Paul's writings does he ever present the spiritual life as one motivated by personal physical, financial, or material benefit.[52] Material benefits may or may not be experienced by people who are faithfully serving the Lord, and while God may increase one's border of influence for his redemptive purpose (1 Chr 4:9–10), the motivation for faith is never personal gain.[53] Instead, the sacrificial love of Christ serves as fuel for Paul's faith-filled obedience: "For the love of Christ controls us, because we have concluded this: that one has died for all, therefore all have died; and he died for all, that those who live might no longer live for themselves but for him who for their sake died and was raised" (2 Cor 5:14–15).[54] The rich reality of Christ's love as demonstrated through his death and resurrection serves as motivation for Paul's ministry. As Paul Barrett comments, "Paul's understanding that Jesus, in his death, loved *him* was now the controlling force in the apostle's life."[55] In 2 Corinthians

---

unique to Paul (1 Pet 2:24; 3:18).

52. Rom 8:32 is no exception. It reads, "He who did not spare his own Son but gave him up for us all, how will he not also with him graciously give us all things?" However, the context is not describing personal benefit as a means of motivation for being faithful to God, but taking of the redemptive reality that God has brought in Christ for the believer. They are not to fear circumstances (8:28) or gospel adversaries (8:31) for in redemption the believer has been made co-heir with Christ (8:17) by which they will be given the universe (Jewett, *Romans*, 538–9; Schreiner, *Romans*, 460–61). But nowhere in the context is personal comfort or gain the motivation for faithfulness. On the contrary, due to their faithfulness, they will suffer (8:17), but their suffering should not cause them to doubt the redemptive promises of God (8:31–39) that find their ultimate expression in "the love of God in Christ Jesus our Lord" (Rom 8:39).

53. As a matter of fact that Bible directly speaks against the use of godliness as a means for personal gain (Acts 8:18–22; 1 Tim 5:1–10; 6:5, 9–11; Jude 11–16; 2 Pet 2:1–19; Eph 5:5–7).

54. While "love of Christ" (ἀγάπη τοῦ Χριστοῦ) could be understood as the believer's love for Christ (objective genitive) or Christ's love for the believer (subjective genitive), it is Christ's love for believers that seems to be in view and that is the interpretation taken here. For more on that discussion, see Harris, *2 Corinthians*, 418–29; Martin, *2 Corinthians*, 128.

55. Barrett, *Second Corinthians*, 289.

5:14–15, Paul describes his motivation for serving God and explains "why a life of self-pleasing was impossible for him."[56]

Starkly contrasting Paul's theocentric approach to faith in the spiritual life is the anthrocentric approach seen in modern proponents of the prosperity gospel often dubbed as "Prosperity Lite."[57] Upfront, it must be established that nothing is wrong with thinking positively or exercising a positive attitude or outlook on life. Nothing is wrong with desiring or anticipating good things from God. After all, the Heavenly Father knows how to give good gifts to his children (Matt 7:11).[58] The problem is when

56. Harris, 2 *Corinthians*, 418. Similarly Thrall states, "Christ's self-sacrificing love restrains Paul from self-seeking" (Thrall, *Second Corinthians*, 1:408).

57. Van Biema, and Chu, "Does God Want You to Be Rich." Also commonly referred to as "Faith theology" or "Health and Wealth gospel." This approach to Christianity finds its roots in positive thinking sometimes called PMA (positive mental attitude) or positive confession. McConnell sees the ego-centric approach within prosperity theologians as a form of "charismatic humanism." He writes, "Biblical faith is always *theocentric* (God-centered) rather than *anthropocentric* (man-centered). Although this phrase 'charismatic humanism' may appear to be a contradiction in terms, its truth-value lies in its expression of the man-centered supernaturalism of PMA and positive confession. PMA and positive confession are humanistic in the sense that they confer upon man the unrestrained power to meet his own self-defined 'needs'" (McConnell, *Different Gospel*, 146). A key proponent of PMA who has great influenced the prosperity movement is Norman Vincent Peale. See Meyer, *Positive Thinkers*. Peale has written dozens of books promoting PMA to include *Amazing Results of Positive Thinking*; *Power of Positive Thinking*; *You Can if You Think*. Some important works critiquing "Prosperity Lite" theology are Barron, *Health and Wealth Gospel*; Bowman Jr., *Word-Faith Controversy*; Hanegraaff, *Christianity in Crisis*; Horton, *Agony of Deceit*; Jones and Woodbridge, *Health, Wealth & Happiness*; McConnell, *Different Gospel*; Perriman, *Faith, Health and Prosperity*; Wilson-Hartgrove, *God's Economy*.

Additionally, it should be noted that this approach to Christianity is not isolated to prosperity theology but is also prevalent within modern-day "Christian" approaches to psychology as Hunt and McMahon reveal, "The Bible never urges self-acceptance, self-love, self-assertion, self-confidence, self-esteem, self-forgiveness, nor any of the other selfisms that are so popular today. The answer to depression is not to accept self, but to turn from self to Christ. A preoccupation with self is the very antithesis of what the Bible teaches, and would be unknown in the church today were it not for the seductive influence of selfist psychologies" (Hunt and McMahon, *Seduction of Christianity*, 195).

58. But again here the focus of the good gifts is not focused on physical, financial, or material blessing as evidenced from this passages parallel in Luke 11:9–13 and the many verses that talk of the fact that riches can serve as a hindrance to one's own pursuit of the gospel (Matt 6:24; 13:22; 16:26; 19:22–24; Mark 4:19; 8:36–37; 10:22–25; Luke 1:53; 6:24; 8:14; 9:24–25; 12:16–21; 16:13, 19–31; 18:23–25),that believers will be persecuted and suffer for Jesus's sake (Matt 5:10–12, 44; 10:23–25; 23:34; 24:9; Mark 4:17; 10:29–31; Luke 11:49; 21:12; John 5:18–21; 13:16; 16:20–24, 33), prayer must be in accordance with the will of the Father and in the name of Jesus (Matt 6:9–10; 26:39, 42; John 6:38; 14:13–14;

personal benefits become (or are portrayed as) a key motivation for faith in the spiritual life. Faith is to be sustained so that believers might be found faithful at the return of Christ (Titus 2:11–14), not so that believers can be physically blessed while on earth. Again, this does not mean that physical blessings are bad, but demonstrates that they are not the motivation that drives faith in the spiritual life.

Proponents of prosperity theology consistently present faith as a tool one wields in order to receive physical and material blessings. Such an approach stands in opposition to the role of faith as presented by Paul. One prominent and popular example of this approach within prosperity theology is seen in the writings of Joel Osteen.[59] Osteen in his book *Your Best Life Now* pervasively promotes this false view of faith.[60] In the opening of the book, he states, "To live your best life now, you must start looking at life through eyes of faith, seeing yourself rising to new levels. See your business taking off. See your marriage restored. See your family prospering. See your dreams coming to pass. You must conceive it and believe it is possible if you ever hope to experience it."[61] Notice that in Osteen's system, the individual becomes the object of faith and their personal desires and materialism becomes the fuel for such faith. The quote above is not an isolated example. This ego-centric approach to the spiritual life permeates his book. Osteen often makes comments such as, "Friend, that's what faith is all about. You have to start believing that good things are coming your way, and they will!"[62] And, "Regardless of how many people tell you what you're attempting can't be done, if you'll persevere, declaring the favor of God and staying in an attitude of faith, God will open doors for you and change circumstances on your behalf."[63] Notice that self is the focus. It is

---

15:16; 16:23, 26). The reality of Jesus's death despite his personal desire to have the cup pass from him additionally demonstrates a great issue of submitting to the will of the Father and dismisses the idea that one's own words have creative power (Matt 16:21; 17:12; 26:38–44; Mark 8:31; 9:12; Luke 9:22; 17:23–25; 22:15, 41–44; 24:26, 46; John 18:11–14). It is the power of the Holy Spirit working through one that does the work of God.

59. It is noted that Osteen and others within the prosperity movement do not write for the purpose of research or for the purpose of "peer review." Nevertheless, Osteen and some others are so influential with respect to the current dialogue of spirituality that they are addressed in this book at this point.

60. For a couple of more current examples, see Osteen, *Become a Better You*; idem, *It's Your Time*.

61. Osteen, *Your Best Life Now*, 4.

62. Ibid., 11.

63. Ibid., 20.

for the benefit of self, not the glory of God, not the good of his redemptive purposes, not the promise of the Kingdom, but self. Later he would add, "If you will live with an attitude of faith, then, like the saints of old, before long God's favor is going to show up, and that situation will turn around to your benefit."[64] That statement is categorically inaccurate. Many saints of old, who lived by faith, did not experience the fulfillment of the promises of God in their lifetime; rather, experienced great persecution and painful loss (Heb 11:36–40).

Osteen is not alone in promoting faith as a means of personal benefit instead of the means of living life in continual conformity to Christ. Benny Hinn writes on the financial benefits of faith, "Trust God that this is your year of abundance and liberty from debt. This can be your year of deliverance and divine, supernatural prosperity, in the name of Jesus Christ, when all that has been lost and destroyed will be restored! Sow your seed in faith today and see what God will do with you. Do your part. Give. Be faithful. Get prepared. Then watch what God does next!"[65] Gloria Copeland's focus here is that of physical healing, "If you need a healing, you can't sit back and wait for God to drop it down on you. You have to do what it takes so you can rise up in faith and *take* what rightfully belongs to you! *Taking* requires active faith. Having faith in God and His Word is the bottom-line answer to every problem regardless of what others may say."[66] Despite this false focus of faith, Copeland is right that the promises of God in his Word can and should be prayed with unwavering faith. Bruce Barron helps in tempering the critiques of some by highlighting this positive aspect of the prosperity movement.

> The most important contribution the world view of positive confession has to offer probably concerns the relationship between prayer and God's will. This is a hotly disputed topic, but the faith teachers have plenty of New Testament Scriptures to show that those who seek diligently after God can often find God's will for their lives and then pray for it without wavering. Most Christians seem to pray with little confidence, committing themselves to whatever the Lord desires for them but seldom knowing just what he does desire. In contrast, the faith teachers are serious about teaching people to earnestly seek and consistently receive divine guidance.[67]

64. Osteen, *Your Best Life Now*, 24.
65. Hinn, "Three Keys to Prepare."
66. Copeland, "Take Your Healing."
67. Barron, *Health and Wealth Gospel*, 105–6.

This particular emphasis of these prosperity teachers should be appreciated; however, their approach goes awry due to their confusion that God's promises necessitate personal health and wealth in this life. Instead, the biblical model of the spiritual life is not the pursuit of health and wealth; rather, it is a dying to self so that one can be used for the purposes of promoting the gospel of the kingdom to the nations, even if that means selling all that one has, giving it to the poor, and following Jesus (Matt 10:38; 16:24–26; 19:20–22; 28:19–20; Mark 8:34–38; 10:21–22; Luke 14:25–33; 18:22–23; 2 Cor 11:16–33; Gal 2:20; etc.). It is in such a context that one is to understand promises such as 1 John 5:14–15, "And this is the confidence that we have toward him, that if we ask anything according to his will he hears us. And if we know that he hears us in whatever we ask, we know that we have the requests that we have asked of him." Additionally, God's promises to faithfully answer the believer's requests are not without qualifications such as the request being made in Jesus' name,[68] flowing from a life lived

68. Praying in "the name of Jesus" is a concept easily misunderstood. Keener brings some clarity to its contextual meaning, "More likely, praying 'in one's name' might evoke praying 'on the merits of' or because of another's status before the one entreated. . . . Most likely, asking 'in his name' signifies asking 'as his representative, while about his business,' just as Jesus came in his Father's name (5:43; 10:25). It involves prayer 'in keeping with his character and concerns and, indeed, in union with him.' This usage . . . was common and fits the context (14:26; 15:21; cf. 15:26–27). . . . Such prayer naturally implied desiring the sort of thing that Jesus would desire—hence praying, as best as one knows, according to God's will (cf. 1 John 5:14)" (Keener, *Gospel of John*, 2:948–9). Unfortunately, the name of Jesus within prosperity practice is often used in a manner similar to cultic incantations (Copeland, "I Want My People Well"; idem, "Name Above All Names." McConnell explains why the prominent approach within prosperity practice is inappropriate, "The Faith theology's teaching on Jesus' name violates one of God's primary commandments. In the Decalogue, Yahweh told the people of Israel, 'You shall not take the name of the Lord your God in vain, for the Lord will not leave him unpunished who takes his name in vain' (Ex. 20:7; cf. Lev. 19:12; Deut. 5:11). The intent of the third commandment is far broader than a mere prohibition of cursing or profanity; it also prohibits and threatens to punish any attempt to use the divine name to manipulate or control Yahweh. In Canaanite and Egyptian mythology, to discover a god's secret name is to control the god. The magical arts of the diviners and sorcerers consisted of constant muttering of the divine names of their gods. The diviner-magician usually had selfish goals in mind and had little regard for the will of the deity. After the return from captivity, so great in Israel was the fear of profaning the name of Yahweh that the Jews ceased to use it in conversation. . . . How this Jewish reverence differs from the way Faith teachers use the divine name! They imply that God will answer any egocentric prayer a believer prays if it is accompanied by Jesus' name. The Faith theology's teaching on Jesus' name is dangerously close to the beliefs and practices of the diviner-magicians. Jesus did, indeed, promise his disciples that 'if you ask Me anything in My name, I will do it' (Jn. 16:24). But his promise was not unqualified. It requires believers to abide in him and allow his words to abide in

in obedience to Christ's words, flowing from pure motives, being made in the Spirit, being made in accordance with the will of the Father, etc. (Prov 15:8–9, 28–29; 28:9; Matt 6:10; 26:39, 42; Mark 14:36; Luke 22:42; John 14:13–14; 15:7; 16:23–24; Eph 6:18–19; Col 4:2; Jas 4:1–10; 5:15; 1 John 3:21–2; etc.).[69]

Regrettably, the egocentric approach evidenced within prosperity teaching has created substantial confusion concerning the nature of the spiritual life within the broader Christian community. A 2006 Time Magazine poll shows "A majority (61%) of Christians believe that God wants people to be financially prosperous."[70] When questioned on this impact their theology has had, Joyce Meyer responded, "Who would want to get in on something where you're miserable, poor, broke and ugly and you just have to muddle through until you get to heaven?"[71] Yet, advocates of prosperity theology will admit that it is more about the quality of life than the physical resources one receives, as Creflo Dollar states,

> Fortunately, Jesus' redemptive work on the cross of Calvary made provision for all who would receive Him as their Lord and Savior. This means where poverty once reigned, prosperity is now available for everyone who receives it by faith. . . . I'm not just talking about having a lot of money in the bank, even though God does want us to prosper financially. I'm talking about a quality of life

---

them (Jn. 15:7). It requires them to keep his commandments (1 Jn. 3:22). It requires them to pray according to his will (1 Jn. 5:14, 15). The motives and objects for which one prays are vitally important: 'You ask and do not receive because you ask with wrong motives, so that you may spend it on your pleasures' (Jas. 4:3). Believers who use the name of Jesus for their lusts should expect nothing from God" (McConnell, *Different Gospel*, 143–4).

69. Moo commenting on certain qualifications found in the epistle to James states, "And in both this verse [Jas 1:6] and in 5:15, he makes God's answering of prayer contingent on faith. James is again reflecting the teaching of Jesus, who, in response to the disciples' amazement at the withering of the fig tree, said, 'I tell you the truth, if you have faith and do not doubt, not only can you do what was done to the fig tree, but also you can say to this mountain, "Go, throw yourself into the sea," and it will be done. If you believe, you will receive whatever you ask for in prayer' (Matt 21:21–22). This text is a favorite with those false prophets who claim that God has promised 'health and wealth' to every Christian—if only his or her faith is strong enough. But neither Jesus nor James intends to give to Christians a blank check on which they can write whatever they want and expect God to back it up. The 'whatever you ask' is clearly qualified by Scripture elsewhere to include only what God has promised to give his people . . ." (Moo, *James*, 60).

70. Regan, "Wealth and Theology." The poll also revealed that 35% of Protestants believe that if you give away money to God, God will bless you with more money.

71. Biema and Chu, "Does God Want You to Be Rich?"

that is marked by an overflow of peace, health, wholeness, and provision. . . . It is through our faith in the Word of God that this truth will become a reality in our lives.[72]

Nevertheless, the focus is significantly, though not exclusively, physical in nature with the benefits for self as the primary motivator for faith as Dollar consistently demonstrates, "When you have faith, you are able to see everything Heaven has to offer you without 'seeing' it in front of you first. By tapping into faith, you gain access to the abundant wealth, riches, health, and blessings available to you. Anything you find in the Word of God is available to you in Heaven's storehouses; from wisdom to finances."[73] Such a focus stands in opposition to the consistent themes presented throughout Scripture concerning the nature of and motivation for the spiritual life. As Paul declares, the life of faith (i.e., the spiritual life) is to be lived in devotion to Jesus who as the Son of God lovingly and sacrificially laid down his life. The reality of who Jesus is and the reality of his great sacrificial love for those who have received him is the motivation for faithful living in this life.

Conclusion

Galatians 2:20 serves as an important summary of the spiritual life. The last part of the verse, "I live by faith in the Son of God, who loved me and gave himself for me," demonstrates that though every believer will continue to live physically in this world, they do so within a new context. Their life is now to be lived under the directives of Christ by faith and not the impulses of the flesh. Faith is necessary for the beginning and the continued living of one's spiritual life (Gal 2:16; 2:20). In this verse, Paul refutes the notion of a bifurcated faith. Faith is not merely a momentary act, but a decision that continually governs the course of one's spiritual experience throughout their life. Such governance is not without evidence. Genuine faith will bring about a change and be manifested in the course of one's spiritual journey. Faith in Christ brings evidences of its existence, and is to be motivated by an appreciation of Christ's sacrificial love. The motivating factor for faithfulness is not personal physical benefit, although some may come; rather, it is the acknowledgment that God in his infinite mercy sent his Son to die so that all who would believe might become sons and be co-heirs of glory

---

72. Dollar, "Total Life Prosperity."
73. Idem, "Living the Faith."

(John 1:12; 3:14–18; Rom 5:8; 8:16–17; Gal 3:29; 4:7; Eph 1:3–14; Titus 3:4–7; Jas 2:5). Thus, when Galatians 2:20 is contextually understood, it reveals that the believer's life this side of heaven has a spiritual focus and motivation. This spiritually focused life is sustained by faith in continual submission to Christ, and it is motivated by the reality that Christ has redeemed them and brought them out of darkness and into the kingdom of light (Col. 1:13–14).

Conclusion

What counts in the Church is not progress but reformation—its existence as ecclesia semper reformanda. Semper reformari, however, does not mean always to go with the time, to let the current spirit of the age be the judge of what is true and false, but in every age, and in controversy with the spirit of the age, to ask concerning the form and doctrine and order and ministry which is in accordance with the unalterable essence of the Church.[1]

ALWAYS REFORMING HAS BEEN a major battle cry within the Protestant church since the Reformation.[2] However, always reforming does not necessarily mean that one is always changing, but that, as a community, believers are always seeking to be more faithful to God's revealed will: always examining every aspect of life in light of what the Bible says. *Sola Scriptura.*

Today, as much as ever, the Bible is being questioned as the standard for the spiritual life. Spencer Burke and Barry Taylor exemplify such a challenge to the authority of God's Word, specifically its reliability and relevance. "When it comes to texts, the institutional church needs to let go of its rigid interpretations. Words—even in the Bible—are fluid and unstable, and their meanings shift and change."[3] Thus, for them, "What counts is not a belief system but a holistic approach of following what you feel, experience, discover, and believe; it is a willingness to join Jesus in his vision for a transformed humanity."[4] Yet, this declaration by Burke and Taylor

1. Barth, *CD*, 4:1:705.
2. Olson, *Reformed and Always Reforming*, 39.
3. Burke, and Taylor, *Heretic's Guide to Eternity*, 140.
4. Ibid., 131.

is in itself the promotion of a belief system: it is just a belief system based on the preference of self rather than any objective standard, and this is a major problem within Christian spirituality in America over the last fifty years. Christian spirituality loses its bearings and thus its identification as "Christian" when it is not grounded in the source that gave it its birth. As a result, a need has arisen within Christian spirituality to bring greater clarity concerning the authority of the Bible.

This book involves such an effort. Ultimately, the Scriptures, not tradition, reason, or culture, must be the foundation for gauging the proper expressions of the spiritual life for the follower of Christ. This thought in no way undermines or dismisses the role of the Spirit in guiding the spiritual life of the Christian, but acknowledges that Scripture is the primary revelation by which the Spirit has already revealed his will for the spiritual life. The apostle Paul understood that one's spiritual life could not be based upon one's natural inclinations or cultural norm. Consequently, using himself as an example, he wrote Galatians 2:20 for the purpose of directing the church at Galatia to the proper focus, source, and power of the spiritual life. What he knew to be normative for himself, he provided as normative for all believers. Recognizing, therefore, the inspired nature of Galatian 2:20 as a part of the revelation of God, it is employed in this book as but one example of the ability of the Scriptures to be a corrective guide to the diverse and sometimes erroneous expressions of Christian spirituality found in American Protestantism. The goal in this approach is to allow the biblical text to constantly serve as a corrective guide to theologies seeking to explain or encourage the Christian in the proper expression of the spiritual life empowered by faith in the finished work of Christ.

Context: Galatians 2:15–19

Introduction

GALATIANS 2:15–21 STANDS AS the hinge upon which the entire Galatian epistle turns and is the theological lynchpin for understanding the gospel Paul advocates.[1] Its importance is hard to overstate. The passage presents a defense of Paul's gospel and covers several important theological topics such as justification, sanctification, and the law.

The first half of the epistle establishes the precedence of the true gospel, Paul's defense of that gospel, and his credentials as an apostle to the Gentiles. Immediately, the reality of Jesus as the one who sacrificed himself so that believers would be delivered from the present evil age, and the proclamation that there is only one true gospel is pressed (Gal 1:3–9). From there, the opening of the epistle grows to a climax with Paul's profound declaration concerning justification in 2:15–19. Then, in 2:20, Paul takes the language of justification, established in 2:15–19, and encapsulates in it a summary of the spiritual life. Considering this, the following is designed to establish an appropriate context for understanding the emphasis of Galatians 2:20 regarding justification and sanctification in the life of the believer by examining 2:15–19.

---

1. (Longenecker, *Galatians*, 83). Pauline authorship is preferred. Additionally, the work assumes the Southern Gal Hypothesis. For more on authorship and audience, see Bruce, *Galatians*, 1–18.

Galatians 2:15-19

Galatians 2:15-19: We ourselves are Jews by birth and not Gentile sinners; yet we know that a person is not justified by works of the law but through faith in Jesus Christ, so we also have believed in Christ Jesus, in order to be justified by faith in Christ and not by works of the law, because by works of the law no one will be justified. But if, in our endeavor to be justified in Christ, we too were found to be sinners, is Christ then a servant of sin? Certainly not! For if I rebuild what I tore down, I prove myself to be a transgressor. For through the law I died to the law, so that I might live to God.

Verse 15

Galatians 2:11-14 recounts Paul's confrontation with Peter and other Jews in Antioch revealing the hypocrisy of their actions and expectations in relation to their Gentile brothers in Christ.[2] Paul then transitions back in 2:15 "resuming his polemic against the Galatians opponents."[3] After presenting a rhetorical question (v.14), Paul proceeds by acknowledging the privileged

2. Galatians 2:11-14: But when Cephas came to Antioch, I opposed him to his face, because he stood condemned. For before certain men came from James, he was eating with the Gentiles; but when they came he drew back and separated himself, fearing the circumcision party. And the rest of the Jews acted hypocritically along with him, so that even Barnabas was led astray by their hypocrisy. But when I saw that their conduct was not in step with the truth of the gospel, I said to Cephas before them all, "If you, though a Jew, live like a Gentile and not like a Jew, how can you force the Gentiles to live like Jews?"

3. Scacewater, "Galatians 2:11-21," 309. Scacewater presents a convincing argument for seeing 2:11-14 as Paul's address from Antioch and a shift in 2:15 back to the Galatian opponents, contra Schreiner, *Galatians*, 150. In doing so, he provides a compelling refutation of the New Perspective on Paul's (NPP) view concerning seeing the term "works of the law" as sociological rather than soteriological. Scacewater appropriately argues that the term is soteriological in refuting the Galatians opponents. Even if, as the NPP proponents do, it is argued that 2:15-16 presents the conversation between Paul and Peter in Antioch, this conversation is presented to the Galatian opponents to refute their subversion of Paul's teaching regarding faith in Christ. Although those creating problems in Galatia apparently sought to reinstitute the law and diminish the role of Christ, such did not appear to be the intention of the Jews at Antioch. After all, the Jews in Antioch previously rejoiced and glorified God acknowledging that God had granted the Gentiles repentance that brings life (Acts 11:18). Nonetheless, their actions were wrong and Paul addresses the implications of their behavior, despite any misconceived intentions, and in doing so, corrects a false understanding of justification and the Christian life in the Galatian churches.

status of the Jew: "We are Jews by nature and not sinners from the Gentiles." He is not arguing that the Jews were without sin; nevertheless, his thought does speak to a larger Jewish mindset regarding their perceived superiority under the law. Such a statement was a familiar way in which the Jews understood themselves in distinction from the Gentiles.[4]

Calling them "Jews by nature" might be a subtle reference to circumcision.[5] The continued emphasis of the Abrahamic covenant (Gal 3:5–9, 14–18, 29; 4:22–28)[6] and circumcision (Gal 2:3, 7–9, 12; 5:2–3, 6, 11–12; 6:12–15)[7] in Galatians would support this theory. This idea is further strengthen when seen in light of the thought that the false gods by nature in 4:8 could be a reference to idols made by hands, and finally, in light of the connection between natural status (nature; "φύσις") and circumcision in Romans 2:26–27.

"Jews by nature" in contrast with "Gentile sinners" might also be a reference to their reception of the law.[8] Romans 2:12–14 and 1 Corinthians 9:21 speak of the non-Jew as "lawless." The law of God made the Jew unique. This thought also flows well with the contrast in verse 16 between "faith" and "the works of the law."

An argument could also be made that this statement is not that involved but is a familiar way of speaking of the unique status into which the Jews were born, in which case, both circumcision and the law (as well as other elements) are probably in view, in light of Romans 3:1–2, since these elements were inherently connected to the birth status of the Jew (Rom 9:4–5).

All things considered, however, Paul does seem to have the reception of the law in view. This decision in great part rests on the interpretation of verses 17 and 18. The correlation between the use of "sinner"/"transgressor" there and "sinners" here (v. 15) builds the connection. Verse 17 seems to be drawing from the idea of "sinners" found in verse 15, where a distinction between "sinner" and "Jew" rests, in part, upon attitudes related to the law. Verse 18 furthers that conclusion by talking about the true transgressor as the one who returns to the law that was destroyed in coming to Christ. In

---

4. For a similar cultural expression, see Matt 15:26–27 (Mark 7:27–28), where the Canaanite woman and daughter are referenced as "dogs."

5. In contrast to Gentile sinners.

6. Possible reference in Gal 4:7. See also Gen 15:4–21; 17:1–13.

7. Possible reference in Gal 3:3. See also Gen 17:10–11; Eph 2:11–12.

8. See also Bruce, *Galatians*, 137; Burton, *Galatians*, 119; Fung, *Galatians*, 113; Matera, *Galatians*, 92; Martyn, *Galatians*, 248.

any case, it is evident that Paul uses a familiar cultural expression, identifying the privileged natural status of the Jew, as a starting point for developing his argument concerning justification.

Verse 16

Paul then transitions to remind them that even though they had a privileged status as Jews, they still required faith in Jesus Christ for the remission of sin. That which they received through promise was not fulfilled through compliance to the law. If this reality was true for them, to whom the law was entrusted, how much more is this true for the Gentiles? Part of the irony of the entire passage is seen in the fact that they, as Jews, required the same means of salvation as the Gentiles. Several questions immediately arise as a result of this verse.[9]

Justification

First, what is justification (δικαιόω)? Justification is the decisive declaration[10] of God whereby Christ's righteousness is imputed to a sinner as a gracious gift by means of faith through union with Christ, and the sinner's status is declared to be righteous.[11] Notice a judicial concept is behind the

---

9. Due to the importance of v. 16 in properly understanding not only the context, but Gal 2:20 itself, and due to the many interpretive difficulties this verse presents, a significant portion of this appendix will be dedicated to this verse.

10. One question that persists is whether this declarative act is transformative. In other words, does God simply declare someone righteous in justification or does he also make that person righteous. In short, while justification and regeneration are related and to some degree interdependent (Titus 3:4-7), the issue of being declared righteous should be primarily limited to discussions of justification and the issue of being made righteous should be primarily limited to discussions of regeneration and sanctification. For further discussion on the connection between justification and sanctification, see Snider, "Sanctification and Justification," 159-78. For an alternative view that forensic justification should not be distinguished so sharply from the renewed life, see Leithart, "Justification as Verdict and Deliverance," 56-72. Leithart argues that while justification is a legal term it "is extended in a number of places to settings that are not strictly legal" (ibid., 58).

11. Gal 2:16-17; 3:8, 11, 24; 5:4 (cf. Col 2:13-14). See also Snider, "Sanctification and Justification," 159, and question 60 of *The Heidelberg Catechism*, 191-3). Due to the extensive range of the justification debate and the limited space available here, providing a summary of the essence of justification will be the focus in this section.

imagery of justification. It carries the idea of a legal (forensic) declaration (Deut 25:1; 1 Kngs 8:32; Prov 17:15; Isa 43:26; Col 2:13–14). This declaration is made by God as the judicial authority for it is God who justifies the ungodly (Gen 15:6; Isa 45:25; Rom 3:21–22, 26; 4:3–8; 8:33–34; Gal 3:6–8; Col 2:13–14).

Additionally, justification comes from union with Christ and involves the imputation of Christ's righteousness (Isa 53:4–6; Rom 3:24–25; 5:1, 9–11; 18–21; Gal 2:20; 3:26–28; 5:4–6; Eph 1:11–14; Col 2:13–14; 2 Cor 5:21; 1 Pet 2:24; 3:18). Believers in Christ are not merely declared righteous, they are declared righteous based on the righteousness of Christ. As a result, justification is soteriological and eschatological (Isa 13:9; Obad 15–18; Matt 12:36–37; Acts 17:30–31; Rom 2:15–16; 8:18–23; 14:10; 2 Cor 5:10),[12] but it must be remembered that the eschatological emphasis is for soteriological purposes; thus, the gracious justified status is received by means of faith and not "the works of the law" (Gen 15:6; Rom 3:25–36, 28, 30; 4:16–27; 5:1–2; 9:30; 10:4, 6, 10; Gal 2:16; 3:7–9, 24; Eph 1:13; 2:8–9; Phil 3:9; Titus 3:7; Jas 2:24–26).[13]

12. An argument can also be made for seeing both a soteriological and ecclesiological emphasis in justification; nevertheless, in the end "justification is fundamentally soteriological" (Schreiner, "Justification," 22–28. Contra Wright, *Justification*, 132–4; idem, *What Saint Paul Really Said*, 125).

13. Jas 2:21, 24–26 does not present a contradiction or conflict but in actuality supports this position. In the context of James, "works" are presented as the fruition of faith. They are the evidence of true faith (Hab 2:4 [cited in Rom 1:17; Gal 3:11; Heb 10:38]; Matt 3:8; Luke 3:8; Acts 26:20). James distinguishes between a faith of profession and a faith of possession. This truth does not deny the reality that often times works are shown to be the basis of judgment (Exod 15:26; 19:5–6; Ps 25:10; Ezek 5:11; 11:21; 18:5–9; Matt 3:10; 12:36–37; 25:31–46; Luke 12:41–48; John 3:36; 5:28–29; Acts 10:34–35; Rom 2:5–11; 6:23; 2 Cor 5:10; Eph 5:6; Col 3:6; 1 John 2:9–11, 17; Rev 20:13; 21:8). Godly works are a necessary byproduct of the new life (Ezek 11:19–20; Matt 12:33; John 3:36; 14:23; Acts 6:7; 1 Cor 7:19; Titus 1:16; Heb 10:32–39; Jas 2:14; 1 Pet 1:22–23; 1 John 2:3–6; Rev 14:12). "Works" serve as a means of justification only to the degree in which these works are produced by and demonstrate genuine faith (Jas 2:21, 24–26). "Works of the law" are sufficient to condemn but not to save since no one obeys perfectly. Rom 2:5–11 affirms that for those who do "good" there will be "glory and honor"; however, no one is righteous on their own accord (Ps 14:3; 53:3; Rom 3:10) and all fall short of God's standard, a point clarified in the next two verses (Rom 2:12–13; cf. Rom 3:9–25). John Frame furthers the argument of "good works," and the lost's inability to perform them, stating that in order for an action to be "good" or "righteous" it must contain the "right standard," "right motive," and "right action" (Frame, "Doctrine of Man").

Works of the law

Second, what are the works of the law (ἐξ ἔργων νόμου)?[14] As previously noted, the subject of circumcision is critical to the conversation of Galatians, and circumcision relates most directly to the ceremonial aspect of the law (Lev 12:3; Josh 5:2–9). Does this then imply that Paul only has the ceremonial scope of the law in view or does he have a more inclusive perspective? Additionally, what is meant by the "works of the law" in general?

Preliminarily, it must be noted that Paul is not attacking the morality of the law, but the sufficiency of it.[15] Elsewhere, the apostle affirms the goodness of the law (Rom 3:31; 7:7–12; 1 Tim 1:8); however, he consistently exposes the fact that the law is insufficient if used as a means of salvation (Rom 2:12–29; 3:20–24, 27–28; 4:13–15; 8:3–4; Gal 3:10–14).[16] The law was never intended to save; rather, the law bears witness to one's need to be made righteous (Acts 16:38–39; Rom 3:21; 5:20–21; 7:5; Gal 3:19–24; 1 Tim 1:8–11).[17]

Thus, the scope of the law in this passage[18] should not be limited to one aspect of the law (i.e., ceremonial)[19] or the boundary markers of the law,[20] but should be understood in the broader sense of all that the Mosaic

14. For a good concise summary of the arguments, see Schreiner, *Galatians*, 157–61.

15. The law is primarily insufficient, because of man's insufficiency to keep all that the law demands (Rom 1–3).

16. The law highlights one's sinfulness while demanding perfect adherence. It reveals that no one perfectly keeps the law and that everyone stands in condemnation under the law. The fact that those without the law obey the law proves the validity of the law and brings further condemnation to those who have the law. See also Mounce, *Romans*, 111; Schreiner, *Romans*, 173.

17. Dwight Pentecost argues that there was a ten-fold purpose of the law. While Pentecost's conclusion that the law was temporary and has been completely done away may be debated, his concise summary is helpful. Pentecost, "Purpose of the Law," 176–80.

18. "Law" appears 32 times in Gal: 2:16, 19, 21; 3:2, 5, 10–13, 17–19, 21, 23–24; 4:4–5, 21; 5:3–4, 14, 18, 23; 6:2, 13.

19. "The logic of Paul's argument [in Gal] prohibits a neat distinction of moral and ceremonial law . . ." (Moo, "'Law,' in Paul," 84). See also George, *Galatians*, 195. Nor should this text be limited to the moral law (specifically the ten commands). Moo argues that there are times that Paul "singles out 'moral' commandments when discussing the demand of the law (Rom 7:7–8; 13:8–11), but this is done in order to point up the depths of the law's requirement, not to separate out these commandments as fundamentally distinct from other commandments" (Moo, "'Law,' in Paul," 85). Contra Godet, *Romans*, 144.

20. Dunn, *Theology of Paul*, 354–9; McKnight, "Ego and 'I,'" 276–8; Sanders, *Paul and Palestinian Judaism*; idem, *Paul, the Law, and the Jewish People*; Wright, *Paul for*

law commands.[21] The context of Galatians itself helps clarify the issue. Galatians 3:10–14 connects the "works of the law" to everything written within the book of the law.[22] Galatians 3:17–19 and 4:21–24 shows the law in relation to that which was given at Mount Sinai, and Galatians 5:3 connects the ceremonial aspects of the law to the rest of the law. The point in 5:3 is the converse of that which is presented in James 2:10, which explains that whoever fails in one aspect of the law is guilty of the whole law. In the same way, if someone seeks justification through any aspect of the law, be it circumcision or otherwise, they are obligated to keep the whole law.[23]

Considering these things, "works of the law" should be understood in the broader sense of all that the law commands. As Moo highlights, these "works" are "actions performed in obedience to the law, works which are commanded by the law."[24] The emphasis is not so much on doing various aspects of the law, but fulfilling all demands of the law (Gal 5:3, 14).[25] In the end, Paul explains that no one can be justified through the law. Faith is the sole means of justification.

Everyone, 32; idem, *What Saint Paul Really Said*, 132. Das has an interesting article refuting Sanders showing that this "was not just a matter of ethnic exclusion but also its demand for rigorous obedience" (Das, "Beyond Covenantal Nomism," 235).

21. See also Boer, "Paul's Use and Interpretation," 197–201; Byrne, *Romans*, 120; Das, "Beyond Covenantal Nomism," 244; George, *Galatians*, 193, 195; Ladislav, "Christ in Paul," 43; Lange, *Galatians*, 48; Lightfoot, *Galatians*, 118; Moo, "'Law' in Paul," 76; Schreiner, "Justification," 27–28; idem, "Paul and Perfect Obedience," 245–78; idem, *Romans*, 173; idem, "'Works of Law,'" 221–31; Witherington III, *Grace in Galatia*, 176–7; Westerholm, *Israel's Law and the Church's Faith*, 109–20. The argument that "law" in "works of the law" (ἐξ ἔργων νόμου) should be understood as a subjective genitive (Owen, "'Works of the Law,'" 553–77; Gaston, "Works of Law," 39–46) is attractive, but insufficient and unsustainable (Lindsay, "Works of Law," 80–81; Schreiner, *Galatians*, 158–9; idem, "'Works of Law,'" 231); therefore, it will not be discussed in this section.

22. Whether the author has in mind Deuteronomy, the Pentateuch, or something else, it is clear that the scope is broader than the ceremonial aspects of the law.

23. The text will go on to argue in 6:13 that even those who have been circumcised and press that false standard upon others, themselves fall short of the law. The scope of "law" extends beyond ceremonial requirements.

24. Moo, "'Law' in Paul," 92.

25. Note the emphasis in Gal 5:3, 14 on "the whole law:" as would be argued for those who see this primarily as an indictment against Jewish legalism.

ἐὰν μή

ἐὰν μή poses continued problems for interpreters of this passage. The primary tension is whether *ἐὰν μή* should be understood as exceptive,[26] partially exceptive,[27] or adversative.[28]

If exceptive, Galatians 2:16a would read, "Nevertheless, we know that a person is not justified by the works of the law, *except* through faith in Jesus Christ . . . ." A glaring problem immediately arises. Under this translation, the verse would seem to teach that someone can be justified by such works so long as they are accompanied by faith, which is a direct contradiction to Paul's teaching throughout Galatians (2:16b, 21; 3:2, 5, 10–14, 18, 21–22, 24–25; 5:4). Dunn and Das acknowledge this apparent contradiction and defend the exceptive position by arguing that this passage is part of the progression of Paul's beginning thoughts and does not reflect his final conclusion on the matter.[29] The exceptive position is initially attractive in light of the fact that *ἐὰν μή* is most commonly used in the exceptive sense and is exclusively used as exceptive in its other occurrences within Paul's writings;[30] however, that attraction does not outweigh the problems. Since Dunn and Das's view relies heavily upon speculation,[31] since taking *ἐὰν μή* as exceptive of the entire preceding phrase presents an immediate contradiction in

---

26. Das, "Another Look at *ἐὰν μή*," 537–9; Dunn, "New Perspective on Paul," 116–22; idem, *Jesus, Paul, and the Law*, 195–7; Tarazi, *Galatians*, 84–85.

27. Burton, *Galatians*, 121; Lightfoot, *Galatians*, 115; Walker, "Translation and Interpretation of *ἐὰν μή*," 516–20.

28. Bruce, *Galatians*, 138; Carson, *Love in Hard Places*, 162; Dunn, *Jesus, Paul, and the Law*, 195–97; Hunn, "Ἐὰν μή in Galatians 2:16," 288–90; Ridderbos, *Galatia*, 99; Schreiner, *Galatians*, 163; Fung, *Galatians*, 115; Witherington, *Grace in Galatia*, 169; Martyn, *Galatians*, 251. Other views exist that present an alternative distinct from the traditional debate; however, these views do not seem as likely as the traditional views and do not have as strong grammatical support; thus, they will not be discussed. For example, Gaston argues that "works of law" should be taken as a subjective genitive (Gaston, *Paul and the Torah*, 100–06). Seifrid argues that "works of the law" modify the noun "person" and not the verb "justified" (Seifrid, "Paul, Luther, and Justification," 217–9). While this view has some appeal, it has been reasonably refuted by Schreiner who points out that "in every other instance where the phrase 'works of the law' occurs, it modifies a verb (see Gal 3:2, 5, 10; cf. Rom 3:20, 28)" (Schreiner, *Galatians*, 163).

29. Das, "Another Look at *ἐὰν μή*," 534–8; Dunn, "New Perspective on Paul," 116–22; idem, *Galatians*, 137–40.

30. Das, "Another Look at *ἐὰν μή*," 530–32. He cites Rom 10:15; 11:23; 1 Cor 8:8; 9:16; 13:1; 14:6–7, 9, 11, 28; 15:36.

31. See also Schreiner, *Galatians*, 162.

Paul's argument (2:16b), and since ἐὰν μή can function grammatically as partially exceptive or adversative,[32] the partially exceptive and adversative positions are preferred.

The partially exceptive view and the adversative view essentially communicate the same point, differing more in emphasis than meaning. The partially exceptive view sees ἐὰν μή as being exceptive, but only to the main part of the verse. Thus, the verse reads, "Nevertheless, we know that a person is not justified by the works of the law, *a person is not justified except* through faith in Jesus Christ . . . ." As a result of the division "works of the law" causes between "justified" and the exceptive ἐὰν μή, an ellipsis occurs, whereby the beginning of the sentence is repeated in translation for the sake of clarification. This view retains the more common use of ἐὰν μή without presenting the contextual problems of the previous exceptive position.

The adversative view translates ἐὰν μή as "but" showing contrast between "works of the law" and "faith in Jesus Christ." The verse would then read, "Nevertheless, we know that a person is not justified by the works of the law, *but* through faith in Jesus Christ . . . ."[33] While "except" may be the more general use of ἐὰν μή, it is not the only use (John 5:19; 15:4).[34] "But" is a legitimate translation for ἐὰν μή.

In this situation, the context becomes most helpful in quickly limiting if not altogether dismissing the exclusive view. While Dunn and Das provide thoughtful solutions to the problems presented by taking ἐὰν μή as exceptive of the entire preceding portion of the verse, in the end, their solutions seem deficient. At the same time, the partially exclusive view avoids the major problems and still leaves the more general use of ἐὰν μή; nevertheless, contrast caused by the insertion of "works of the law" between "justified" and ἐὰν μή makes the adversative position most probable.[35]

---

32. Hunn, "Ἐὰν μή in Galatians 2:16," 281–90. Instead of just criticizing Dunn and Das or arguing from tradition, Hunn argues from grammar to show that "ἐὰν μή" can function as partially exceptive or adversative and provides guidelines for understand when it should be taken as adversative rather than partially exceptive. See also Gal 1:7 where εἰ μή is clearly adversative.

33. Or "but only."

34. Acknowledged in Das, "Another Look at ἐὰν μή," 530–31, and demonstrated convincingly in Hunn by looking at John as well as other early Greek works "Ἐὰν μή in Galatians 2:16," 286–8.

35. "If the extra word or phrase in the main clause is important enough to serve as a point of contrast, ἐὰν μή is adversative. If not, it is exceptive" (Hunn, "Ἐὰν μή in Galatians 2:16," 288).

Faith of Jesus Christ

The next difficulty presented in this passage is determining whether "faith of Jesus Christ" (πίστεως Ἰησοῦ Χριστοῦ) should be understood as a subjective genitive[36] (Jesus's faithfulness) or an objective genitive[37] (faith in Jesus). This topic has been heavily debated, in part, due to the fact that grammatically both are legitimate uses of the phrase and the fact that each side of the debate generally acknowledges that the other truth is necessary for salvation.[38] In other words, the faithfulness of Christ does not negate the necessity for faith in Christ as expressed elsewhere in Paul's writings (Eph 1:15; Col 1:4; 2 Tim 3:15), nor does placing faith in Christ negate the reality that faith is based upon Christ's faithfulness in redemption (Rom 5:19; Phil 2:5–8; Heb 5:8–10; 12:2). Despite the legitimacy of each position, which did the apostle seek to present?

Regarding Galatians 2:16, the objective genitive position seems most reasonable for the following four reasons.[39] First, despite the potential attraction of the subjective genitive, the primary reason for taking the "faith

---

36. Hays, *Faith of Jesus Christ*, 141–62. Among other supporters, see also Boer, "Paul's Use and Interpretation," 201–05; Choi, "ΠΙΣΤΙΣ in Galatians 5:5–6," 467–90; Cousar, *Theology of the Cross*, 39–40; Davis, *Structure of Paul's Theology*, 62–72; Donaldson, "'Curse of the Law,'" 94–112; Gorman, *Cruciformity*, 113–4, 134–5, 137; Hays, "ΠΙΣΤΙΣ and Pauline Christology," 4:35–60; Hooker, *Adam to Christ*, 165–86; Howard, *Paul*; Jervis, *Galatians*, 21–22, 68–69; Longenecker, "ΠΙΣΤΙΣ in Romans 3:25," 478–80; Longenecker, *Galatians*, 87–88, 93–94; Matera, *Galatians*, 94, 100–02; Martyn, *Galatians*, 251–2; Witherington, *Grace in Galatia*, 179–83; idem, "Influence of Galatians on Hebrews," 146–52.

37. Porter and Pitts, "Πίστις with a Preposition," 33–53. See also Barnes, *Study on Galatians*, 111–2; Betz, *Galatians*, 117; Boles, *Galatians*, 66; Bruce, *Galatians*, 138–9; Burton, *Galatians*, 121; Carson, *Love in Hard Places*, 162; Dunn, "Once More, ΠΙΣΤΙΣ ΧΡΙΣΤΟΥ," 4:61–81; idem, *Galatians*, 138–9; Fung, *Galatians*, 115; George, *Galatians*, 195–6; Fee, *Pauline Christology*, 223–26; Hansen, *Abraham in Galatians*; Harrisville, "ΠΙΣΤΙΣ ΧΡΙΣΤΟΥ," 233–41; Hultgren, "*Pistis Christou*," 262–3; Hunn, "ΠΙΣΤΙΣ ΧΡΙΣΤΟΥ," 23–33; Johnson, "Paradigm of Abraham," 179–99; Ladislav, "Christ in Paul," 42; Ngewa, *Galatians*, 81; Schreiner, *Galatians*, 164–6; Tarazi, *Galatians*, 84–85; Westerholm, *Israel's Law and the Church's Faith*.

38. BDAG, 6th ed., s.v. "πίστις." Lindsay argues for a more generic attributive genitive which encompasses a subjective and an objective aspect (Lindsay, "Works of Law," 87). He cites Hultgren as part of his support; however, Hultgren concluded that while there is a strong attributive aspect to the genitive that must be considered in interpretation, the genitive is ultimately an objective genitive (Hultgren, "*Pistis Christou*," 262–3).

39. For a good and concise summary of the arguments and a defense of the objective genitive position, see Schreiner, *Galatians*, 163–6.

of Jesus Christ" as an objective genitive is the context of the verse itself.[40] Regardless of possible grammatical uses, Galatians 2:16b provides a compelling context, which seems to force the objective genitive. The use of "καὶ" immediately after "Jesus Christ" (διὰ πίστεως Ἰησοῦ Χριστοῦ, καὶ ἡμεῖς) presents an association whereby the Jews have met the condition of the previous clause of "being justified through faith." As a result, "καὶ" is translated as "even" or "also." Therefore, it reads, "even we have believed in Christ Jesus" (καὶ ἡμεῖς εἰς Χριστὸν Ἰησοῦν ἐπιστεύσαμεν). "Believe" (πιστεύω) is the verb form of the noun "faith" (πίστις); thus, the passage is saying that one is justified, not by the works of the law, but only through faith *in* Jesus Christ.[41] The Jews then, in order to be justified, "believed" in (i.e., placed their faith *in*) Jesus. This point is further emphasized by the fact that "believe" as an activity of faith is never used of Jesus.[42] This interpretation fits most naturally with the flow of the text.

Second, "works of the law" and "faith" are set in contrast to one another.[43] Throughout Galatians, works and faith serve as an essential contrast (Gal 2:16; 3:2, 5, 11–2, 24–25; 5:2–5) to such an extent that the apostle says that if anyone rests in their works, whatever faith they presume to have is worthless (Gal 5:3–4).[44] Since "works of the law" are actions expected of the audience and not of Christ, it seems most reasonable to understand that to which it stands in contrast to refer to the audience and not to Christ as well. Thus, justification is not achieved through one's engagement in the "works of the law," but only through one's expressed faith in Jesus Christ.

Third, in addition to the immediate context, taking "faith of Jesus" as a subjective genitive creates confusion in regards to the larger context of Galatians. Throughout the rest of Galatians the emphasis in regards to faith is the necessity of the personal expression of faith (Gal 3:22, 24; 3:5–6, 8–9, 22 ["faith" and "believe" are used together]; 5:5). This seems, in part, why

---

40. Betz, *Galatians*, 117.

41. See also Bruce, *Galatians*, 139.

42. In John 2:24, πιστεύω is used of Jesus but as an expression of him not "entrusting" himself to the disciples.

43. Contra Dunn, *Galatians*, 137.

44. See also Rom 4:14. This same type of contrast is seen in Rom 3:28; 4:2–5, 13–14. Such a view in no way conflicts with James. James is arguing that works is the natural and necessary byproduct for those who have genuinely placed their faith in Christ. He is not saying that Abraham or anyone else trusted in their works, but that their faith was evidenced through works. With both James and Paul the object of faith is the same.

Paul refers to believers at the end of the letter as "the household of faith" (τοὺς οἰκείους τῆς πίστεως) (Gal 6:10).

Finally, in Galatians, the concept of faith is predicated upon Abraham's example. When a model of expressing faith (believing) is given as an example for believers, it is Abraham, not Christ (Gal 3:5–9; see also Rom 4:9, 11–12, 16–17). This emphasis of the text presses further the point of Galatians regarding the necessity of one's personal expression of faith and brings further evidence that the "faith of Jesus" should be understood as an objective genitive.

Verses 17–19

In continuing to demonstrate the inadequacy of the law as a means of justification, Paul transitions the conversation (v. 17) to use the pre–conversion status of these Jews (himself included) as a proof that justification came through faith in Christ apart from the works of the law. In so doing, Paul addresses a misconception about the implications of such justification. Though Gentiles were viewed as sinners, both literally and as those without the God–given law, these Jews in seeking justification in Christ acknowledged that while under the law, they were still sinners.[45] The law revealed their need for justification, while being insufficient to provide such justification. In order to be justified in Christ, they had to acknowledge the insufficiency of the law and their need to be justified, i.e., that they were sinners before God just as the Gentiles were (see also, Phil 3:4–11). Does this mean that Christ promotes sin? Absolutely not! Paul continues to argue that it is the law that promotes the reality of sin (v. 18). Christ redeemed them from that sin by bringing about their death in relation to the law (v. 19–20a; Rom 7:1). For the law does not have jurisdiction over the dead. The condemnation brought by the law ceases at death. Therefore, Paul died to the law through union with Christ in order to live to God (v. 19; Rom 7:4, 6).

Verse 17

A critical component of the debate surrounding this verse is whether it describes the pre- or post–conversion status of the Jew. The continuation of

---

45. Hunn, "Christ Versus the Law," 539–42.

the first person plural (we/our) indicates that the same group of Christian Jews from verse 15 are still in view. The tension primarily revolves around whether or not their status as "sinners" is a reference to the literal acknowledgment of their position under the law before Christ, or is it an accusation posed by those who see them abandoning the law as converted Jews. Strong arguments exist for both.

If the apostle is reiterating the accusation of other Jews, possible who have "slipped in to spy out their freedoms" (Gal 2:4),[46] that they are sinners, then their post-conversion status is in view. This argument has a lot in favor of it, and can be developed in a couple of different ways. For the first approach, of particular importance is the connection between the law and the status of "sinner" in verses 15 and 17. As argued previously, verse 15 seems to indicate that the Jews referenced Gentiles specifically as sinners in part because they did not have the law. While other factors may have been involved, this factor seems to be a key element behind that cultural phrase. Since therefore, these Christian Jews were abandoning the custom of the law,[47] those watching could see them as abandoning their Jewishness, and identifying with Gentile sinners.[48] It would appear from their perspective that, without the law, no standard of righteousness could exist; thus, one would have the freedom to live however they wanted while still receiving justification.[49] The logical question that would then formulate is, "If you are identifying with sinful Gentiles, doesn't that mean that Christ promotes sinfulness?" Paul's response is, "Certainly not!" The abandonment of the law is not sinful; rather, returning to the law and establishing it as a means of justification is (vv. 16, 18).

Another approach within the post-conversion perspective is to see this verse as an accusation of those who observe continued traces of sin in the lives of these Jews who have abandoned the law and have claimed

---

46. Freedom is a strong theme for Paul in Gal (2:4; 5:1, 13).

47. It seems clear that a critical issue would be the ceremonial aspects of the law, or more specifically the boundary markers; however, as noted in the conversation related to the "works of the law" in v. 16, the argument should not be limited to those.

48. So Burton, *Galatians*, 125; McKnight, "Ego and 'I,'" 277; Witherington, *Grace in Galatia*, 185.

49. A concern repeatedly addressed by Paul (Rom 6:1, 15; Gal 5:13–26). Others who hold the view that this is a post-conversion accusation, such as McKnight ("Ego and 'I,'" 277), argue that the concern is that Jews are violating the covenant in their table fellowship with the Gentiles.

justification in Christ.[50] If they continue to sin, doesn't this mean that Christ promotes sin? In this argument, the apostle responds by saying, "No, absolutely not!" Your failure to walk in the law of love doesn't denote a failure on Christ's part or a promotion of sin (Gal 5:13–4; 6:2).

Though the post–conversion status of the Jew has merit, the text seems to be arguing from the pre–conversion status of these Jewish Christians.[51] Paul accepts as true the initial condition of the argument that they were in fact found to be sinners in seeking justification in Christ.[52] The verse reveals that it was under the law that these Jews came to realize their need for Christ (Gal 3:24).[53] They came to realize that they were in fact sinners, just as the Gentiles were. As Schreiner explains, "Paul accepts in the 'if' clause the reality of the charge. In other words, Peter and Paul had been found to be sinners in seeking to be justified in Christ, and they recognized that they were no better than Gentiles."[54] Though they had the advantage of the law, they could not maintain the demands of the law. The law then drove them to seek redemption outside the law (v. 19) in Christ.[55] They saw the law's inability to justify them. Thus, in a sense, they both acknowledged themselves to be sinners and in doing so, abandoned the law as a means of justification.

So, in seeking to be justified (pre–conversion) in Christ, they acknowledged that they were sinners. The misconception that Paul then addresses is, "Does that mean that Christ promotes sin?" This rhetorical question is immediately dismissed by the apostle, "Absolutely not!"[56]

---

50. So Betz, *Galatians*, 120; Longenecker, *Galatians*, 89–90; O'Neill, *Recovery of Paul's Letter*, 43.

51. See also Bruce, *Galatians*, 140–1; Hunn, "Christ Versus the Law," 540; Matera, *Galatians*, 95; Schreiner, *Galatians*, 169; Shauf, "Galatians 2:20 in Context," 89–90.

52. Contra Dunn, *Galatians*, 141, who argues that Paul was falsely accused of being a sinner on account of eating with Gentiles.

53. "Some scholars object at this point that first–century Judaism never taught that the law condemns everyone. Paul, however, is not teaching the tenets of Judaism. To say that mainstream Judaism never taught that the law condemned everyone under it is to begin to understand Paul's point: it surprised the Jews to be found sinners" (Hunn, "Christ Versus the Law," 544).

54. Schreiner, *Galatians*, 167–8.

55. "ἐν" could be translated as "by" (instrumental) or in (locative). The locative use seems most probably here, since Christ is the sphere in which one finds his justification. See also Matera, *Galatians*, 95; Witherington, *Grace in Galatia*, 185. Contra Fung and Longenecker who argue for a dual understanding whereby both instrumental and locative uses are in view. Fung, *Galatians*, 119; Longenecker, *Galatians*, 89.

56. Some discussion exists whether or not "αρα" should have a circumflex. With the

Verse 18

Paul continues the dismissal of the false accusation that Christ promotes sin by grounding his argument in verse 18.[57] In contrast to Christ being a promoter of sin, using architectural language, the apostle argues that ironically enough, it is the very law they were defending that brings one back into bondage and promotes sin. Paul argues that if he, or anyone else, re-introduces the law as the standard of living then they stand in violation of the will of God.[58] What makes one a sinner is not the abandonment of the law for justification in Christ, but rather turning back to the law despite the work of Christ.

One question that persists is, "Why does the apostle shift from the first-person plural (vv. 15–17) to the first-person singular (vv. 18–21)?" While this change may in part be "a rhetorical feature that allows Paul to make his point in more diplomatic fashion,"[59] in the end, in this shift, Paul presents himself as an example of a truth that is applicable to all who believe in Jesus Christ in order to be justified by faith, to the Jew first and also to the Gentile.[60]

---

circumflex, a question is intended. Without the circumflex a statement is intended. Due to the next phrase "Certainly not!" (μὴ γένοιτο), which normally follows a rhetorical question in Paul's writing (Rom 3:4, 6, 31; 6:2, 15; 7:7, 13; 9:14; 11:1, 11; 1 Cor 6:15; Gal 3:21), the circumflex is preferred. For further brief interaction with the conversation surrounding "αρα" in this text, see Bruce, *Galatians*, 141; Burton, *Galatians*, 126 footnote "*"; Lightfoot, *Galatians*, 117.

57. The "γὰρ" continues Paul's argument to explain why he declares that Christ does not promote sin.

58. For example, this idea is also shown in the declaration that all foods are now clean (Mark 7:19; Acts 11:4–10). To declare the food laws as a sign of the covenant or of righteousness stands opposed to God's declared will. This statement is true whether someone was seeking to argue someone's righteousness based on their adherence to the law, or whether someone was arguing that the law represents the way someone should live (i.e., a necessary standard of living). Witherington states it well when he says, "Here Paul is using the [architectural] metaphor negatively to of the reconstruction of a Torah-observant lifestyle and community, after that sort of approach was dismantled by the death of Christ . . . " (Witherington, *Grace in Galatia*, 187).

59. Longenecker, *Galatians*, 90.

60. As Shauf writes, "The reason for the change probably comes down to both generalization and tact" (Shauf, "Galatians 2:20 in Context," 91).

Verse 19

Paul grounds his argument by explaining that it was through the law that he died to the law.[61] The law itself pointed Paul to Christ (Gal 3:22-24). The law itself created unachievable demands, because of the sinfulness of man, causing man to abandon it in search of justification by faith. Paul, then, is not arguing for anything other than what the law itself advocates in pointing to Christ (Luke 24:27; John 5:39-40).[62] It was through the law that Paul found his need for Christ (i.e., was found to be a sinner), and accepted Christ, dying to the law through union with Christ (v. 20), for the intended purpose that he might have true life with and for God.[63] Jesus bore the curse of the law, so that in identifying with his death through faith, believers are reckoned righteous and released from the penalty of sin and the curse of the law (Gal 3:10-14). The law has jurisdiction, and brings condemnation, so long as one is living, but in death, the legal requirements of the law are broken. Therefore, Paul died to the law by abandoning it, seeking justification in Christ outside the works of the law, and being united with Christ's death through faith in Christ.

This law is now dead to the apostle, because his identity is now found in the crucified Savior (vv. 19-20a). It is not the law that has died, but the apostle himself. Those who are dead are no longer bound to the law (Rom 7:2; 1 Cor 7:39). Paul shows how in Christ, the requirement of the law have been met through spiritual crucifixion. His identity with Christ

---

61. Two points on the continuation of his argument should be noted. First, it is further grounded with the use of another "γὰρ." Second, it should be remembers that Paul used an initial argument from Antioch presented to Jewish Christians (vv. 11-14) in order to communicate truths that are applicable to every believer in Christ. Thus, dying to the law through the law, should be understood first and foremost from the perspective of the Jew and then the implications are carried over to the Gentile community.

62. As pointed to in the fall (Gen 3:15), in the picture provided by Melchizedeck (Ps 110:4; Heb 7), in the Abrahamic Covenant (Gen 17:9-27; cf. Ps 89:4; Gal 3:16), in Abraham's willingness to sacrifice Isaac and God's provision (Gen 22:7-14; cf. John 1:29, 36), in the Passover feast (Exod 12:43-51; cf. Num 9:12; John 19:33-37; 1 Cor 5:7), the rock in the wilderness (Exod 17:6; cf. Num 20:8-12; Neh 9:15; Ps 78:16-20; 105:41; 114:8; Isa 48:2; 1 Cor 10:3-4), in God's promise to raise up his prophet (Deut 18:15-22), in the curse of the hanged man (Deut 21:22-23; Gal 3:13-14). Paul presses to make this most clear in speaking of the faith of Abraham being before the giving of the law (Rom 4; Gal 3).

63. Rom 3:20; 5:20; 7:4, 6-10. Paul found his need for Christ in one sense on the road to Damascus (Acts 9) through an encounter with the risen Savior; however, later Paul explains that he came to understand what the true purposes of the law were. One of the purposes of the law is to reveal sin (Rom 7:6-10).

is an identity through death into new life. Thus, the beginning of verse 20 explains how Paul died to the law while transitioning the reader to the implications of this justified life that now exists. The law has been abolished in the sense that the apostle died to it. Therefore, to reintroduce its prominence is to come alive to it again and fall back into the status of "sinner" before God (v. 18).

Furthermore, for the believer, the law as it once stood has now been overshadowed by a new and fuller law (John 13:34; 2 Cor 3:6; Eph 2:14–16; Heb 8:7, 13; 10:1, 10; 1 John 2:7–8; 2 John 5). This new law may be called the "law of love" (Gal 5:13–14); "the law of the Spirit" (Gal 5:22–23); or "the law of Christ" (Gal 6:2). It is a law that brings freedom: freedom to serve God and others. Such a law summarizes the intentions of God and when followed serves in a capacity against which no other law can stand (Gal 5:23). As George explains, "However, he [Paul] was not saying here that the law of God had lost all meaning or relevance for the Christian believer. This is the error of antinomianism, which Paul was at pains to refute both here in Galatians as well as in Romans . . . There is an ethical imperative in the Christian life that flows from a proper understanding of justification."[64] This point is important to note, for the apostle continues on to argue that this crucified life still lives (v. 20), and the life produced should be one that is godly; however, godliness is not measured in relation to the law, but in relation to Christ.

Conclusion

"Works of the law" are insufficient to make one right before God. Regardless of what advantage or disadvantage one may have ethnically, religiously, or in any other way, everyone falls short of God's standard of righteousness (Rom 3:23). Thus, despite the privileged status the Jews had in possessing the law, the faith in Jesus Christ for the remission of sin was still required for justification. If this was true for Jews, who had the advantage of the law, how much more was it true for the Gentiles. Therefore, Paul is emphatically rejecting any notion that in order to be justified one has to comply with the law. Justification is obtained solely through faith in Jesus Christ and not by the works of the law, for no one is justified by works.

Having established this principle of justification, Paul proceeds in Galatians 2:20 to argue that the believer has died to the law through

---

64. George, *Galatians*, 198.

union with Christ. In that spiritual death, the believer resigns their life to Christ and experiences new life through the presence of the Spirit of Christ living through him. Thus, the context (vv. 15–19) helps show that Galatians 2:20 presents, in condensed fashion, Paul's understanding of the spiritual life that proceeds forth out of one who has been justified through union with Christ.

Ephesians 3:14–19

Ephesians 3:14–19: For this reason I bow my knees before the Father, from whom every family in heaven and on earth is named, that according to the riches of his glory he may grant you to be strengthened with power through his Spirit in your inner being, so that Christ may dwell in your hearts through faith—that you, being rooted and grounded in love, may have strength to comprehend with all the saints what is the breadth and length and height and depth, and to know the love of Christ that surpasses knowledge, that you may be filled with all the fullness of God.

Introduction

EPHESIANS 3:14–19 RANKS AMONG the more remarkable passages in the epistles if not the entire New Testament. After establishing how those who were once far away from God have been brought near to God through the priceless sacrifice of Christ Jesus (2:13), the author[1] of Ephesians prays his second prayer of the epistle (3:14–21).[2] In this prayer, the audience is presented to their Father so that they might be empowered to know the love of Christ in such a way that they would be filled up to all the fullness of God.

1. Discussions of authorship are beyond the scope of this section; however, Pauline authorship is preferred. For a defense of Pauline authorship, see O'Brien, *Ephesians*, 4–47.

2. The first prayer is provided in 1:15–23.

The purpose of this appendix is to provide a contextual interpretation of Ephesians 3:14–19.

Ephesians 3:14–15

Verse 14

After a brief theological aside (3:2–13),[3] the repetition of "For this reason" (Τούτου χάριν) reconnects the reader with the author's prayer for the Gentiles he began in 3:1. This grammatical link with 3:1 pulls the contextual ground for the pending prayer to include both 3:2–13 and 2:11–22.[4] Thus, he can pray in this way for the Gentiles because they have been brought into God's family and united with Jews in order to make the two into "one new man" (2:15).

The reality that the author is entering into prayer is further expressed by the fact that he "bows his knee before the Father." The idea of kneeling in prayer should not be emphasized over and against standing in prayer.[5] Even though standing was the primary posture of prayer,[6] kneeling was certainly not an unfamiliar one (1 Kgs 8:54; 2 Chr 6:13; Ezra 9:5; Dan 6:10; Acts 7:60; 21:5). Additionally, falling on one's knees historically had been a sign of respect, submission or even worship (2 Kgs 1:13; Ps 95:6; Isa 45:23; Matt 17:14; 27:29;[7] Mark 1:40; Luke 5:8; Rom 14:11; Phil 2:10), which coincide with the act of praying. Thus, the statement that he is kneeling before the Father is designed to express that he is entering into prayer on their behalf, and in the process showing reverence for the one before whom he approaches in prayer: "the Father."[8]

3. This statement in no way implies that the information provided in 3:2–13 is superfluous. Addressing the Gentiles compelled the biblical author to interrupt the prayer in order to elaborate upon the mystery of the inclusion of the Gentiles into the people of God through the gospel, and his role, as commission by God, in bringing the gospel to the Gentiles.

4. Hoehner, *Ephesians*, 472.

5. So Jeal, *Integrating Theology and Ethics*, 112–3. Such an overemphasis may be seen in Lenski, *Ephesians*, 489–90; Lincoln, *Ephesians*, 202.

6. Ibid.; Abbott, *Ephesians*, 93; O'Brien, *Ephesians*, 255.

7. Here the soldiers are mocking "King Jesus"; however, their actions reveal actions that would be expected to show honor to greatness. See also Mark 15:19.

8. Regardless of whether one prefers to understand πρὸς as "to" or "before," the focus of the wording is on relationship and presence. Hoehner, *Ephesians*, 473; Lenski, *Ephesians*, 490.

"Father" is a title used in reference to God throughout New Testament epistles (Rom 1:7; 6:4; 8:15; 15:6; 1 Cor 1:3; 8:6; 15:24; 2 Cor 1:2, 3; 6:18; 11:31; Gal 1:1, 3, 4; 4:6; Eph 1:2, 3, 17; 2:18; 3:14; 4:6; 5:20; 6:23; Phil 1:2; 2:11; 4:20; Col 1:2, 3, 12; 3:17, 21; 1 Thess 1:1, 3; 3:11, 13; 2 Thess 1:1, 2; 2:16; 1 Tim 1:2; 2 Tim 1:2; Titus 1:4; Phlm 3; Heb 1:5; 12:7, 9; Jas 1:17, 27; 3:9; 1 Pet 1:2, 3, 17; 2 Pet 1:17; 1 John 1:2, 3; 2:1, 13, 15, 16, 22, 23, 24; 3:1; 4:14; 2 John 3, 4, 9; Jude 1). Inherent within the title is an understanding of the authority and paternity of God.[9] God is shown as the sovereign creator of the world, and as such, he is the Father of all (Eph 3:9; 1 Cor 8:6). As creator, God provides oversight and he sustains his creation (Col 1:15–17). These aspects of God's fatherhood apply to all men more generally. More narrowly, by virtue of their covenant relationship with God through the Son, believers are adopted as sons; thus, becoming children of God (John 1:12; Rom 8:15; Gal 4:6).

Verse 15

While the first two chapters of Ephesians (1:2, 3; 2:18) highlight the more narrow perspective on fatherhood, the modifying phrase "from whom every family in heaven and earth derives its name" seems to imply that the more general usage is in view: referring to God's authority over all human and angelic beings. The strongest argument in opposition to this view is the fact mentioned above that the first two chapters clearly highlight "fatherhood" in relationship to the believer's adoption as sons through the Son of God, Jesus the Christ (1:2, 3; 2:18). Contextually, then, God should be seen as the Father over all those who belong to the household of God. Thus, it would be argued that the translation should read "from whom the whole family . . . derives its name" versus "every family." Two factors, however, when taken cumulatively, seem to negate this more narrow understanding of fatherhood in favor of the broader connotation that God is being presented as the Father over all.

First, no article is provided to limit the scope of the family in reference.[10] Generally, an article would be needed in order to read πᾶσα[11] πατρια

---

9. While "authority" and "paternity" do not exhaust the implications of the fatherhood of God, they are certainly shown within New Testament literature to be contained within the idea.

10. So Salmond, "Ephesians," 312; Wuest, *Ephesians,* 1:87.

11. πᾶς is used 52 times in 38 verses throughout Eph: 1:3, 8, 10–11, 15, 21–23; 2:3,

as "the whole family"; thus, the absence of the article should result in the more natural translation of "every family."[12] In response to this reasoning, Lenski argues that 2:21 does not use an article and is clearly to be understood as "the whole building" in contrast with "every building."[13] While his observation of 2:21 is correct, the connection of 3:15 with 2:21 is unwarranted for two reasons. First, within certain manuscripts, scribes added the article in 2:21 demonstrating that historically the text had been understood as referring to "the whole building."[14] No such textual variant exists in 3:15. Second, the immediate context of 2:21 allows for "the whole building" to be the more natural reading, while the immediate context of 3:15 does not provide the same restrictions.

Second, the theological aside provided in 3:2-13 is significant and adds an additional contextual element, which the author deemed necessary for properly understanding the prayer. Verses 9 and 10 contain the most immediate and direct references to God. In verse 9, God is described as the one "who created all things" (τῷ τὰ πάντα κτίσαντι). This statement provides a significant shift in the discussion in order to prepare the reader to understand at least one way in which God is the "Father, from whom every family . . . derives its name." Verse 10 follows within the same sentence to show God's purpose in allowing the wisdom of God to be revealed through the church to the "rulers and authorities in the heavenly places" (ταῖς ἀρχαῖς καὶ ταῖς ἐξοθσίαις ἐν τοῖς ἐπουρανίοις). These rulers and authorities encompass both preserved and fallen angels (6:12). In light of these factors, the broader understanding of God as the Father who names "every family" is favored.

Finally, God's authority as Father is ultimately demonstrated in the naming of these families. While the exact means by which God names

---

21; 3:8-9, 15, 18-21; 4:2, 6, 10, 13-16, 19, 29, 31; 5:3, 5, 9, 13-14, 20, 24; 6:16, 18, 21, 24.

12. "The anarthrous adjective πᾶσα could be translated 'all' or 'whole' family (AV, NIV), as in 2:21, but in this phrase it seems more appropriate to accept the normal grammatical usage meaning 'every' family (RV, ASV . . .)" (Hoehner, *Ephesians*, 475).

13. Lenski, *Ephesians*, 491.

14. ℵ A C P 6 81 326 1739c 1881 have πᾶσα ἡ οἰκοδομήν, while ℵ* B D F G Γ 33 1739* M have πᾶσα οἰκοδομή. This defense was adapted from Barth, *Ephesians*, 381. He writes, "If it is presupposed that 3:15 contains the same grammatical mistake as 2:21, i.e., the omission of the article before the noun qualified by *pas* ('each,' 'all,' or 'whole'), then 3:15 can be translated with the American Version as referring to the one 'whole' family that embraces heaven and earth. But the Greek text of all MSS speaks, correctly translated, of 'each family,' not of 'the whole family.'"

every family cannot be definitively proven,[15] the varying views available all function to highlight the authority of God over his creation, to include both Jew and Gentile. Thus in the end, regardless of whether verse 15 is seen as describing every family or the whole family and regardless of how God is seen as naming every family, the entire dependent clause serves to demonstrate the authority of God as Father before whom the author is submitting his prayer.

Ephesians 3:16-17a

Verse 16

After introducing the prayer, the content of the prayer is provided.[16] The initial component of the prayer is that God,[17] would grant them "to be strengthened."[18] This strengthening is to be granted "according to the riches of his [God's] glory," which prefaces the main thrust of the request for strengthening.[19] As such, it provides the source from which the author is requesting the prayer to be granted, and also asks that God's "giving corresponds to the inexhaustible riches of that glory."[20]

The prayer continues to request that these saints be strengthened "with power" by means of "his Spirit." This power is God's power. It is the same power attributed to God in the middle of the epistle's first prayer in 1:19. Now, that power, previously attributed solely to God, is requested to be bestowed upon these believers by means of the Spirit. Such a request

15. Barth presents four possible views concerning how every family derives its name from God. View three seems most convincing (Barth, *Ephesians*, 382–4).

16. Hoehner, *Ephesians*, 477. ἵνα usually denotes purpose; however, in the context of praying, the purpose for the prayer is often expressed in terms of the actual content of the prayer. Therefore, in this case, ἵνα conjoins the one to whom the author prays with the content of what is actually prayed. See Matt 24:20 as another example.

17. The implied subject "he" of δῷ is a reference to "Father" in v. 14, which is a title given to God.

18. "To be strengthened" (κραταιωθῆναι) is a complementary divine passive infinitive. The request is that they would be strengthened by God in accordance with the riches of his glory.

19. Similar statements have been made throughout Eph: 1:7, 12, 14, 18; 2:4, 7; 3:8. For a brief exposition on the glory of God, see Bruce, *Ephesians,* 326; Hodge, *Ephesians,* 181.

20. O'Brien, *Ephesians,* 257.

implies the divinity of the Spirit as the One who is able to bring the power of God into the life of the believer.[21]

The "inner man," where this strengthening with power by the Spirit is to take place, is best understood as the immaterial inner part of man's moral being paralleling the author's references to the "heart" of a person, which is found elsewhere throughout the epistle (1:18; 3:17; 4:18; 5:19; 6:5, 22). Two factors support the view that "inner man" and "heart" in this context are interchangeable.

First, other passages demonstrate this same usage. "Inner" (ἔσω) is used eight other times in the New Testament (Matt 26:58; Mark 14:54, 15:16; John 20:26; Acts 5:23; Rom 7:22; 1 Cor 5:12; 2 Cor 4:16). Of those, only Romans 7:22 and 2 Corinthians 4:16 are used in the same way as Ephesians 3:16.[22] While Romans 7:22 is a more heavily debated context, 2 Corinthians 4:16 proves most significant for these purposes.[23] Within that setting, the "inner man" of 4:16 is contextually paralleled with "heart" in both 4:6 and 5:12.[24] Additionally, though the words "inner man" are not used, 1 Peter 3:4 ("the hidden person of the heart") provides an interesting parallel to Ephesians 3:16 as well, further supporting the view that "inner man" is to be understood as being synonymously with "heart" in this context.[25]

Second, and more convincingly, the content portion of the prayer (3:16–19) is structured so that 3:17a clarifies and restates 3:16, while 3:19a clarifies and restates 3:18. Both verses 16 and 18 begin with a content clause (ἵνα + the subjunctive) followed by two infinitives which explain one another.[26] As a result of the pattern, "to be strengthened with power through

21. Lenski, *Ephesians*, 493. Such an implication of the divinity of the Spirit is not unique in Eph. As Lincoln explains, "Power is to be mediated to believers by the Spirit, who has previously mentioned as the one by whom believers are sealed, as the guarantee of the full salvation of the age to come (1:13, 14), and as the means by which God is present in the church (2:22). Spirit and power of the age to come, and that association is continued here" (Lincoln, *Ephesians*, 205).

22. All other references deal with the idea of being "within" or "inside" various structures; though, all references show the inward emphasis of the word.

23. Rom 7:22 does not provide the clear grammatical links that 2 Cor does for understanding more specifically what Paul means by "inner man."

24. O'Brien, *Ephesians*, 258.

25. Lincoln, *Ephesians*, 205–6. Additionally, John 7:37–39 shows that the Spirit of Christ will reside and flow out of the hearts of believers (i.e., their inner being), and John 14:16–17 states that the Spirit will be in believers.

26. In other words, the second infinitive in each of these cases is taken as an "epexegetical" infinitive versus a "purpose/result" infinitive. Contra Hoehner, *Ephesians*, 481.

his Spirit in the inner man" is explained as "Christ dwelling in your hearts through faith" and this is requested so that (purpose) "you, being rooted and grounded in love, may be able to comprehend what is the breadth and length and height and depth," which is explained as "knowing the love of Christ which surpasses knowledge."[27]

Verse 17a

Thus, the next infinitive clause (v. 17a: "in other words, that Christ may dwell in your hearts through faith") serves to explain exactly what is meant by the request that the readers be "strengthened with power by his Spirit in the inner man."[28] This indwelling of Christ (i.e., the empowerment of the Spirit) should not be confused with the initial indwelling of the Spirit of Christ at salvation; rather, the author is praying that Christ would be "at the very center of or deeply rooted in believers' lives."[29] He is praying that they would walk in faith under the abiding rule of Christ similar to Galatians 5:16, 25 where believers are encouraged to walk in the Spirit so that they will not carry out the desires of the flesh. Thus, believers need the sustaining presence of Christ. This presence of Christ is facilitated by the indwelling work of his Spirit.[30] Therefore, to experience the Spirit is to experience the presence of Christ.[31] As Lincoln explains, "Believers do not experience Christ except as Spirit and do not experience the Spirit except

27. For other arguments for seeing this structure, see Witherington III, *Ephesians*, 273; Bouttier, *L'Épître De Saint Paul Aux Éphésiens*, 153–4.

28. So, Abbott, *Ephesians*, 96; Bruce, *Ephesians*, 326–27; Hendriksen, *Ephesians*, 171; Hodge, *Ephesians*, 184; Lincoln, *Ephesians*, 206; O'Brien, *Ephesians*, 258; Westcott, *Ephesians*, 51–52. Contra Hoehner who sees it as result, "The strengthening in the inner person results in the deep indwelling of Christ by means of faith . . ." (Hoehner, *Ephesians*, 481).

29. Hoehner, *Ephesians*, 481. See also O'Brien, "The focus of this request is not the initial indwelling of Christ but on his continual presence . . ." (O'Brien, *Ephesians*, 258–59).

30. Referencing the Spirit as the "Spirit of Christ" is seen elsewhere in Scripture (Rom 8:9–11; Gal 2:20; 4:6), but is most clearly developed throughout the Gospel of John (1:33; 7:37–39; 14:16–17, 26; 15:26; 16:13; 20:22).

31. Developing or elaborating upon the doctrine of the Trinity is beyond the scope of this section; however, these statements are in no way indicating that there is not distinction of person among the Trinity. While the Spirit is the Spirit of Christ, there are still distinctions of roles among their persons. For an examination of the doctrine of the Trinity, see Ware, *Father, Son, and Holy Spirit*.

as Christ. The implication, as far as this prayer is concerned, is that greater experience of the Spirit's power will mean the character of Christ increasingly becoming the hallmark of believers' lives."[32] A beautiful picture of the Trinity exists here showing how "all three persons of the Trinity are very involved in the redemption and growth of believers."[33] This habitation of Christ in the heart of the believer is by means of faith. The same faith that was integral in procuring salvation (2:5, 8) is now described as necessary in abiding in relationship with Christ.

Ephesians 3:17b-19

Verse 17b

The next two participles, "being rooted and grounded in love" (ἐν ἀγάπῃ ἐρριζωμένοι καὶ τεθεμελιωμένοι),[34] now pull the reader forward by provide the foundation for the second part of the prayer.[35] It is this rooting and grounding in the love of God in Christ provided by the presence of Christ through his Spirit (16b, 17a) that enables one to be strengthened (16) with the power to comprehend the unfathomable and inexhaustible love granted to them in Christ Jesus.[36]

32. Lincoln, *Ephesians*, 206.

33. Hoehner, *Ephesians*, 482. Here and throughout Eph: 1:4–14, 17; 2:18, 22; 3:4–5, 14–17; 4:4–6; 5:18–20. List taken from Hoehner (ibid.).

34. While "love" could go with either the preceding thought (Christ may dwell in your hearts through faith in love) or the following clause (being rooted and grounded in love), it seems most likely that "love" serve as the soil and foundation of their rooting and grounding (being rooted and grounded in love). In the end, this conclusion was reached because it seemed to match the flow of the text best and fit within the overall theological framework of Eph. Additionally, the ideas of "rooting" and "grounding" seemed to necessitate something in which that "rooting" and "grounding" would take place, while the preceding clause already provided the sphere (in their hearts) and means (through faith) of Christ's sustained presence. So, Lenski, *Ephesians*, 494–9; Westcott, *Ephesians*, 52; Witherington, *Ephesians*, 274–5.

35. So, Foulkes, *Ephesians*, 112; Hoehner, *Ephesians*, 482; Lenski, *Ephesians*, 494–5; Westcott, *Saint Paul's Ephesians*, 52. Contra Robinson, *Ephesians*, 175; Salmond, "Ephesians," 314–15. Categorizing these participles is difficult. They could easily be temporal or causal. Ultimately, they are being taken as causal.

36. So Bruce, *Ephesians*, 327; O'Brien, *Ephesians*, 260. Contra Abbott, *Ephesians*, 98; Hodge, *Ephesians*, 187; Stoeckhardt, *Ephesians*, 170. The "love" referenced can be seen as God's love (1:4) or brotherly love among the saints (4:2). Those appealing to the brotherly love view argue that the lack of a genitive modifier implies that it is not God's love;

While the more instinctive reading may be to take these participles (rooted and grounded) with the preceding clause (that Christ may dwell in your hearts through faith), grammatically it is not plausible since the case of the participles (nominatives) does not match the case required of the preceding infinitive (accusative).[37] Since there is nothing in the preceding section that these participles could naturally modify, they should be seen as part of the following purpose clause, which would provide agreement with the nominative case.[38]

Verse 18

The underlying purpose of the initial request is revealed at this point. The author desires that they might "be able to comprehend with all the saints what is the breadth and length and height and depth." But, what exactly is it that they are supposed to comprehend? In other words, to what does the breadth, length, height, and depth refer? The lack of specificity has led to many speculations ranging from the four arms of the cross, the cosmos, and the wisdom of God[39] to the spiritual building[40] or the heavenly city.[41]

Romans 8:35–39 provides a remarkable resemblance to the current passage.[42] In that context, these spatial dimensions are linked to the love

however, in the end, this argument seems unpersuasive. Regardless of the view taken, the two ultimately should not be neatly separated for those who have experienced God's love should manifest brotherly love, which then serves as a mark of their salvation.

37. Nor could they refer to the dative ὑμῶν.

38. So Hendriksen, *Ephesians*, 172; Hoehner, *Ephesians*, 483–4; O'Brien, *Ephesians*, 259–60. Contra Abbott, *Ephesians*, 97; Barth, *Ephesians*, 371–2; Bruce, *Ephesians*, 327; Lincoln, *Ephesians*, 197.

39. Bruce, *Ephesians*, 329. It should be noted that Bruce does not dismiss the fact that the "love of Christ" is involved; rather, he sees the love of Christ as but one component in seeking to grasp the divine purpose. He states that "it is impossible to grasp the divine purpose in all its dimensions without knowing the love of Christ—and this cannot be other than an experimental knowledge" (Bruce, *Ephesians*, 329).

40. Stoeckhardt, *Ephesians*, 173.

41. See Barth, *Ephesians*, 395–7; Lincoln, *Ephesians*, 208–13 for a survey of these and other views along with their citations.

42. "Who shall separate us from the love of Christ? Shall tribulation, or distress, or persecution, or famine, or nakedness, or danger, or sword? As it is written, 'For your sake we are being killed all the day long; we are regarded as sheep to be slaughtered.' No, in all these things we are more than conquerors through him who loved us. For I am sure that neither death nor life, nor angels nor rulers, nor things present nor things to come, nor powers, nor height nor depth, nor anything else in all creation, will be able to separate us

of God manifested through Christ, which fits ideally with the present context; however, there (Rom 8), they are described as categories which cannot serve as lasting obstacles to keep the true believer from experiencing God's love. Thus, despite the similarity in language, the usage serves a different purpose. In Romans, the terms are potential obstacles while in Ephesians they are descriptive of the immensity of something unspecified. Nonetheless, the statements in Ephesians also refer to the love of Christ, not because of the linguistic connections with Romans, but because of the immediate context in which the statements reside. Just as the infinitives in verses 16 and 17 are descriptive of one another[43] so are the infinitives of verses 18 and 19.[44] Therefore, the "love of Christ" does not have to be spelled out in connection with these spatial dimensions, because it is clarified in the following parallel clause (v. 19). As Hodge rightly develops, "The effect of the inward strengthening by the Spirit, or of the indwelling of Christ, is this confirmation of love; and the effect of the confirmation of love, is the ability to comprehend (in our measure) the love of Christ."[45] Such dimensions provide significance because they show the vastness of this love, which cannot be exhaustively known or experienced.

Verse 19a

Accordingly, this knowledge of the love of Christ that the author requests for these believers will not be an exhaustive knowledge for it is a love that

from the love of God in Christ Jesus our Lord."

43. "Descriptive" means that they describe one another, further clarify, are expexegetical, etc.

44. See the explanation of structure of the passage mentioned above. The pattern of the passage is:
Subjunctive (v. 16a–Introduces the first request of the prayer).
Infinitive\(v. 16b). These explain one another. They are parallel, providing the same request.
Infinitive/(v. 17a–epexegetical).
Subjunctive (Introduces the purpose for the first request and provides the second request).
Infinitive\(v. 18a). These explain one another. They are parallel, providing the same request.
Infinitive/(19a–epexegetical).
Subjunctive (Provides the purpose of the second request and the final desired result for the prayer).

45. Hodge, *Ephesians*, 187.

"surpasses knowledge." This thought in no way diminishes the knowledge that believers do experience. It is not a negation of their knowledge but an exaltation of the expansiveness and inexhaustibleness of Christ's love.[46] The author is simply acknowledging the fact that while they are to know the love of Christ, that same love, which comes from the eternal God of the universe, is so magnificent that it exceeds the limits of anyone's ultimate understanding. Lincoln explains, "As elsewhere in the letter (cf. 1:9, 17, 18; 3:3-5, 9; 4:13; 5:17), revealed knowledge is of utmost importance to the writer and it is something that he desires as a primary goal for his readers' growth, requesting it twice in this prayer (v 18 and v 19a). It is simply that the supreme object of Christian knowledge, Christ's love, is so profound that its depths will never be sounded and so vast that its extent will never be encompassed by the human mind."[47]

Verse 19b

The ultimate purpose of the prayer is now reached: that they "may be filled up with all the fullness of God."[48] All of the preceding content was presented and prayed so that they might ultimately be filled up with all the fullness of God. In attempting to understand what it means for someone to be filled with all the fullness of God, it is important to examine the immediate context that was established so that this final purpose could be expressed. Initially, the desire was that the saints might be strengthened by the Spirit. This strengthening was to be within the life of the believer and was explained as the continual habitation of Christ in their hearts through faith. As a result, they would be rooted and grounded in love and ready to grow in their comprehension of the magnitude of the Christ's love for them. Finally, as a result of knowing this love, which can never be exhausted, they could be filled with all the fullness of God.[49]

46. The "love of Christ" (ἀγάπην τοῦ Χριστοῦ) should be taken as a subjective (or possessive) genitive. It is Christ's love not the believer's love for Christ. So Abbott, *Ephesians*, 101; Hoehner, *Ephesians*, 489; Lenski, *Ephesians*, 497-8.

47. Lincoln, *Ephesians*, 213.

48. See Lenski and Lincoln in reference to why the εἰς is not take as directive (i.e., 'into' or 'towards') but is taken to mean 'with respect to' (Lenski, *Ephesians*, 498; Lincoln, *Ephesians*, 214).

49. The genitive τοῦ θεοῦ should be seen as subjective or possessive "and thus refers to God in all his perfection, including his presence, life, and power" (O'Brien, *Ephesians*, 265).

As saints grow in their understanding of God's love for them in Christ, they should be enraptured in that love, filled with that love, and be surrendered more fully to the one who bestows that love upon them (5:1-2). Thus, the being "filled with all the fullness of God" is directly connected to their understanding of the love God has bestowed upon them through the ministry of Jesus the Christ (Rom 5:8). Certainly, these believers were already filled with Christ (1:23);[50] however, the fullness of Christ expressed in 1:23 is the unifying presence of Christ within his corporate body, the universal, invisible church. Believers are also called to continue to be filled with the Spirit (5:18), which, is also an expression of Christ's presence in the life of the individual believer.[51] Thus, the first fullness of Christ (1:23) is the corporate unity of the body, while the second (5:18) is the continued filling that each individual believer needs as they journey through this fallen world. It is this later idea that penetrates the intent of this prayer. As O'Brien articulates,

> Paul's predominantly Gentile readers have already been united with Christ in his death, resurrection, and exaltation (Eph. 2:5, 6). Yet they are still to walk in newness of life, and need to attain to this fullness (4:13; cf. 5:18). They are to become what they already are. Divine enabling is essential for them (3:19) in the midst of the tension as they live between the two ages, and being filled by the Spirit is an important means in the process (5:18). When the apostle desires that his readers may be strengthened through the Spirit and experience the effects of Christ's indwelling so that they may be *filled to the measure of all the fullness of God*, he is praying that they may 'be all that God wants them to be', that is, spiritually mature.[52]

The prayer is beseeching the Father that these saints, each one of them, might continue to grow in their experience of God's love in such a way that their lives are continually shaped into a new person (4:24). As they are filled with the fullness of God, understanding with growing clarity the love with which they have been loved, their lives are to be continually transformed into greater conformity with the will of God (5:1-2). Thus, from this final prayer of the epistle, the author begins to build upon the expression of the

50. 4:14-16 reveals a similar idea.

51. This command is also stated in the negative in 4:30 where they are told not to grieve the Holy Spirit.

52. O'Brien, *Ephesians*, 265-6.

nature and character of God that should flow from their lives as a result of having experience such unfathomable love.

Conclusion

As a result of this prayer, the author proceeds to challenge the audience to live their lives in a manner that reflects the love they have experienced (4:1) and thus, walk unified in the Spirit (4:2). The acknowledgement and experience of this love should translate into a life submitted before God, filled up with all the fullness of who he is and the wonder of his love. Such love can be comprehended only from a life inhabited by Christ through faith that is empowered by God's Spirit. Thus, the author prays a remarkable prayer so that through the working of God in the innermost part of his saints, they might be transformed through full submission to him in faith.

Bibliography

Abbott, T. K. *Critical and Exegetical Commentary on the Epistles to the Ephesians and to the Colossians.* The International Critical Commentary. Edinburgh: T & T Clark, 1946.

"About Craig Keener." No pages. Online: http://www.craigkeener.com/about-craig/.

"About Union." No pages. Online: http://www.utsnyc. edu/page.aspx?pid=282.

Achtemeier, Paul J. *1 Peter.* Minneapolis: Fortress, 1996.

———. "Apropos the Faith of/in Christ: A Response to Hays and Dunn." In *Pauline Theology: Looking Back, Pressing On,* ed. E. Elizabeth Johnson and David M. Hay, 4:82–92. Atlanta: Scholars Press, 1997.

Adam, Peter. *Hearing God's Word: Exploring Biblical Spirituality.* Edited by D. A. Carson. New Studies in Biblical Theology, vol. 16. Downers Grove, IL: InterVarsity, 2004.

Adeyemi, Femi. "The New Covenant Law and the Law of Christ." *Bibliotheca Sacra* 163 (2006): 438–52.

Allan, John A. *The Epistle of Paul the Apostle to the Galatians.* London: SCM, 1951.

Ambrosii. *In Epistolam Beati Pauli ad Galatas.* Edited 1866. PL 27:358–94.

Anders, Max. *Galatians, Ephesians, Philippians & Colossians.* Holman New Testament Commentary. Nashville: Broadman & Holman, 1999.

Anderson, Jeffrey K. "The Holy Spirit and Justification: A Pneumatological and Trinitarian Approach to Forensic Justification." *Evangelical Review of Theology* 32 (2008): 292–305.

Aquinas, Thomas. *Commentary on Saint Paul's Epistle to the Galatians.* Translated by F. R. Larcher. Albany, NY: Magi Books, 1966.

Arnold, Clinton E. *Ephesians.* Zondervan Exegetical Commentary on the New Testament. Grand Rapids: Zondervan, 2010.

Arrington, French L. *Unconditional Eternal Security: Myth or Truth?* Cleveland, TN: Pathway, 2005.

"Articles of Faith." No pages. Online: http://nazarene.org/ministries/administration/visitorcenter/articles/display.html.

Askwith, E. H. *The Epistle to the Galatians: An Essay on Its Destination and Date.* New York: Macmillan, 1899.

Atkinson, William. *Baptism in the Spirit: Luke-Acts and the Dunn Debate.* Eugene, OR: Pickwick, 2011.

———. "Pentecostal Responses to Dunn's Baptism in the Holy Spirit: Luke-Acts." *Journal of Pentecostal Theology* 3 (1995): 87–131.

Augustine, S. Aurelii. *Epistolæ ad Galatas.* Edited 1864. PL 35:2106–48.

Bachmann, Michael. *Sünder oder Übertreter: Studien zur Argumentation in Gal 2,15ff.* Tübingen: Mohr, 1992.

Bahnsen, Greg L., ed. *Five Views on Law and Gospel.* Grand Rapids: Zondervan, 1996.

Bailey, George. "Entire Sanctification and Theological Method." In *New Perspective for Evangelical Theology: Engaging with God, Scripture and the World,* ed. Tom Greggs, 63–77. New York: Routledge, 2010.

"Baptism in the Holy Spirit." No pages. Online: http://www.ag.org/top/beliefs/position_ papers/pp_downloads/PP_Baptism_In_the_Holy_Spirit.pdf.

Barclay, John M. G. *"Christ in You:" A Study in Paul's Theology and Ethics.* New York: University Press of America, 1999.

———. *Flesh and Spirit: An Examination of Galatians 5.19–23.* London: SCM, 1962.

———. "Mirror-Reading A Polemical Letter: Galatians as a Test Case." *Journal for the Study of the New Testament* 31 (1987): 73–93.

———. *Obeying the Truth: A Study of Paul's Ethics in Galatians.* Edited by John Riches. Edinburgh: T. & T. Clark, 1988.

———. *The Letter to the Galatians.* Edinburgh: Saint Andrew, 1958.

Barnes, Peter. *A Study on Galatians.* Webster, NY: Evangelical, 2006.

Barrett, C. K. *Freedom and Obligation: A Study of the Epistle to the Galatians.* Philadelphia: Westminster, 1985.

———. *The Second Epistle to the Corinthians.* Black's New Testament Commentary. Peabody, MA: Hendrickson, 1993.

Barron, Bruce. *The Health and Wealth Gospel: What's Going on Today in a Movement that has Shaped the Faith of Millions?* Downers Grove, IL: InterVarsity, 1987.

Barth, Karl. *Church Dogmatics.* Vol. 4. Edited by G. W. Bromiley, and T. F. Torrance. Edinburgh: T & T Clark, 1985.

———. *Community, State, and Church.* Garden City, NY: Doubleday & Company, 1960.

———. *The Epistle to the Romans.* Translated by Edwyn C. Hoskyns. London: Oxford University, 1950.

Barth, Markus. *Ephesians: Introduction, Translation, and Commentary on Chapters 1–3.* The Anchor Bible. Garden City, NY: Doubleday, 1974.

———. "Justification: From Text to Sermon on Galatians 2:11–21." *Interpretation* 22 (1968): 147–57.

Basham, Don. *A Handbook on Holy Spirit Baptism.* New Kensington, PA: Whitaker House, 1969.

Bateman, Herbert W., IV, ed. *Four Views on the Warning Passages in Hebrews.* Grand Rapids: Kregel Academic & Professional, 2007.

Bates, Maurice L. *Saved Forever!* Nashville: Broadman, 1968.

Baxter, Batsell Barrett. "Who are the Churches of Christ and What do They Believe in?" No pages. Online: http://church-of-christ.org/who.html#baptism.

Bayer, Oswald. "Justification." *Lutheran Quarterly* 24 (2010): 337–42.

———. "Justification: Basis and Boundary of Theology." In *By Faith Alone: Essays on Justification in Honor of Gerhard O. Forde,* 67–85. Grand Rapids: Eerdmans, 2004.

Beale, G. K. *1–2 Thessalonians.* The IVP New Testament Commentary. Downers Grove, IL: InterVarsity, 2003.

Bebbington, D. W. "British Baptist Crucicentrism Since the Late Eighteenth Century." Paper presented at the annual meeting of The Andrew Fuller Conference, Louisville, KY, 30 August 2010.

———. *Evangelicalism in Modern Britain: A History from the 1730s to the 1980s.* Winchester, MA: Allen & Unwin, 1989.

Beker, Johan Christiaan. *Paul the Apostle: The Triumph of God in Life and Thought.* Philadelphia: Fortress, 1980.

Bell, Rob. *Love Wins: A Book about Heaven, Hell, and the Fate of Every Person Who Ever Lived.* New York: HarperOne, 2011.

Bence, Clarence L. *Romans: A Bible Commentary in the Wesleyan Tradition.* Indianapolis: Wesleyan, 1996.

Bennett, Dennis, and Rita Bennett. *The Holy Spirit and You.* Plainfield, NJ: Logos International, 1971.

Betz, Hans Dieter. *Galatians.* Philadelphia: Fortress, 1979.

———. "The Concept of the 'Inner Human Being' (ὁ ἔσω ἄνθρωπος) in the Anthropology of Paul." *New Testament Studies* 46 (2000): 315–41.

Berkhof, Louis. *Systematic Theology.* Grand Rapids: Eerdmans, 1996.

Biema, David Van, and Jeff Chu. "Does God Want You to Be Rich?" No pages. Online: http://www.time.com/time/magazine/article/0,9171, 1533448,00.html.

Bing, Charles C. *Lordship Salvation: A Biblical Evaluation and Response.* Burleson, TX: Grace Life Ministries, 1997.

Blauvelt, Livingston, Jr. "Does the Bible Teach Lordship Salvation." *Bibliotheca Sacra* 143 (1986): 37–45.

Bligh, John. *Galatians.* Householder Commentaries, vol. 1. London: St Paul Publications, 1969.

———. *Galatians in Greek: A Structural Analysis of St. Paul's Epistle to the Galatians with Notes on the Greek.* Detroit: University of Detroit, 1966.

Bloesch, Donald G. *Spirituality Old & New.* Downers Grove, IL: IVP Academic, 2007.

Blumhofer, Edith L., et al., eds. *Pentecostal Currents in American Protestantism.* Urbana: University of Illinois, 1999.

Blunt, A. W. F. *The Epistle of Paul to the Galatians.* London: Oxford University, 1960.

Bock, Darrell L. *Luke.* Baker Exegetical Commentary on the New Testament. 2 vols. Grand Rapids: Baker, 1994.

Boer, Martinus C de. "Paul's Use and Interpretation of a Justification Tradition in Galatians 2.15–21." *Journal for the Study of the New Testament* 28 (2005): 189–216.

Boice, James Montgomery. *Christ's Call to Discipleship.* Chicago: Moody, 1986.

———. *Ephesians: An Expositional Commentary.* Grand Rapids: Baker, 1997.

———. *Galatians.* In vol. 10 of *The Expositor's Bible Commentary.* Edited by Frank E. Gæbelein, 407–508. Grand Rapids: Zondervan, 1976.

Boles, Kenneth L. *Galatians & Ephesians.* The College Press NIV Commentary. Joplin, MO: College, 1996.

Borchert, Gerald L. *Assurance and Warning.* Nashville: Broadman, 1987.

Borse, Udo. *Der Standort des Galaterbriefes.* Köln-bonn: Peter Hanstein, 1972.

Bouttier, Michel. *L'Épître De Saint Paul Aux Éphésiens.* Commentaire Du Nouvea Testament. Geneva: Labor et Fides, 1991.

Bouyer, Louis. *La Spiritualité du Nouveau Testament et des Péres.* Vol. 1 in *Histoire de la Spiritualité Chrétienne.* Paris: Aubier, 1960.

Bowman Jr., Robert M. *The Word-Faith Controversy: Understanding the Health and Wealth Gospel.* Grand Rapids: Baker, 2001.

Boys, Mary C. "The Cross: Should a Symbol Betrayed be Reclaimed?" *Cross Currents* 44 (1994), 5–27.

BIBLIOGRAPHY

Brand, Chad Owen, ed. *Perspectives on Election.* Nashville: B&H Academic, 2006.

———, ed. *Perspectives on Spirit Baptism.* Nashville: Broadman & Holman, 2004.

Bredfeldt, Gary. *Great Leader Great Teacher: Recovering the Biblical Vision for Leadership.* Chicago: Moody, 2006.

Bridge, William. *The Works of William Bridge, sometime fellow of Emmanuel Colledge in Cambridge, now preacher of the Word of God at Yarmouth.* Vol. 3. London: Printed by Peter Cole, 1649.

Bring, Ragnar. *Commentary on Galatians.* Translated by Eric Wahlstrom. Philadelphia: Muhlenberg, 1961.

Brister, C. W. *Pastoral Care in the Church.* New York: Harper and Row, 1964.

Brock, Rita Nakashima, and Rebecca Ann Parker. *Proverbs of Ashes: Violence, Redemptive Suffering, and the Search for What Saves Us.* Boston: Beacon, 2001.

Brock, Rita Nakashima. *Journeys by Heart: A Christology of Erotic Power.* New York: Crossroad, 1991.

Brown, Joanne Carlson and Carole R. Bohn, "For God so Love the World?" In *Christianity, Patriarchy, and Abuse: A Feminist Critique,* eds. Joanne Carlson Brown and Rebecca Parker, 1–30. New York: Prilgrim, 1989.

Brown, John. *The Epistle of Paul the Apostle to the Galatians.* Minneapolis: Klock & Klock Christian, 1957.

Brown, Keith. "Is Mitt Romney a Christian?" No pages. Online: http://www.examiner. com/lds-church-in-baltimore/is-mitt-romney-a-christian.

Bruce, F. F. *Paul: Apostle of the Free Spirit.* Exeter: Paternoster, 1977.

———. *The Book of Acts.* The New International Commentary on the New Testament. Grand Rapids: Eerdmans, 1988.

———. *The Epistles to the Colossians, to Philemon, and to the Ephesians.* The New International Commentary on the New Testament. Grand Rapids: Eerdmans, 1984.

———. *The Epistle to the Galatians: A Commentary on the Greek Text.* The New International Greek Testament Commentary. Grand Rapids: Eerdmans, 1982.

———. *The Epistle to the Hebrews.* The New International Commentary on the New Testament. Rev. ed. Grand Rapids: Eerdmans, 1990.

Bultmann, Rudolf. *Theologie des Neuen Testaments.* 8th ed. Tübingen: J. C. B. Mohr, 1980.

———. *Theology of the New Testament.* 2 vols. Translated by Kendrick Grobel. New York: Charles Scribner's Sons, 1951.

Burge, Gary M. *The Anointed Community: The Holy Spirit in the Johannine Tradition.* Grand Rapids: Eerdmans, 1987.

Burke, Spencer, and Barry Taylor. *A Heretic's Guide to Eternity.* San Francisco: Jossey-Bass, 2006.

Burton, Ernest DeWitt. *A Critical and Exegetical Commentary on the Epistle to the Galatians.* The International Critical Commentary. New York: Charles Scribner's Sons, 1920.

———. *Spirit, Soul, and Flesh: The Usage of Πνεῦμα, Ψυχή, and Σάρξ in Greek Writing and Translated Works from the Earliest Period to 225 A.D.; and of their Equivalents ר‎ נֶמֶשׁ, תָה, and בָּשָׂר in the Hebrew Old Testament.* Chicago: University of Chicago, 1918.

Byrne, Brendan S. J. *Romans.* Sacra Pagina, vol. 6. Collegeville, MN: Liturgical, 2007.

Caldwell, Patricia. "Antinomian Language Controversy." *Harvard Theological Review* 69 (1976): 345–67.

Callen, Barry L. *Authentic Spirituality: Moving Beyond Mere Religion.* Grand Rapids: Baker Academics, 2001.

Campbell, William S. *Paul and the Creation of Christian Identity*. New York: T&T Clark, 2006.

Capps, Donald. "Norman Vincent Peale, Smiley Blanton and the Hidden Energies of the Mind." *Journal of Religion and Health* 48 (2009): 507–27.

———. "Relaxed Bodies, Emancipated Minds, and Dominant Calm." *Journal of Religion and Health* 48 (2009): 368–80.

Carson, D. A. *A Call to Spiritual Reformation: Priorities from Paul and His Prayers*. Grand Rapids: Baker, 1992.

———. *Love in Hard Places*. Wheaton: Crossway, 2002.

———. *Scandalous: The Cross and Resurrection of Jesus*. Wheaton: Crossway, 2010.

———. *The Difficult Doctrine of the Love of God*. Wheaton: Crossway, 2000.

———. *The Gagging of God: Christianity Confronts Pluralism*. Grand Rapids: Zondervan, 1996.

Carson, D. A., et al., eds. *Justification and Variegated Nomism: Fresh Appraisal of Paul and Second Temple Judaism*. 2 vols. Grand Rapids: Baker Academic, 2001.

Chafer, Lewis Sperry. *He That is Spiritual: A Classic Study of the Biblical Doctrine of Spirituality*. Grand Rapids: Zondervan, 1967.

Chalke, Steve. "Redeeming the Cross from Death to Life." In *Consuming Passion: Why the Killing of Jesus Really Matters*, ed. Barrow, Simon and Jonathan Bartley, 19–26. London: Darton, Longman and Todd, 2005.

Charry, Ellen T. "The Grace of God and the Law of Christ." *Interpretation* 57 (2003): 34–44.

Chester, Stephen J. "It Is No Longer I Who Live: Justification by Faith and Participation in Christ in Martin Luther's Exegesis of Galatians." *New Testament Studies* 55 (2009): 315–37.

———. "When Old Was New: Reformation Perspectives on Galatians 2:16." *Expository Times* 119 (2008): 320–29.

Chia, Roland. "Salvation as Justification and Deification." *Scottish Journal of Theology* 64 (2011): 125–39.

Choi, Hung-Sik. "ΠΙΣΤΙΣ in Galatians 5:5–6: Neglected Evidence for the Faithfulness of Christ." *Journal of Biblical Literature* 124 (2005): 467–90.

Christensen, Michael J., and Jeffery A. Wittung, eds. *Partakers of the Divine Nature: The History and Development of Deification in the Christian Traditions*. Grand Rapids: Baker, 2008.

Chrysostom, John. ΥΠΟΜΝΗΜΑ ΕΙΣ ΤΗΝ ΠΡΟΣ ΓΑΛΑΤΑΣ ΕΠΙΣΤΟΛΗΝ. Edited 1859. PG 61:611–82.

Claybrook, Frederick W., Jr. *Once Saved, Always Saved? A New Testament Study of Apostasy*. New York: University Press of America, 2003.

Cole, R. Alan. *Galatians*. The Tyndale New Testament Commentaries, vol. 9. Downers Grove, IL: InterVarsity, 1989.

Cone, James H., and Gayraud S. Wilmore, eds. *Black Theology: A Documentary History*. Maryknoll, NY: Orbis, 1993.

Cone, James H. "An African-American Perspective on the Cross and Suffering." In *The Scandal of a Crucified World: Perspective on the Cross and Suffering*, ed. Yacob Tesfai, 48–60. Maryknoll, NY: Orbis, 1994.

———. "Calling the Oppressors to Account: God and Black Suffering." In *Toward a New Heaven and a New Earth: Essays in Honor of Elisabeth Schüssler Fiorenza*, ed. Fernando F. Segovia. Maryknoll, NY: Orbis, 2003.

Cooey, Paula M., et al., eds. *After Patriarchy: Feminist Transformations of the World Religions*. Maryknoll, NY: Orbis, 1992.

Cooey, Paula M. "The Redemption of the Body: Post-Patriarchal Reconstruction of Inherited Christian Doctrine." In *After Patriarchy: Feminist Transformations of the World Religions*, ed. Paula M. Cooey, William R. Eakin, and Jay B. McDaniel, 106–30. Maryknoll, NY: Orbis, 1992.

Copeland, Gloria. *God's Will is Prosperity*. Fort Worth, TX: Kenneth Copeland, 1996.

———. "Take Your Healing – By Faith!" No pages. Online: http://www.kcm.org/real-help/article/take-your-healing-faith.

Copeland, Kenneth. "Applying Faith in Prayer." No pages. Online: http://www.kenneth-copeland-ministries.com/98/applying-faith-in-prayer-by-kenneth-copeland/.

———. "I Want My People Well." No pages. Online: http://www.kcm.org.uk/images/I_Want_You_Well1.pdf.

———. *The Laws of Prosperity*. Fort Worth, TX: Kenneth Copeland, 1974.

———. "The Name Above All Names." No pages. Online: http://www.kcm.org/real-help/article/name-above-all-names.

Copeland, Kenneth, and Gloria Copeland. *Healing Promises*. Tulsa, OK: Harrison House, 2012.

Corduan, Winfried. *Mysticism: An Evangelical Option?* Grand Rapids: Zondervan, 2009.

Cosgrove, Charles H. "The Mosaic Law Preaches Faith: A Study in Galatians 3." *Westminster Theological Journal* 41 (1978): 146–64.

Cousar, Charles B. *A Theology of the Cross: The Death of Jesus in the Pauline Letters*. Minneapolis: Fortress, 1990.

———. *Galatians*. Atlanta: John Knox, 1982

Craig, William Lane. "'Lest Anyone Should Fall': A Middle Knowledge Perspective on Perseverance and Apostolic Warnings." *International Journal for Philosophy of Religion* 29 (1991): 65–74.

Cranfield, C. E. B. *A Critical and Exegetical Commentary on the Epistle to the Romans*. Vol. 2. Edinburgh: T&T Clark, 1979.

Cranford, Lorin L. "A Rhetorical Reading of Galatians." *Southwestern Journal of Theology* 37 (1994): 4–10.

Crow, Earl P. "Wesley and Antinomianism." *Duke Divinity School Review* 31 (1966): 10–19.

Cullmann, Oscar. *Christ and Time: The Primitive Christian Conception of Time and History*. Translated by Floyd V. Filson. Philadelphia: Westminster, 1950.

Dabney, Robert L. *Christ our Penal Substitute*. Harrisonburg, VA: Sprinkle, 1985.

Daly, Mary. *Beyond God the Father: Toward a Philosophy of Women's Liberation*. Boston: Beacon, 1973.

Das, A. Andrew. "Another Look at ἐὰν μή in Galatians 2:16." *Journal of Biblical Literature* 119 (2000): 529–39.

———. "Beyond Covenantal Nomism: Paul, Judaism, and Perfect Obedience." *Concordia Journal* 27 (2001): 234–52.

Davies, W. D. *Paul and Rabbinic Judaism: Some Rabbinic Elements in Pauline Theology*. New York: Harper & Row, 1948.

———. *Torah in the Messianic Age and/or the Age to Come*. Philadelphia: Society of Biblical Literature, 1952.

Davis, Christopher A. *The Structure of Paul's Theology: "The Truth which is the Gospel."* Lewiston, NY: Mellen Biblical, 1995.

Day, Alan. "The Lordship Salvation Controversy." *Theological Educator* 45 (1992): 23–29.

Day, Richard B. "Incarnational Christian Psychology and Psychotherapy: What Do We Believe and What Do We Do?" *Pastoral Psychology* 54 (2006): 535–44.

Dayton, Wilber T. "The New Testament Conception of Flesh." *Wesleyan Theological Journal* 2 (1967): 7–17.

Decker, William B. "The Early Dating of Galatians." *Restoration Quarterly* 2 (1958): 132–38.

Delio, Ilia. "Is Spirituality the Future of Theology? Insights from Bonaventure." *Spiritus* 8 (2008): 148–55.

DeSilva, D. A. "Exchanging Favor for Wrath: Apostasy in Hebrews and Patron-Client Relationships." *Journal of Biblical Literature* 115 (1996): 91–116.

———. "Honor and Shame." In *Dictionary of New Testament Background*, ed. Craig A. Evans and Stanley E. Porter. Downers Grove, IL: InterVarsity, 2000.

Dieter, Melvin E., et al. *Five Views on Sanctification*. Grand Rapids: Zondervan, 1987.

Dillow, Joseph C. *The Reign of the Servant Kings: A Study of Eternal Security and the Final Significance of Man*. Miami Springs, FL: Schoettle, 1992.

Dodd, C. H. *Gospel and Law: The Relation of Faith and Ethics in Early Christianity*. New York: Columbia University, 1951.

———. *The Epistle of Paul to the Romans*. London: Hodder and Stoughton, 1954.

Dollar, Creflo. "Living the Faith." No pages. Online: http://www.creflodollarministries.org/BibleStudy/Articles.aspx?id=323.

———. *Total Life Prosperity*. Nashville: Thomas Nelson, 1999.

———. "Total Life Prosperity: God's Will." No pages. Online: http://www.creflodollarministries.org/BibleStudy/Articles.aspx?id= 401.

———. *Winning in Troubled Times: God's Solution for Victory over Life's Toughest Challenges*. New York: FaithWords, 2010.

Donaldson, Terence L. "The 'Curse of the Law' and the Inclusion of the Gentiles: Galatians 3:13–14." *New Testament Studies* 32 (1986): 94–112.

Douglas, Kelly Brown. *The Black Christ*. Maryknoll, NY: Orbis, 1994.

Drury, Keith. *Holiness for Ordinary People*. Indianapolis: Wesleyan, 2004.

Du Plessis, Paul Johannes. ΤΕΛΕΙΟΣ: *The Idea of Perfection in the New Testament*. Kampen: J. H. Kok, *n.d.*

Duffield, Guy P., and Nathaniel M. Van Cleave. *Foundations of Pentecostal Theology*. Los Angeles: LIFE Bible College, 1983.

Duncan, George S. *The Epistle of Paul to the Galatians*. The Moffatt New Testament Commentary. New York: Harper and Brothers, 1934.

Dunn, James D. G. *Baptism in the Holy Spirit: A Re-examination of the New Testament Teaching on the Gift of the Spirit in relation to Pentecostalism Today*. Philadelphia: Westminster, 1970.

———. "Baptism in the Holy Spirit: A Response to Pentecostal Scholarship on Luke-Acts." *Journal of Pentecostal Theology* 3 (1993): 3–27.

———. "Baptism in the Holy Spirit: Yet Once More." *Journal of Pentecostal Theology* 18 (1998): 3–25.

———. "Baptism in the Holy Spirit: Yet Once More—Again." *Journal of Pentecostal Theology* 19 (2010): 32–43.

———. "Echoes of Intra-Jewish Polemic in Paul's Letter to the Galatians." *Journal of Biblical Literature* 112 (1993): 459–77.

————. *Jesus, Paul, and the Law: Studies in Mark and Galatians*. Louisville, Westminster/ John Knox, 1990.

————. *Jesus and the Spirit: A Study of the Religious and Charismatic Experience of Jesus and the First Christians as Reflected in the New Testament*. Philadelphia: Westminster, 1975.

————. "Once More, ΠΙΣΤΙΣ ΧΡΙΣΤΟΥ." In *Pauline Theology: Looking Back, Pressing On*, ed. E. Elizabeth Johnson and David M. Hay, 4:61–81. Atlanta: Scholars, 1997.

————. ed. *Paul and the Mosaic Law*. Grand Rapids: Eerdmans, 2001.

————. "Rom. 7:14–21 in the Theology of Paul," *Theologische Zeitschrift* 31 (1975): 257–73.

————. *Romans 9–16*. Word Biblical Commentary, vol. 38B. Dallas: Word Books, 1988.

————. *The Epistle to the Galatians*. Black's New Testament Commentary. Peabody, MA: Hendrickson, 1993.

————. *The New Perspective on Paul*. Rev. ed. Grand Rapids: Eerdmans, 2008.

————. "The New Perspective on Paul." *Bulletin of the John Rylands University Library of Manchester* 65 (1983): 95–122.

————. "The New Perspective on Paul." In *Jesus, Paul, and the Law: Studies in mark and Galatians*. Louisville: Westminster, 1990.

————. *The Theology of Paul the Apostle*. Grand Rapids: Eerdmans, 1998.

————. *Unity and Diversity in the New Testament: An Inquiry into the Character of Earliest Christianity*. London: SCM, 2006.

Dunning, H. Ray. *Grace, Faith, and Holiness: A Wesleyan Systematic Theology*. Kansas City, MO: Beacon Hill, 1988.

Earle, Ralph, et al. *Matthew – Mark – Luke – John – Acts*. The Wesleyan Bible Commentary, vol. 4. Grand Rapids: Eerdmans, 1967.

Earle, Ralph. *2 Timothy*. In vol. 11 of *The Expositor's Bible Commentary*. Edited by Frank E. Gæbelein, 391–418. Grand Rapids: Zondervan, 1981.

Eaton, Michael A. *No Condemnation: A New Theology of Assurance*. Downers Grove, IL: InterVarsity, 1997.

Ebeling, Gerhard. *The Truth of the Gospel: An Exposition of Galatians*. Translated by David Green. Philadelphia: Fortress, 1981.

————. *Word and Faith*. London: SCM, 1963.

Erdman, Charles R. *The Epistle of Paul to the Galatians*. Philadelphia: Westminster, 1930.

Erickson, Millard J. *Christian Theology*. 2nd ed. Grand Rapids: Baker, 2000.

Eriksson, Bart A. "Luther, Paul and the New Perspective." Th.M. thesis, Toronto School of Theology, 2004.

Ervin, Howard M. *Conversion-Initiation and the Baptism in the Holy Spirit: A Critique of James D. G. Dunn, Baptism in the Holy Spirit*. Peabody, MA: Hendrickson, 1984.

Esler, Philip F. *Galatians*. New Testament Readings. New York: Routledge, 1998.

Estelle, Bryan D., et al., eds. *The Law Is Not of Faith: Essays on Works and Grace in the Mosaic Covenant*. Phillipsburg, NJ: P&R, 2009.

Fanning, Buist M. "A Classical Reformed View." In *Four Views on the Warning Passages in Hebrews*, ed. Herbert W. Bateman IV, 172–219. Grand Rapids: Kregel Academic & Professional, 2007.

Farnell, F. David. "The New Perspective on Paul: Its Basic Tenets, History, and Presuppositions." *Master's Seminary Journal* 16 (2005): 189–243.

Fee, Gordon D. *God's Empowering Presence: The Holy Spirit in the Letters of Paul*. Peabody, MA: Hendrickson, 1994.

BIBLIOGRAPHY

———. *Gospel and Spirit: Issues in New Testament Hermeneutics.* Peabody, MA: Hendrickson, 1991.

———. *Listening to the Spirit in the Text.* Grand Rapids: Eerdmans, 2000.

———. "On Getting the Spirit Back into Spirituality." In *Life in the Spirit: Spiritual Formation in Theological Perspective*, ed. Jeffrey P. Greenman and George Kalantzis, 36–44. Downers Grove, IL: InterVarsity, 2010.

———. *Paul, the Spirit, and the People of God.* Peabody, MA: Hendrickson, 1996.

———. *Pauline Christology: An Exegetical-Theological Study.* Peabody, MA: Hendrickson, 2007.

Finlan, Stephen and Vladimir Kharlamov. *Theōsis: Deification in Christian Theology.* Eugene, OR: Pickwick, 2006.

Fiorenza, Elisabeth Schüssler. *Jesus: Miriam's Child Sophia's Prophet: Critical Issues in Feminist Christology.* New York: Continuum, 1994.

Fletcher, D. K. "The Singular Argument of Paul's Letter to the Galatians." Ph.D. diss., Princeton Theological Seminary, 1982.

Flew, R. Newton. *The Idea of Perfection in Christian Theology: An Historical Study of the Christian Ideal for the Present Life.* London: Oxford University, 1934.

Forde, Gerhard O. "Fake Theology: Reflections on Antinomianism Past and Present." *Dialog* 22 (1983): 246–51.

Foulkes, Francis. *The Letter of Paul to the Ephesians: an Introduction and Commentary.* The Tyndale New Testament Commentaries. Grand Rapids: Eerdmans, 1989.

Frame, John. *The Doctrine of God.* Phillipsburg, NJ: P&R, 2002.

———. *The Doctrine of the Knowledge of God.* Phillipsburg, NJ: P&R, 1987.

Fuller, Andrew. *The Complete Works of Andrew Fuller.* Edited by Andrew Gunton Fuller. Revised by Joseph Belcher. 3 vols. 1845 ed. Reprint, Harrisonburg, VA: Sprinkle, 1988.

Fung, Ronald Y. K. *The Epistle to the Galatians.* Grand Rapids: Eerdmans, 1988.

Furnish, Victor Paul. *Theology and Ethics in Paul.* Louisville: John Knox, 2009.

Garlington, Don B. "'Even We Have Believed': Galatians 2:15–16 Revisited." *Criswell Theological Review* 7 (2009): 3–28.

———. "Paul's 'Partisan ἐχ' and the Question of Justification in Galatians." *Journal of Biblical Literature* 127 (2008): 567–89.

———. "The New Perspective on Paul: An Appraisal Two Decades Later." *Criswell Theological Review* 2 (2005): 17–38.

Garrett, James Leo, Jr. *Systematic Theology: Biblical, Historical, and Evangelical.* Vol. 2. North Richland Hills, TX: Bibal, 2001.

Gaston, Lloyd. *Paul and the Torah.* Vancouver: University of British Columbia, 1987.

———. "Works of Law as a Subjective Genitive." *Studies in Religion* 13 (1984): 39–46.

Gavrilyuk, Paul. "The Retrieval of Deification: How a Once-Despised Archaism Became and Ecumenical Desideratum." *Modern Theology* 25 (2009): 647–59.

Geisler, Norman L. "A Moderate Calvinist View." In *Four Views on Eternal Security*, ed. Pinson, Matthew J., 61–134. Grand Rapids: Zondervan, 2002.

———. *Chosen but Free: A Balanced View of God's Sovereignty and Free Will.* 3rd ed. Minneapolis: Bethany, 2010.

———. *Systematic Theology.* Vol. 3. Minneapolis: Bethany House, 2004.

George, Carol V. R. *God's Salesman: Norman Vincent Peale & the Power of Positive Thinking.* New York: Oxford University, 1993.

George, Timothy. *Galatians*. The New American Commentary, vol. 30. Nashville: Broadman, 1994.

Godet, Frederic Louis. *Commentary on Romans*. Grand Rapids: Kregel Publications, 1977.

Gorman, Michael J. *Cruciformity: Paul's Narrative Spirituality of the Cross*. Grand Rapids: Eerdmans, 2001.

———. *Inhabiting the Cruciform God: Kenosis, Justification and Theosis in Paul's Narrative Soteriology*. Grand Rapids: Eerdmans, 2009.

Grant, Jacquelyn. *White Women's Christ and Black Women's Jesus: Feminist Christology and Womanist Response*. Atlanta: Scholars, 1989.

Grayston, Kenneth. *The Epistles to the Galatians and to the Philippians*. London: Epworth, 1957.

Greathouse, William M., and George Lyons. *Romans: A Commentary in the Wesleyan Tradition*. 2 vols. New Beacon Bible Commentary. Kansas City, MO: Beacon Hill, 2008.

Greathouse, William M. *Wholeness in Christ: Toward a Biblical Theology of Holiness*. Kansas City, MO: Beacon Hill, 1998.

Green, Gene L. *The Letters to the Thessalonians*. The Pillar New Testament Commentary. Grand Rapids: Eerdmans, 2002.

Green, Joel B. *Reading Scripture as Wesleyans*. Nashville: Abingdon, 2010.

———. *Salvation*. St. Louis: Chalice, 2003.

Green, Michael. *I Believe in the Holy Spirit*. Grand Rapids: Eerdmans, 1975.

Greene-McCreight, Kathryn. *Feminist Reconstruction of Christian Doctrine*. New York: Oxford University, 2000.

Grenz, Stanley J. *The Social God and the Relational Self: A Trinitarian Theology of the Imago Dei*. Louisville: Westminster John Knox, 2001.

Grider, J. Kenneth. *A Wesleyan-Holiness Theology*. Kansas City, MO: Beacon Hill, 1994.

Grudem, Wayne A. *Systematic Theology: An Introduction to Biblical Doctrine*. Grand Rapids: Zondervan, 2000.

Habets, Myk. "Reforming Theōsis." In *Theōsis: Deification in Christian Theology*, ed. Stephen Finlan and Vladimir Kharlamov, 146–67. Eugene, OR: Pickwick, 2006.

Haldane, James A. *An Exposition of the Epistle to the Galatians Showing that the Present Divisions Among Christians Originate in Blending the Ordinances of the Old and New Covenants*. The Newport Commentary. Springfield, MO: Particular Baptist, 2002.

Hallonsten, Gösta. "*Theosis* in Recent Research." In *Partakers of the Divine Nature: The History and Development of Deification in the Christian Traditions*, ed. Michael J. Christensen and Jeffery A. Wittung, 281–93. Grand Rapids: Baker, 2008.

Hanegraaff, Hank. *Christianity in Crisis: 21st Century*. Nashville: Thomas Nelson, 2009.

Hansen, G. Walter. *Abraham in Galatians: Epistolary and Rhetorical Contexts*. Sheffield, England: JSOT, 1989.

———. *Galatians*. The IVP New Testament Commentary. Downers Grove, IL: InterVarsity, 1994.

Harrington, Daniel J. *The Gospel of Matthew*. Sacra Pagina, vol. 1. Collegeville, MN: Liturgical, 1991.

Harris, Murray J. *2 Corinthians*. In vol. 10 of *The Expositor's Bible Commentary*. Edited by Frank E. Gæbelein, 299–406. Grand Rapids: Zondervan, 1976.

Harrisville, Roy A. "ΠΙΣΤΙΣ ΧΡΙΣΤΟΥ: Witness of the Fathers." *Novum Testamentum* 36 (1994): 233–41.

Haykin, Michael A. G., and Kenneth J. Stewart, eds. *The Emergence of Evangelicalism: Exploring Historical Continuities.* Downers Grove, IL: InterVarsity, 2008.

Haykin, Michael A. G. "'A Great Thirst for Reading': Andrew Fuller the Theological Reader." *Eusebia* 9 (2008): 5–25.

———. "Andrew Fuller (1754–1815) – and the Free Offer of the Gospel." *Reformation Today* 182 (2001): 19–26.

———. "Andrew Fuller (1754–1815) – and the Free Offer of the Gospel: Part 2." *Reformation Today* 183 (2001): 29–32.

———. "Fuller, Andrew (1754–1815)." In *Biographical Dictionary of Evangelicals*, ed. Timothy Larsen, 241–44. Downers Grove, IL: InterVarsity, 2003.

———. "Particular Redemption in the Writing of Andrew Fuller (1754–1815)." In *The Gospel in the World: International Baptist Studies*, ed. David Bebbington, 107–28.

———., ed. *The Armies of the Lamb: The Spirituality of Andrew Fuller.* Dundas, Ontario: Joshua, 2001.

———. *The God Who Draws Near: An Introduction to Biblical Spirituality.* Webster: Evangelical, 2007.

Hays, Richard B. "Christology and Ethics in Galatians: The Law of Christ." *Catholic Biblical Quarterly* 49 (1987): 268–90.

———. "ΠΙΣΤΙΣ and Pauline Christology: What Is at Stake?" In *Pauline Theology: Looking Back, Pressing On*, ed. E. Elizabeth Johnson and David M. Hay, 4:35–60. Atlanta: Scholars, 1997.

———. *The Faith of Jesus Christ: The Narrative Substructure of Galatians 3:1—4:11.* Grand Rapids: Eerdmans, 2002.

Healey, Charles J. *Christian Spirituality: An Introduction to the Heritage.* New York: Alba House, 2008.

Hendriksen, William. *Exposition of Galatians, Ephesians, Philippians, Colossians, and Philemon.* Grand Rapids: Baker, 2007.

Hinn, Benny. *Good Morning Holy Spirit.* Nashville, TN: Thomas Nelson, 1997.

———. *Prayer that Gets Results: The Key to Your Survival.* Kaduna, Nigeria: Clarion Call, 2005.

———. *This is Your Day for a Miracle: Experiencing God's Supernatural Healing Power.* Lake Mary, FL: Creation House, 1996.

———. "Three Keys to Prepare You for the Coming Wealth Transfer." No pages. Online: http://www.bennyhinn.org/articles/8650/three-keys-to-prepare-you-for-the-coming-wealth-transfer.

Hodge, Charles. *A Commentary on the Epistle to the Ephesians.* Grand Rapids: Eerdmans, 1950.

———. *Commentary on the Epistle to the Romans.* Grand Rapids: Eerdmans, 1977.

———. *Systematic Theology.* 3 vols. Grand Rapids: Eerdmans, 1979.

Hodges, Zane C. *Absolutely Free! A Biblical Reply to Lordship Salvation.* Grand Rapids: Zondervan, 1989.

———. *The Gospel Under Siege: Faith and Works in Tension.* 2nd ed. Dallas: Redención Viva, 1992.

———. "Dead Faith—What is It?" No pages. Online: http://www.freegraceresources.org/deadfaithhodges.pdf.

Hoehner, Harold W. *Ephesians: An Exegetical Commentary.* Grand Rapids: Baker, 2002.

Hoekema, Anthony A. *Holy Spirit Baptism.* Grand Rapids: Eerdmans, 1972.

———. *Saved by Grace.* Grand Rapids: Eerdmans, 1989.

BIBLIOGRAPHY

Hollenweger, W. J. *Pentecostalism: Origins and Developments Worldwide.* Peabody, MA: Hendrickson, 1997.

————. *The Pentecostals: The Charismatic Movement in the Churches.* Translated by R. A. Wilson. Minneapolis: Augsburg, 1972.

Holmes, Urban T., III. *A History of Christian Spirituality: An Analytical Introduction.* Harrisburg, PA: Morehouse, 2002.

Holt, Bradley P. *Thirsty for God: A Brief History of Christian Spirituality.* 2nd ed. Minneapolis: Fortress, 2005.

Hooker, Morna D. *From Adam to Christ: Essays on Paul.* New York: Cambridge University Press, 1990.

Horton, Michael, ed. *The Agony of Deceit.* Chicago: Moody, 1990.

Horton, Michael S. "A Classical Calvinist View." In *Four Views on Eternal Security,* ed. Matthew J. Pinson, 22–42. Grand Rapids: Zondervan, 2002.

Howard, Evan B. *The Brazos Introduction to Christian Spirituality.* Grand Rapids: Brazos, 2008.

Howard, George. *Paul: Crisis in Galatia.* New York: Cambridge University Press, 1990.

Howard, James M. *Paul, the Community, and Progressive Sanctification: An Exploration into Community-Based Transformation within Pauline Theology.* New York: Peter Lang, 2007.

Hubbard, David Allan. *Galatians: Gospel of Freedom.* Waco: Word Books, 1977.

Hudson, Nancy J. *Becoming God: The Doctrine of Theosis in Nicholas of Cusa.* Washington, DC: The Catholic University of America, 2007.

Hughes, Jack. "The New Perspective's View of Paul and the Law." *Master's Seminary Journal* (2005): 261–76.

Hultgren, Arland J. "The *Pistis Christou* Formulation in Paul." *Novum Testamentum* 22 (1980): 248–63.

Hunn, Debbie. "Christ Versus the Law: Issues in Galatians 2:17–18." *Catholic Biblical Quarterly* 72 (2010): 537–55.

————. "Ἐὰν μή in Galatians 2:16: A Look at Greek Literature." *Novum testamentum* 49 (2007): 281–90.

————. "ΠΙΣΤΙΣ ΧΡΙΣΤΟΥ in Galatians 2:16: Clarification from 3:1–6." *Tyndale Bulletin* 57 (2006): 23–33.

————. "Pleasing God or Pleasing People? Defending the Gospel in Galatians 1–2." *Biblica* 91 (2010): 24–49.

Hunt, Dave, and T. A. McMahon. *The Seduction of Christianity: Spiritual Discernment in the Last Days.* Eugene, OR: Harvest House, 1985.

Hunter, Harold. *Spirit-Baptism: A Pentecostal Alternative.* Lanham, MD: University Press of America, 1983.

Husbands, M., and Daniel J. Treier, eds. *Justification: What's at Stake in the Current Debates.* Downers Grove, IL: InterVarsity, 2004.

Jakes, T. D. *64 Lessons for a Life without Limits.* New York: Atria, 2011.

Jeal, Roy R. *Integrating Theology and Ethics in Ephesians: The Ethos of Communication.* Lewiston, NY: Edwin Mellen, 2000.

Jerome, Eusebii. *Commentarius in Epistolam S. Pauli ad Galatas.* Edited 1866. PL 26:331–467.

Jersak, Brad, and Michael Hardin, eds. *Stricken by God? Nonviolent Identification and the Victory of Christ.* Grand Rapids: Eerdmans, 2007.

Jervis, L. Ann. *Galatians*. New International Biblical Commentary. Peabody, MA: Hendrickson, 1999.

Jewett, Robert. *Paul's Anthropological Terms: A Study of Their Use in Conflict Settings*. Leiden: E. J. Brill, 1971.

―――. *Romans*. Minneapolis: Fortress, 2007.

Johnson, Arthur L. *Faith Misguided: Exposing the Dangers of Mysticism*. Chicago: Moody, 1988.

Johnson, Ben Campbell. "The Theological Implications of the Pauline Concept of 'Flesh' (Σάρξ)." B.Div. thesis, Asbury Theological Seminary, 1955.

Johnson, H. Wayne. "The Paradigm of Abraham in Galatians 3:6–9." *Trinity Journal* 8 (1987): 179–99.

Jones, David W., and Russell S. Woodbridge. *Health, Wealth & Happiness: Has the Prosperity Gospel Overshadowed the Gospel of Christ?* Grand Rapids: Kregel, 2011.

Jones, Major J. *Black Awareness: A Theology of Hope*. Nashville: Abingdon, 1971.

Jones, Serene. *Trauma and Grace: Theology in a Ruptured World*. Louisville: Westminster John Knox, 2009.

Kalusche, Martin. "'Das Gesetz als Thema biblischer Theologie': Anmerkungen zu einem Entwurf Peer Stuhlmachers." *Zeitschrift für die neutestamentliche Wissenschaft und die Kunde der älteren Kirche* 77 (1986): 194–205.

Kärkkäinen, Veli-Matti, ed. *Holy Spirit and Salvation: The Sources of Christian Theology*. Louisville: Westminster John Knox, 2010.

―――. *One with God: Salvation as Deification and Justification*. Collegeville, MN: Liturgical, 2004.

―――. *Toward a Pneumatological Theology: Pentecostal and Ecumenical Perspectives on Ecclesiology, Soteriology, and Theology of Mission*. Edited by Amos Yong. New York: University Press of America, 2002.

Kay, William K. *Pentecostalism: A Very Short Introduction*. New York: Oxford University, 2011.

Keathley, Kenneth. *Salvation and Sovereignty: A Molinist Approach*. Nashville: B&H, 2010.

Keener, Craig S. *3 Crucial Questions about the Holy Spirit*. Grand Rapids: Baker, 1996.

―――. *Gift & Giver: The Holy Spirit for Today*. Grand Rapids: Baker, 2001.

―――. *The Gospel of John: A Commentary*. 2 vols. Peabody, MA: Hendrickson, 2003.

Kendall, R. T. *Once Saved, Always Saved*. Chicago: Moody, 1985.

Kepler, Thomas S., ed. *Christian Perfection as Believed and Taught by John Wesley*. New York: World, 1954.

Kertelge, Karl. "Gesetz und Freiheit im Galaterbrief." *New Testament Studies* 30 (1984): 382–94.

Kim, Seyoon. *Paul and the New Perspective: Second Thoughts on the Origin of Paul's Gospel*. Grand Rapids: Eerdmans, 2002.

Klopfenstein, W. O. *1 & 2 Thessalonians*. The Wesleyan Bible Commentary, vol. 5. Grand Rapids: Eerdmans, 1967.

Knight, George W., III. *The Pastoral Epistles: A Commentary on the Greek Text*. The New International Greek Testament Commentary, vol. 14. Grand Rapids: Eerdmans, 1992.

Köstenberger, Margaret Elizabeth. *Jesus and the Feminists: Who Do They Say that He Is?* Wheaton: Crossway, 2008.

Kumar, Anugrah. "Pat Robertson: Mitt Romney an 'Outstanding Christian.'" No pages. Online: http://www.christianpost.com/news/pat-robertson-mitt-romney-an-outstanding-christian-57017/.

Ladd, George Eldon. *The Presence of the Future: The Eschatology of Biblical Realism.* Grand Rapids: Eerdmans, 1974.

Ladislav, Tichy. "Christ in Paul: The Apostle Paul's Relation to Christ Viewed through Galatians 2:20a." In *Testimony and Interpretation: Early Christology in its Judeo-Hellenistic Milieu,* ed. Jirí Mrázek and Jan Roskovec, 40–48. New York: T&T Clark, 2004.

Lampe, G. W. H. *The Seal of the Spirit: A Study of the Doctrine of Baptism and Confirmation in the New Testament and the Fathers.* 2nd ed. London: SPCK, 1967.

Lane, William L. *The Gospel According to Mark.* Grand Rapids: Eerdmans, 1974.

Lange, John Peter. *Galatians, Ephesians, Philippians, Colossians: Commentary on the Holy Scriptures Critical, Doctrinal and Homiletical.* Edited and translated by Philip Schaff. Grand Rapids: Zondervan, 1949.

Larsen, David L. *Biblical Spirituality: Discovering the Real Connection Between the Bible and Life.* Grand Rapids: Kregel, 2001.

Lategan, Bernard C. "Is Paul Defending His Apostleship in Galatians: The Function of Galatians 1:11–12 and 2:19–20 in the Development of Paul's Argument." *New Testament Studies* 34 (1988): 411–30.

Leclerq, Jean. "Spiritualitas." *Studi medievali* 3 (1962): 279–96.

Leiter, Charles. *Justification and Regeneration.* Hannibal, MO: Granted Ministries, 2009.

Leithart, Peter J. "Justification as Verdict and Deliverance: A Biblical Perspective." *Pro Ecclesia* 16 (2007): 56–72.

Lenski, R. C. H. *The Interpretation of St. Paul's Epistles to the Galatians to the Ephesians and to the Philippians.* Columbus: Wartburg, 1937.

Letham, Robert. *The Work of Christ.* Downers Grove, IL: InterVarsity, 1993.

Lightfoot, J. B. *St. Paul's Epistle to the Galatians.* Peabody, MA: Hendrickson, 1987.

Lightner, Robert P. *Sin, the Savior, and Salvation: The Theology of Everlasting Life.* Nashville: Thomas Nelson, 1991.

Lincoln, Andrew T. *Ephesians.* Word Biblical Commentary, vol. 42. Waco: Word Books, 1990.

Lindsay, Dennis R. "Works of Law, Hearing of Faith and Πίστις Χριστοῦ in Galatians 2:16—13:5." *Stone-Campbell Journal* 3 (2000): 79–88.

Lloyd-Jones, D. Martyn. *Romans: An Exposition of Chapter 8:17–39: The Final Perseverance of the Saints.* Grand Rapids: Zondervan, 1976.

———. *The Cross: The Vindication of God.* Carlisle, PA: The Banner of Truth Trust, 2009.

———. *The Unsearchable Riches of Christ: An Exposition of Ephesians 3.* Grand Rapids: Baker, 1979.

———. *Unsearchable Riches of Christ: An Exposition of Ephesians 3.* Vol. 8. Grand Rapids: Baker, 1979.

Lombaard, Christo. "What is Biblical Spirituality? Perspectives from a Minor Genre of Old Testament Scholarship." *Journal of Theology for Southern Africa* 135 (1009): 85–99.

Long, Zeb Bradford, and Douglas McMurry. *Receiving the Power: Preparing the Way for the Holy Spirit.* Grand Rapids: Chosen, 1996.

Longenecker, Bruce W. "ΠΙΣΤΙΣ in Romans 3:25: Neglected Evidence for the 'Faithfulness of Christ'?" *New Testament Studies* 39 (1993): 478–80.

Longenecker, Richard N. *Acts*. In vol. 9 of *The Expositor's Bible Commentary*. Edited by Frank E. Gæbelein, 207–573. Grand Rapids: Zondervan, 1981.

———. *Galatians*. Word Biblical Commentary, vol. 41. Nashville: Thomas Nelson, 1990.

———. "New Testament Social Ethics for Today." In *Understanding Paul's Ethics: Twentieth Century Approaches*, ed. Rosner, Brian S., 337–50. Grand Rapids: Eerdmans, 1995.

———. *Paul: Apostle of Liberty*. New York: Harper & Row, 1964.

———. *Studies in Paul, Exegetical and Theological*. Sheffield, England: Sheffield Phoenix, 2004.

———. "The Pedagogical Nature of the Law in Galatians 3:19—14:7." *Journal of the Evangelical Theological Society* 25 (1982): 53–61.

———., ed. *The Road from Damascus: the Impact of Paul's Conversion on His Life, Thought, and Ministry*. Grand Rapids: Eerdmans, 1997.

Lovelace, Richard F. "Evangelical Spirituality: A Church Historian's Perspective." *Journal of the Evangelical Theological Society* 31 (1988): 25–35.

Luther, Martin. *Commentary on the Epistle to the Romans*. Translated by J. Theodore Mueller. Grand Rapids: Zondervan, 1954.

———. *Lectures on Galatians 1535*. In *Luther's Works*. Edited by Jaroslav Pelikan. Vol. 26. Saint Louis: Concordia, 1963.

Maas, Robin. *Crucified Love: The Practice of Christian Perfection*. Nashville: Abingdon, 1989.

MacArthur, John F. *Faith Works: The Gospel According to the Apostles*. Dallas: Word, 1993.

———. *Galatians*. The MacArthur New Testament Commentary. Chicago: Moody, 1987.

———. *Romans 1–8*. The MacArthur New Testament Commentary. Chicago: Moody, 1991.

———. *The Gospel According to Jesus*. Grand Rapids: Zondervan, 2008.

Macchia, Frank D. "Babel and the Tongues of Pentecost: Reversal or Fulfilment? – A Theological Perspective." In *Speaking in Tongues: Multi-Disciplinary Perspectives*, ed. Mark J. Cartledge, 34–51. Waynesboro, GA: Paternoster, 2006.

Machen, J. Gresham. *Machen's Notes on Galatians: Notes on Biblical Exposition and Other Aids to the Interpretation of the Epistle to the Galatians from the Writings of J. Gresham Machen, D. D., Litt. D. Late Professor of New Testament in Westminster Theological Seminary, Philadelphia*. Edited by John H. Skilton. Nutley, NJ: P&R, 1977.

Manual of the Church of the Nazarene: History Constitution and Government Ritual. Kansas City, MO: Nazarene, 1952.

Marquart, Kurt E. "Antinomian Aversion to Sanctification?" *Concordia Theological Quarterly* 67 (2003): 379–81.

Marshall, Bruce D. "Justification as Declaration and Deification." *International Journal of Systematic Theology* 4 (2002): 3–28.

Marshall, I. Howard. *Kept by the Power of God: A Study of Perseverance and Falling Away*. 2nd ed. Minneapolis: Bethany, 1974.

———. "Living in the 'Flesh.'" *Bibliotheca Sacra* 159 (2002): 387–403.

Martin, D. Michael. *1, 2 Thessalonians*. The New American Commentary, vol. 33. Nashville: Broadman & Holman, 1995.

Martin, Ralph P. *2 Corinthians*. Word Biblical Commentary, vol. 40. Waco, TX: Word, 1986.

Martyn, J. Louis. *Galatians: A New Translation with Introduction and Commentary*. The Anchor Bible, vol. 33A. Garden City, NY: Doubleday, 1997.

———. *Theological Issues in the Letters of Paul*. Nashville: Abingdon, 1997.

Matera, Frank J. *Galatians*. Sacra Pagina, vol. 9. Collegeville, MN: Liturgical, 1992.

————. "The Culmination of Paul's Argument to the Galatians: Gal. 5:1—6:17." *Journal for the Study of the New Testament* 32 (1988): 79–91.

Matlock, R. Barry. "Detheologizing the ΠΙΣΤΙΣ ΧΡΙΣΤΟΥ Debate: Cautionary Remarks from a Lexical Semantic Perspective." *Novum Testamentum* 42 (2000): 1–23.

————. "The Rhetoric of πίστις in Paul: Galatians 2.16, 3.22, Romans 3.22, and Philippians 3.9." *Journal for the Study of the New Testament* 30 (2007): 173–203.

Mattes, Mark C. "Beyond Impasse: Re-examining the Third Use of the Law." *Concordia Theological Journal* 69 (2005): 271–91.

McClendon, Adam. "The Crucicentrism of Andrew Fuller (1754–1815)." *Churchman* 4 (2013): 311–22.

————. "Defining the Role of the Bible in Spirituality: '3 Degrees of Spirituality' in American Culture." *Journal of Spiritual Formation & Soul Care* 5 (2012): 207–25.

————. "A Puritan's Perspective of Galatians 2:20." *Puritan Reformed Journal* 3 (2011): 56–80.

————. "Galatians 2:20 as a Corrective to Selected Contemporary Views of Christian Spirituality" (Ph.D. Diss., The Southern Baptist Theological Seminary, 2012).

McConnell, D. R. *A Different Gospel: A Historical and Biblical Analysis of the Modern Faith Movement*. Peabody, MA: Hendrickson, 1988.

McDonnell, Kilian, and George T. Montague. *Christian Initiation and Baptism in the Holy Spirit: Evidence from the First Eight Centuries*. Collegeville, MN: Liturgical, 1991.

McGinn, Bernard, and John Meyendorff, eds. *Christian Spirituality: Origins to the Twelfth Century*. World Spirituality: An Encyclopedic History of the Religious Quest, vol. 16. New York: Crossroad, 1987.

McGinn, Bernard, ed. *The Essential Writings of Christian Mysticism*. New York: Random House, 2006.

McGrath, Alister E. *Christian Spirituality: An Introduction*. Malden, MA: Blackwell, 2003.

————. *Iustitia Dei: A History of the Christian Doctrine of Justification from 1500 to the Present Day*. 2 vols. Cambridge: Cambridge University Press, 1986.

McKnight, Scot. "The Ego and 'I': Galatians 2:19 in New Perspective." *Word & World* 20 (2000): 272–80.

McLaren, Brian D. *A Generous Orthodoxy*. Grand Rapids: Zondervan, 2004.

————. *A New Kind of Christian: A Tale of Two Friends on a Spiritual Journey*. San Francisco: Jossey-Bass, 2001.

————. *The Last Word and the Word After That: A Tale of Faith, Doubt, and a New Kind of Christianity*. San Francisco: Jossey-Bass, 2005.

————. *The Story We Find Ourselves In: Further Adventures of a New Kind of Christian*. San Francisco: Jossey-Bass, 2003.

McWilliams, David B. *Galatians: A Mentor Commentary*. Ross-shire, Scotland: Mentor, 2009.

Meadley, T. D. *Top Level Talks: The Christian Summit Meeting: Studies in Scriptural Holiness or the Doctrine of Entire Sanctification*. London: Epworth, 1969.

Meek, James A. "The New Perspective on Paul: An Introduction for the Uninitiated." *Concordia Journal* 27 (2001): 208–33.

Meyer, Donald. *The Positive Thinkers: A Study of the American Quest for Health, Wealth and Personal Power from Mary Baker Eddy to Norman Vincent Peale*. New York: Doubleday, 1965.

Meyer, Joyce. "Why Do Christians Suffer?" No pages. Online: http://www.joycemeyer.org/articles/ea.aspx?article=why_do_christians_suffer.

Mijoga, Hilary B. P. *The Pauline Notion of Deeds of the Law*. San Francisco: International Scholars, 1999.

Mills, Kevin. *Justifying Language: Paul and Contemporary Literary Theory*. New York: St. Martin's, 1995.

Montague, George T. *The Spirit and His Gifts: The Biblical Background of Spirit-Baptism, Tongue-Speaking, and Prophecy*. New York: Paulist, 1974.

Moo, Douglas J. *Epistle to Romans*. The NIV Application Commentary. Grand Rapids: Zondervan, 2000.

———. "'Law,' 'Works of the Law,' and Legalism in Paul." *Westminster Theological Journal* 45 (1983): 73–100.

———. *The Epistle to the Romans*, The New International Commentary on the New Testament. Grand Rapids: Eerdmans, 1996.

———. *The Letter of James*, The Pillar New Testament Commentary. Grand Rapids: Eerdmans, 2000.

Moody, Dale. *The Word of Truth: A Summary of Christian Doctrine Based on Biblical Revelation*. Grand Rapids: Eerdmans, 1981.

Morris, Leon. *The Epistle to the Romans*. The Pillar New Testament Commentary. Grand Rapids: Eerdmans, 1988.

———. *The First and Second Epistles to the Thessalonians*. The New International Commentary on the New Testament. Grand Rapids: Eerdmans, 1959.

———. *Luke*. The Tyndale New Testament Commentaries. Downers Grove, IL: IVP, 1988.

Mounce, Robert H. *Romans*. The New American Commentary, vol. 27. Nashville: Broadman & Holman, 1995.

Mounce, William D. *Pastoral Epistles*. Word Biblical Commentary, vol. 46. Nashville: Thomas Nelson, 2000.

Murray, John. *Christian Baptism*. Philadelphia: OPC, 1952.

———. *Redemption Accomplished and Applied*. Grand Rapids: Eerdmans, 1955.

———. *The Imputation of Adam's Sin*. Phillipsburg, NJ: P&R, 1959.

Murray, Scott R. *Law, Life, and the Living God: The Third Use of the Law in Modern American Lutheranism*. St. Louis: Concordia, 2002.

———. "The Third Use of the Law: The Author Responds to His Critics." *Concordia Theological Quarterly* 72 (2008): 99–118.

Mursell, Gordon. *The Story of Christian Spirituality: Two Thousand Years from East to West*. Minneapolis: Fortress, 2001.

Naselli, Andrew David. *Let Go and Let God? A Survey and Analysis of Keswick Theology*. Bellingham, WA: Logos Bible Software, 2010.

Needham, David C. *Birthright: Christian, Do You Know Who You Are?* Portland, OR: Multnomah, 1979.

Neill, Stephen. *Christian Holiness: The Carnahan Lectures for 1958*. London: Lutterworth, 1960.

———. *Paul to the Galatians*. New York: Association, 1958.

Nelson, Robert J. *The Realm of Redemption*. London: Epworth, 1951.

Ngewa, Samuel. *Galatians*. Africa Bible Commentary. Nairobi, Kenya: Hippo Books, 2010

Noth, Martin. *The Laws in the Pentateuch and Other Essays*. Translated by D. R. Ap-Thomas. Philadelphia: Fortress, 1967.

Novak, David. "Avoiding Charges of Legalism and Antinomianism in Jewish-Christian Dialogue." *Modern Theology* 16 (2000): 275–91.

Nüssel, Friederike. "'Ich lebe, doch nun nicht ich, sondern Christus lebt in mir' (Gal 2,20a): dogmatische Überlegungen zur Rede vom 'Sein in Christus.'" *Zeitschrift für Theologie und Kirche* 99 (2002):480–502.

O'Brien, Kelli S. "The Curse of the Law (Galatians 3.13): Crucifixion, Persecution, and Deuteronomy 21.22–23." *Journal of the Study of the New Testament* 29 (2006): 55–76.

O'Brien, Peter T. *The Letter to the Ephesians.* The Pillar New Testament Commentary. Grand Rapids: Eerdmans, 1999.

O'Brien, Scott. "Partakers of the Divine Sacrifice: Liturgy and the Deification of the Christian Assembly." *Liturgical Ministry* 18 (2009): 68–76.

O'Day, Gail R. "New Birth as a New People: Spirituality and Community in the Fourth Gospel." *Word & World* 8 (1988): 53–61.

———. "The Ethical Shape of Pauline Spirituality." *Brethren Life and Thought* 32 (1987): 81–92.

O'Gorman, Robert T. "Effect of Theological Orientation on Christian Education in Spiritual Formation: Toward a Postmodern Model of Spirituality." *Review & Expositor* 98 (2001): 351–68.

Olson, Lloyd A. *Eternal Security: Once Saved, Always Saved.* Mustang, OK: Tate, 2007.

Olson, Roger E. "Deification in Contemporary Theology." *Theology Today* 64 (2007): 186–200.

———. *Reformed and Always Reforming: The Post-conservative Approach to Evangelical Theology.* Grand Rapids: Baker Academic, 2007.

O'Neill J. C. *The Recovery of Paul's Letter to the Galatians.* London: SPCK, 1972.

Oropeza, B. J. *Paul and Apostasy: Eschatology, Perseverance, and Falling Away in the Corinth Congregation.* Wissenschaftilche Untersuchungen zum Neuen Testament. Tübingen: Mohr Siebeck, 2000.

Osteen, Joel. *Become a Better You: 7 Keys to Improving Your Life Every Day.* New York: Simon & Schuster, 2007.

———. *It's Your Time: Activate Your Faith, Achieve Your Dreams, and Increase in God's Favor.* New York: Simon & Schuster, 2009.

———. *Your Best Life Now: 7 Steps to Living at Your Full Potential.* New York: Faith Words, 2004.

Owen, Paul. "The 'Works of the Law' in Romans and Galatians: a New Defense of the Subjective Genitive." *Journal of Biblical Literature* 126 (2007): 553–77.

Palma, Anthony D. *The Holy Spirit: A Pentecostal Perspective.* Springfield, MO: Gospel, 2001.

Pannenberg, Wolfhart. *Christian Spirituality.* Philadelphia: The Westminster, 1983.

Parsons, Susan Frank. *Feminism and Christian Ethics.* New York: Cambridge University, 1996.

Peale, Norman Vincent, and Robert Clifford Peale. *Live Longer and Better.* Pawling, NY: Foundation for Christian Living, 1958.

Peale, Norman Vincent. *A Guide to Confident Living.* New York: Fireside, 2003.

———. *A Prayer for Every Need.* Pawling, NY: Foundation for Christian Living, 1964.

———. *Enthusiasm Makes the Difference.* New York: Ballantine, 1982.

———. *Have a Great Day.* New York: Fawcett, 1985.

———. *Overcoming Anxiety and Fear.* Pawling, NY: Foundation for Christian Living, 1967.

————. *Positive Imaging: The Powerful Way to Change Your Life.* New York: Fawcett, 1982.

————. *Positive Thinking Everyday.* New York: Fireside, 1993.

————. *Positive Thinking for a Time Like This.* Englewood Cliffs, NJ: Prentice-Hall, 1975.

————. *Power of the Plus Factor.* New York: Fawcett, 1988.

————. *Stay Alive All Your Life.* Englewood Cliffs, NJ: Prentice-Hall, 1957.

————. *The Amazing Results of Positive Thinking.* New York: Fireside, 2003.

————. *The Art of Real Happiness.* New York: Prentice-Hall, 1950.

————. *The New Art of Living.* New York: Hawthorn, 1971.

————. *The Positive Power of Jesus Christ.* London: Hodder and Soughton, 1980.

————. *The Positive Principle Today: How to Renew and Sustain the Power of Positive Thinking.* Greenwich, CT: Fawcett, 1976.

————. *The Power of Positive Thinking.* New York: Prentice-Hall, 1952.

————. *The Tough-Minded Optimist.* Englewood, NJ: Prentice-Hall, 1961.

————. *Thought Conditioners.* Pawling, NY: Sermon, 1951.

————. *What to Do When.* Pawling, NY: Foundation for Christian Living, 1956.

————. *Why Some Positive Thinkers Get Powerful Results.* Nashville: Oliver-Nelson, 1986.

————. *You Can Have God's Help with Daily Problems.* Pawling, NY: Foundation for Christian Living, 1980.

————. *You Can if You Think You Can.* New York: Fireside, 1992.

————. *You Can Win.* New York: Abingdon, 1938.

Peck, George. *The Scripture Doctrine of Christian Perfection Stated and Defended: With a Critical and Historical Examination of the Controversy, both Ancient and Modern.* New York: G. Lane & P. P. Sanford, 1842.

Pentecost, J. Dwight. "The Purpose of the Law." In *Vital Theological Issues: Examining Enduring Issues of Theology,* ed. Roy B. Zuck, 174–80. Grand Rapids: Kregel Resources, 1994.

————. *Things Which Become Sound Doctrine.* Grand Rapids: Zondervan, 1965.

Perkins, Harold William. *The Doctrine of Christian or Evangelical Perfection.* London: Epworth, 1927.

————. *A Commentary on Galatians.* Pilgrim Class Commentaries. New York: Pilgrim, 1989.

Perowne, E. H. *The Epistle to the Galatians with Introduction and Notes.* Cambridge: Cambridge University, 1892.

Perriman, Andrew, ed. *Faith, Health and Prosperity: A Report on 'Word of Faith' and 'Positive Confession' Theologies by ACUTE (the Evangelical Alliance Commission on Unity and Truth among Evangelicals).* Waynesboro, GA: Peternoster, 2003.

Peters, John Leland. *Christian Perfection and American Methodism.* Grand Rapids: Francis Asbury, 1985.

Picirilli, Robert E. *Grace, Faith, Free Will: Contrasting Views of Salvation: Calvinism & Arminianism.* Nashville: Randall House, 2002.

Pink, Arthur W. *Eternal Security.* La Vergne, TN: Lightening Source, 2001.

————. *Studies on Saving Faith.* Orlando: Northampton, 2010.

Pinson, Matthew J., ed. *Four Views on Eternal Security.* Grand Rapids: Zondervan, 2002.

Piper, John. *A Godward Life: Savoring the Supremacy of God in All of Life.* Sisters, OR: Mulnomah, 1997.

————. *Contending for Our All: Defending Truth and Treasuring Christ in the Lives of Athanasius, John Owen, and J. Gresham Machen.* Wheaton: Crossway, 2006.

————. *Counted Righteous in Christ: Should We Abandon the Imputation of Christ's Righteousness?* Wheaton: Crossway, 2002.

————. *The Future of Justification: A Response to N. T. Wright.* Wheaton: Crossway, 2007.

————. *What Jesus Demands from the World.* Wheaton: Crossway, 2006.

Plummer, Alfred. *A Commentary on St. Paul's First Epistle to the Thessalonians.* London: Robert Scott, 1918.

Polhill, John B. *Acts.* The New American Commentary, vol. 26. Nashville: Broadman & Holman, 1992.

Popkes, Wiard. "Two interpretations of 'Justification' in the New Testament: Reflections on Galatians 2:15–21 and James 2:21–25." *Studia theologica* 59 (2005): 129–46.

Porter, Stanley. *Idioms of the Greek New Testament.* 2nd ed. London: Sheffield Academic, 2007.

Porter, Stanley E., and Andrew W. Pitts. "Πίστις with a Preposition and Genitive Modifier: Lexical, Semantic, and Syntactic Considerations in the πίστις Χριστοῦ Discussion." In *The Faith of Jesus Christ: Exegetical, Biblical and Theological Studies,* ed. Michael F. Bird and Preston M. Sprinkle, 33–53. Peabody, MA: Hendrickson, 2009.

Porter, Stanley E., and Anthony R. Cross, eds. *Dimensions of Baptism.* Journal for the Study of the New Testament Supplement. New York: Sheffield Academic, 2002.

Powers, Thomas E. *Invitation to a Great Experiment: Exploring the Possibility that God Can Be Known.* New York: Crossroad, 1990.

"Preamble and Articles of Faith." No pages. Online: http://nazarene.org/ministries/administration/visitorcenter/articles/display.html.

Principe, Walter. "Toward Defining Spirituality." In *Exploring Christian Spirituality: An Ecumenical Reader,* ed. Kenneth J. Collins, 43–60. Grand Rapids: Baker, 2000.

Ps. Jérôme. *Epist. 7.* Edited 1865. PL 30:107–18.

Quanstrom, Mark R. *A Century of Holiness Theology: The Doctrine of Entire Sanctification in the Church of the Nazarene 1905 to 2004.* Kansas City, MO: Beacon Hill, 2004.

Quebedeaux, Richard. *The New Charismatics II.* San Francisco: Harper & Row, 1983.

Räisänen, Heikki. *Paul and the Law.* Philadelphia: Fortress, 1983.

Ramsay, W. M. *A Historical Commentary on St. Paul's Epistle to the Galatians.* Grand Rapids: Baker, 1965.

————. *The Teaching of Paul in Terms of the Present Day.* New York: Hodder and Stoughton, 1914.

Randall, Gleason. "The Lordship Salvation Debate." *Evangelical Review of Theology* 27 (2003): 55–72.

Regan, Tara. "Wealth and Theology." No pages. Online: http://on-linesurvey.com/time_poll_arc32.html.

Reisinger, Ernest C. *Lord and Christ: The Implications of Lordship for Faith and Life.* Phillipsburg, NJ: P&R, 1994.

Reitzenstein, Richard. *Die Hellenistischen Mysterienreligionen: nach Ihren Grundgedanken und Wirkungen.* Stuttgart: B. G. Teubner, 1956.

Rendall, Frederic. *The Epistle to the Galatians.* In *The Expositor's Greek Testament,* ed. W. Robertson Nicoll, vol. 3, 121–200. Grand Rapids: Eerdmans, 1976.

Rice, Howard L. *Reformed Spirituality: An Introduction for Believers.* Louisville: John Knox, 1991.

Richard, Earl J. *First and Second Thessalonians.* Sacra Pagina, vol. 11. Collegeville, MN: Liturgical, 1995.

BIBLIOGRAPHY

Richards, Lawrence O. *A Practical Theology of Spirituality*. Grand Rapids: Zondervan, 1987.

Riches, John. *Galatians Through the Centuries*. Blackwell Bible Commentaries. Malden, MA: Blackwell, 2008.

Ridderbos, Herman. *Paul: An Outline of His Theology*. Translated by John Richard De Witt. Grand Rapids: Eerdmans, 1975.

———. *The Epistle of Paul to the Churches of Galatia*. Grand Rapids: Eerdmans, 1953.

Riddlebarger, Kim. "What Is Faith?" in *Christ the Lord: The Reformation and Lordship Salvation*, ed. Michael Horton, 81–106. Grand Rapids: Baker, 1992.

Rierman, T. Wayne. "Spirituality: God's Order of Being (Toward Defining Spirituality)." *Brethren Life and Thought* 34 (1989): 73–81.

Roberts, J. Deotis. *Liberation and Reconciliation: A Black Theology*. Louisville: Westminster John Knox, 2005.

Roberts, Robert C. "What Is Spirituality." *Reformed Journal* 33 (1983): 14–18.

Robertson, A. T. *A Grammar of the Greek New Testament in the Light of Historical Research*. Nashville: Broadman, 1934.

———. *Word Pictures in the New Testament*. Vol. 4. New York: Harper & Brothers, 1931.

Robins, R. G. *Pentecostalism in America*. Santa Barbra, CA: Praeger, 2010.

Robinson, J. Armitage. *St Paul's Epistle to the Ephesians*. London: Macmillan, 1907.

Rondelle, H. K. la. *Perfection and Perfectionism: A Dogmatic-Ethical Study of Biblical Perfection and Phenomenal Perfectionism*. Berrien Springs, MI: Andrews University Press, 1971.

Rusch, William G., ed. *Justification and the Future of the Ecumenical Movement: The Joint Declaration on the Doctrine of Justification*. Collegeville, MN: Liturgical, 2003.

Russell, Letty M. *Human Liberation in a Feminist Perspective—A Theology*. Philadelphia: Westminster, 1974.

Russell, Walter B., III. "Does the Christian Have 'Flesh' in Gal 5:13–26." *Journal of Evangelical Theological Society* 36 (1993): 179–87.

———. "Paul's Use of Sarx and Pneuma in Galatians 5–6 in Light of the Argument of Galatians." Ph.D. diss., Westminster Theological Seminary, 1991.

———. "The Apostle Paul's Redemptive-Historical Argumentation in Galatians 5:13–26." *Westminster Theological Journal* 57 (1995): 333–57.

Ryken, Philip Graham. *Galatians*. Reformed Expository Commentary. Phillipsburg, NJ: P&R, 2005.

Ryrie, Charles C. *Balancing the Christian Life*. Chicago: Moody, 1969.

———. *So Great Salvation: What It Means to Believe in Jesus Christ*. Wheaton: Victor, 1989.

Salmond, S. D. F. *The Epistle to the Ephesians*. In *The Expositor's Greek Testament*, ed. W. Robertson Nicoll, 201–395. Grand Rapids: Eerdmans, 1976.

Sanchez, Juan Ramon, Jr. "The Old Man Versus the New Man in the Doctrine of Sanctification: A Critique of the Two-Nature Theory." Th.M. thesis, The Southern Baptist Theological Seminary, 2002.

Sanders, E. P. *Paul and Palestinian Judaism*. Philadelphia: Fortress, 1977.

———. *Paul, the Law, and the Jewish People*. Philadelphia: Fortress, 1983.

Sanders, John, ed. *Atonement and Violence: A Theological Conversation*. Nashville: Abingdon, 2006.

Scacewater, Todd. "Galatians 2:11–21 and the Interpretive Context of 'Works of the Law.'" *Journal of Evangelical Theological Society* 56 (2013): 307–23.

Scaer, David P. "The Third Use of the Law: Resolving the Tension." *Concordia Theological Quarterly* 69 (2005): 237–57.

Schaeffer, Francis A. *True Spirituality.* Wheaton: Tyndale House, 1971.

Schneiders, Sandra M. *Beyond Patching: Faith and Feminism in the Catholic Church.* Rev. ed. New York: Paulist, 2004.

———. "Biblical Interpretation: The Soul of Theology." *Australian Biblical Review* 58 (2010): 72–82.

———. "Biblical Spirituality." *Interpretations* 56 (2002): 133–42.

———. "Born Anew." *Theology Today* 44 (1987): 189–96.

———. "Christian Spirituality: Definition, Methods and Types." In *The New Westminster Dictionary of Christian Spirituality*, ed. Philip Sheldrake, 1–6. Louisville: Westminster John Knox, 2005.

———. "Contemporary Religious Life: Death or Transformation." *Cross Currents* 46 (1996–97): 510–35.

———. "Death in the Community of Eternal Life: History, Theology, and Spirituality in John 11." *Interpretations* 41 (1987): 44–56.

———. "Experiencing the Direct Presence of God." *Christian Century* 109 (1992): 1070–73.

———. "From Exegesis to Hermeneutics: The Problem of the Contemporary Meaning of Scripture." *Horizons* 8 (1981): 23–39.

———. *New Wineskins: Re-Imagining Religious Life Today.* New York: Paulist, 1986.

———. "Religion vs. Spirituality: A Contemporary Conundrum." *Spiritus* 3 (2003): 163–85.

———. "Spirituality and Scripture." In *The New Westminster Dictionary of Christian Spirituality*, ed. Philip Sheldrake, 62–67. Louisville: Westminster John Knox, 2005.

———. "Spirituality in the Academy." *Theological Studies* 50 (1989): 676–97.

———. "The Impact of the Classics of Western Spirituality Series on the Discipline of Christian Spirituality." *Spiritus* 5 (2005): 97–102.

———. *The Revelatory Text: Interpreting the New Testament as Sacred Scripture.* 2nd ed. Collegeville, MN: Liturgical, 1999.

———. "Theology and Spirituality: Strangers, Rivals or Partners." *Horizons* 13 (1986): 253–74.

———. *With Oil in Their Lamps: Faith, Feminism, and the Future.* New York: Paulist, 2000.

———. *Women and the Word: The Gender of God in the New Testament and the Spirituality of Women.* New York: Paulist, 1986.

———. *Written that You May Believe: Encountering Jesus in the Fourth Gospel.* Rev. ed. New York: Crossroad, 2003.

Schoeps, H. J. *Paul: The Theology of the Apostle in the Light of Jewish Religious History.* London: Lutterworth, 1961.

Schreiner, Thomas R. *1, 2 Peter, Jude.* The New American Commentary, vol. 37. Nashville: Broadman & Holman, 2003.

———. "An Old Perspective on the New Perspective." *Concordia Journal* 35 (2009): 140–55.

———. "Another Look at the New Perspective." *The Southern Baptist Journal of Theology* 14 (2010): 4–18.

———. "Did Paul Believe in Justification by Works? Another Look at Romans 2." *Bulletin for Biblical Research* 3 (1993): 131–55.

———. *Galatians.* Zondervan Exegetical Commentary on the New Testament. Grand Rapids: Zondervan, 2010.

———. "Interpreting the Pauline Epistles." *The Southern Baptist Journal of Theology* 3 (1999): 4–21.

———. *Interpreting the Pauline Epistles.* Grand Rapids: Baker, 1990.

———. "Is Perfect Obedience to the Law Possible: A Re-examination of Galatians 3:10." *Journal of the Evangelical Theological Society* 27 (1984): 151–60.

———. "Israel's Failure to Attain Righteousness in Romans 9:30—10:3." *Trinity Journal* 12 (1991): 209–20.

———. "Justification: The Saving Righteousness of God in Christ." *Journal of the Evangelical Theological Society* 54 (2011): 19–34.

———. "Paul and Perfect Obedience to the Law: An Evaluation of the View of E. P. Sanders." *Westminster Theological Journal* 47 (1985): 245–78.

———. *Paul Apostle of God's Glory in Christ: A Pauline Theology.* Downers Grove, IL: InterVarsity, 2001.

———. "Paul's View of the Law in Romans 10:4–5." *Westminster Theological Journal* 55 (1993): 113–35.

———. *Romans.* Baker Exegetical Commentary on the New Testament. Grand Rapids: Baker, 1998.

———. "Sermon: Loving One Another Fulfills the Law: Romans 13:8–10." *The Southern Baptist Journal of Theology* 11 (2007): 104–9.

———. "The Abolition and Fulfillment of the Law in Paul." *Journal for the Study of the New Testament* 35 (1989): 47–74.

———. *The Law and Its Fulfillment: A Pauline Theology of Law.* Grand Rapids: Baker, 1993.

———. "'Works of Law' in Paul." *Novum Testamentum* 33 (1991): 217–44.

Schreiner, Thomas R., and Ardel B. Caneday. *The Race Set before Us: A Biblical Theology of Perseverance & Assurance.* Downers Grove, IL: InterVarsity, 2001.

Schreiner, Thomas R., and Shawn D. Wright. *Believer's Baptism: Sign of the New Covenant in Christ.* Nashville: B&H Academic, 2006.

Schweitzer, Albert. *Die Mystik des Apostels Paulus.* Tübingen: J. C. B. Mohr, 1954.

Scott, Ian W. "Common Ground? The Role of Galatians 2.16 in Paul's Argument." *New Testament Studies* 53 (2007): 425–35.

Seifrid, Mark A. *Justification by Faith: The Origin and Development of a Central Pauline Theme.* New York: E. J. Brill, 1992.

———. "Paul, Luther, and Justification in Gal 2:15–21." *Westminster Theological Journal* 65 (2003): 215–30.

———. "Romans." In *Commentary on the New Testament Use of the Old Testament.* Edited by G.K. Beale and D.A.Carson, 660–67. Grand Rapids: Baker Academic, 2007.

———. "The New Perspective *from* Paul." *The Southern Baptist Journal of Theology* 14 (2010): 20–35.

Shanks, Monte A. "Galatians 5:2–4 in Light of the Doctrine of Justification." *Bibliotheca Sacra* 169 (2012): 188–202.

Shanks, Robert. *Life in the Son: A Study in the Doctrine of Perseverance.* Minneapolis: Bethany House, 1989.

Shauf, Scott. "Galatians 2:20 in Context." *New Testament Studies* 52 (2006): 86–101.

Sheldrake, Philip. *A Brief History of Spirituality.* Malden, MA: Blackwell, 2007.

―――. "Spirituality and History." In *The New Westminster Dictionary of Christian Spirituality*, ed. Philip Sheldrake, 38–43. Louisville: Westminster John Knox, 2005.

―――. *Spirituality and History: Questions of Interpretation and Method*. London: SPCK, 1991.

―――. *Spirituality and Theology: Christian Living and the Doctrine of God*. Maryknoll, NY: Orbis, 1998.

Simmons, Willard R. *The Biblical Anthology on the Spirit of God: The Spirit of God from Eternity Past to Eternity Future*. West Sacramento: Grace, 2006.

Smiles, Vincent M. *The Gospel and the Law in Galatian: Paul's Response to Jewish-Christian Separatism and the Threat of Galatians Apostasy*. Collegeville, MN: Liturgical, 1998.

Smith, Chuck. *Living Water: The Power of the Holy Spirit in Your Life*. Santa Ana, CA: The Word for Today, 2007.

Smith, Karen E. *Christian Spirituality*. London: SCM, 2007.

Smith, Robert. "Justification in 'The New Perspective on Paul.'" *Reformed Theological Review* 58 (1999): 16–30.

Smith, Timothy L. *Called Unto Holiness: The Story of the Nararenes: The Formative Years*. Kansas City, MO: Nazarene, 1962.

Snider, Andrew V. "Sanctification and Justification: A Unity of Distinctions." *Master's Seminary Journal* 21 (2010): 159–78.

Snodgrass, Klyne. "Introduction to a Hermeneutics of Identity." *Bibliotheca Sacra* 168 (2011): 3–19.

Spross, Daniel Brett. "Sanctification in the Thessalonian Epistles in a Canonical Context." Ph.D. diss., The Southern Baptist Theological Seminary, 1987.

Stanley, Charles F. *Confronting Casual Christianity: A Call to Total Commitment*. Nashville: Broadman, 1985.

―――. *Eternal Security: Can You be Sure?* Nashville: Oliver-Nelson, 1990.

―――. *Understanding Eternal Security*. Nashville: Thomas Nelson, 1998.

Stanton, Graham N. "What Is the Law of Christ?" *Ex Auditu* 17 (2001): 47–59.

Stendahl, Krister. *Paul Among Jews and Gentiles and Other Essays*. Philadelphia: Fortress, 1976.

Stoeckhardt, G. *Commentary on St. Paul's Letter to the Ephesians*. Translated by Martin S. Sommer. Saint Louis: Concordia, 1952.

Stott, John R. W. *Baptism & Fullness: The Work of the Holy Spirit Today*. Downers Grove, IL: InterVarsity, 1975.

Strelan, John G. "Burden-bearing and the Law of Christ: A Re-examination of Galatians 6:2." *Journal of Biblical Literature* 94 (1975): 266–76.

Stubbs, David L. "The Shape of Soteriology and the *Pistis Christou* Debate." *Scottish Journal of Theology* 61 (2008): 137–57.

Stuhlmacher, Peter. *A Challenge to the New Perspective: Revisiting Paul's Doctrine of Justification: With an Essay by Donald A. Hagner*. Downers Grove, IL: InterVarsity, 2001.

Stumme, Wayne C., ed. *The Gospel of Justification in Christ: Where Does the Church Stand Today?* Grand Rapids: Eerdmans, 2006.

Tanner, Kathryn. "Incarnation, Cross, and Sacrifice: A Feminist-inspired Reappraisal." *Anglican Theological Review* 1 (2004): 35–56.

―――. *Jesus, Humanity and the Trinity: A Brief Systematic Theology*. Minneapolis: Fortress, 2001.

Tarazi, Paul Nadim. *Galatians: A Commentary*. Orthodox Biblical Studies. Crestwood, NY: St Vladirmir's Seminary, 1994.

Tenney, Merrill C. *Galatians: The Character of Christian Liberty*. Grand Rapids: Eerdmans, 1954.

"The Baptism in the Holy Spirit." No pages. Online: http://ag.org/top/Beliefs/Statement_of_Fundamental_Truths/sft_full.cfm#7.

"The Confessions of Faith of the Evangelical United Brethren Church." No pages. Online: http://www.umc.org/site/apps/nlnet/content.aspx?c=lwL4KnN1LtH&b=5068507&ct=6466511&notoc=1.

The Heidelberg Catechism: in German, Latin, and English: with an Historical Introduction. New York: M. Kieffer, 1863.

"The Security of the Believer." No pages. Online: http://www.ag.org/top/beliefs/position_papers/pp_downloads/pp_4178_security.pdf.

Thiselton, Anthony C. *New Horizons in Hermeneutics*. Grand Rapids: Zondervan, 1992.

Thompson, Deanna A. *Crossing the Divide: Luther, Feminism, and the Cross*. Minneapolis: Fortress, 2004.

Thrall, Margaret E. *A Critical and Exegetical Commentary on the Second Epistle to the Corinthians*. The International Critical Commentary, 2 vols. Edinburgh, Scotland: T&T Clark, 1994.

Toon, Peter. *What Is Spirituality? And Is It for Me?* London: Daybreak, 1989.

Towner, Philip H. *The Letters to Timothy and Titus*. The New International Commentary on the New Testament. Grand Rapids: Eerdmans, 2006.

Traitler, Reinhild. "Feminist and Orthodox Spiritualities: 'Women's Spirituality.'" *Ecumenical Review* 60 (2008): 16–28.

Tyson, John R. *Charles Wesley on Sanctification: A Biographical and Theological Study*. Grand Rapids: Francis Asbury, 1986.

Tyson, Joseph B. "'Works of Law' in Galatians." *Journal of Biblical Literature* 92 (1973): 423–31.

Udoh, Fabian E. "Paul's Views on the Law: Questions about Origin (Gal 1:6—2:21; Phil 3:2–11)." *Novum testamentum* 42 (2000): 214–37.

Vainio, Olli-Pekka. *Justification and Participation in Christ: The Development of the Lutheran Doctrine of Justification from Luther to the Formula of Concord (1580)*. Boston: Brill, 2008.

Vickers, Brian. *Jesus' Blood and Righteousness: Paul's Theology of Imputation*. Wheaton: Crossway, 2006.

Vogel, Larry M. "A Third Use of the Law: Is the Phrase Necessary?" *Concordia Theological Quarterly* 69 (2005): 191–220.

Volf, Judith M. Gundry. *Paul & Perseverance: Staying in and Falling Away*: Wissenschaftilche Untersuchungen zum Neuen Testament. Louisville: John Knox, 1991.

Vos, Johan S. "Paul's Argumentation in Galatians 1–2." *Harvard Theological Review* 87 (1994): 1–16.

Walker, William O. "Translation and Interpretation of ἐὰν μή in Galatians 2:16." *Journal of Biblical Literature* 116 (1997): 515–20.

Wallace, Daniel B. *Greek Grammar beyond the Basics: An Exegetical Syntax of the New Testament*. Grand Rapids: Zondervan, 1996.

Walls, Jerry L., and Joseph R. Dongell. *Why I'm Not a Calvinist*. Downers Grove, IL: InterVarsity, 2004.

Walters, John R. *Perfection in New Testament Theology: Ethics and Eschatology in Relational Dynamic*. Lewiston, NY: Edwin Mellen, 1995.

Wanamaker, Charles A. *The Epistles to the Thessalonians: A Commentary on the Greek Text*. The New International Greek Testament Commentary. Grand Rapids: Eerdmans, 1990.

Ware, Bruce A. *Father, Son, & Holy Spirit: Relationships, Roles, & Relevance*. Wheaton: Crossway, 2005.

———. "The Man Christ Jesus." *Journal of the Evangelical Theological Society* 53 (2010): 5–18.

Warfield, Benjamin Breckinridge. *Biblical Doctrines*. Carlisle, PA: The Banner of Truth Trust, 1988.

———. *Perfectionism*, 2 vols. New York: Oxford University, 1931–32.

Warrington, Keith. *Pentecostal Theology: A Theology of Encounter*. New York: T&T Clark, 2008.

Waters, Guy Prentiss. *Justification and the New Perspectives on Paul: A Review and Response*. Phillipsburg, NJ: P&R, 2004.

Weatherly, Jon A. *1 & 2 Thessalonians*. The College Press NIV Commentary. Joplin, MO: College Press, 1996.

Weaver, J. Denny. *The Nonviolent Atonement*. Grand Rapids: Eerdmans, 2001.

Weinrich, M., and John P. Burgess, eds. *What Is Justification About? Reformed Contributions to an Ecumenical Theme*. Grand Rapids: Eerdmans, 2009.

Weiss, Johannes. *The History of Primitive Christianity*. 2 vols. New York: Wilson-Erickson, 1937.

Welker, Michael, ed. *The Work of the Spirit: Pneumatology and Pentecostalism*. Grand Rapids: Eerdmans, 2006.

Wenham, David. "The Christian Life: A Life of Tension? A Consideration of the Nature of Christian Experience in Paul." In *Pauline Studies: Essays Presented to Professor F. F. Bruce on His 70th Birthday*, ed. Donald A. Hagner, 80–94. Grand Rapids: Eerdmans, 1980.

Wesche, Kenneth Paul. "The Doctrine of Deification: A Call to Worship." *Theology Today* 65 (2008): 169–79.

Wesley, John. *A Plain Account of Christian Perfection*. London: Epworth, 1970.

West, Traci C. *Disruptive Christian Ethics: When Racism and Women's Lives Matter*. Louisville: Westminster John Knox, 2006.

Westcott, Brooke Foss. *Saint Paul's Epistle to the Ephesians: The Creek Text with Notes and Addenda*. New York: Macmillan, 1906.

Westerholm, Stephen. *Israel's Law and the Church's Faith: Paul and His Recent Interpreters*. Grand Rapids: Eerdmans, 1988.

White, R. "Antinomianism and Christian Ethics." *Theology* 67 (1964): 202–7.

Whitney, Donald S. *Spiritual Disciplines for the Christian Life*. Colorado Springs: Navpress, 1991.

———. *How Can I Be Sure I'm a Christian? What the Bible Says about Assurance of Salvation*. Colorado Springs: NavPress, 1994.

Wierwille, Victor Paul. *Receiving the Holy Spirit Today*. New Knoxville, OH: American Christian, 1972.

Wiley, H. Orton. *Christian Theology*. 3 vols. Kansas City, MO: Beacon Hill, 1953.

Williams, Delores S. "Black Women's Surrogacy Experience and the Christian Notion of Redemption." In *After Patriarchy: Feminist Transformations of the World Religions*, ed. Cooey, Paula M., William R. Eakin, and Jay B. Mcdaniel, 1–14. Maryknoll, NY: Orbis, 1992.

Williams, Sam K. "Again *Pistis Christou*." *Catholic Biblical Quarterly* 49 (1987): 431–47.

Wilmore, Gayraud S. *Black Religion and Black Radicalism: An Interpretation of the Religious History of African Americans*. Maryknoll, NY: Orbis, 1998.

Wilson-Hartgrove, Jonathan. *God's Economy: Redefining the Health & Wealth Gospel*. Grand Rapids: Zondervan, 2009.

Wilson, Todd A. "The Law of Christ and the Law of Moses: Reflections on a Recent Trend in Interpretation." *Currents in Biblical Research* 5 (2006): 123–44.

———. "The Leading of the Spirit and the Curse of the Law: Reassessing Paul's Response to Galatian Crisis." *Tyndale Bulletin* 1 (2006): 157–60.

———. "'Under Law' in Galatians: A Pauline Theological Abbreviation." *Journal of Theological Studies* 56 (2005): 362–92.

Wise, Carroll A. *The Meaning of Pastoral Care*. New York: Harper and Row, 1966.

Witherington, Ben, III. *1 and 2 Thessalonians: A Socia-Rhetorical Commentary*. Grand Rapids: Eerdmans, 2006.

———. *Grace in Galatia: A Commentary on St Paul's Letter to the Galatians*. Grand Rapids: Eerdmans, 1998.

———. "The Influence of Galatians on Hebrews." *New Testament Studies* 37 (1991): 146–52.

———. *The Letters to Philemon, the Colossians, and the Ephesians: A Socio-Rhetorical Commentary on the Captivity Epistles*. Grand Rapids: Eerdmans, 2007.

———. *The Paul Quest: The Renewed Search for the Jew of Tarsus*. Downers Grove, IL: InterVarsity, 1998.

Wood, Laurence W. *Pentecostal Grace*. Wilmore, KY: Francis Asbury, 1980.

Wright, N. T. *Climax of the Covenant: Christ and the Law in Pauline Theology*. Minneapolis: Fortress, 1991.

———. *Justification: God's Plan & Paul's Vision*. Downers Grove, IL: IVP Academic, 2009.

———. "Justification: Yesterday, Today, and Forever." *Journal of the Evangelical Theological Society* 54 (2011): 49–64.

———. "One God, One Lord, One People: Incarnational Christology for a Church in a Pagan Environment." *Ex Auditu* 7 (1991): 45–58.

———. *Paul for Everyone: Galatians and Thessalonians*. Louisville: Westminster, 2004.

———. *Paul for Everyone: Romans*. 2 vols. Louisville: Westminster John Knox, 2004.

———. *Paul: In Fresh Perspective*. Minneapolis: Fortress, 2009.

———. "Romans." In vol. 10 of *The New Interpreter's Bible*. Edited by Leander E. Keck, 393–770. Nashville: Abingdon, 1994.

———. *What Saint Paul Really Said: Was Paul of Tarsus the Real Founder of Christianity?* Grand Rapids: Eerdmans, 1997.

Wroblewski, Sergius. *Christian Perfection for the Layman*. Chicago: Franciscan Herald, 1963.

Wuest, Kenneth S. *Wuest's Word Studies From the Greek New Testament For the English Reader*. Vol. 1 and 3. Grand Rapids: Eerdmans, 1999.

Wyckoff, John W. "The Baptism in the Holy Spirit." In *Systematic Theology*, ed. Stanley M. Horton, 423–55. Springfield, MO: Logion, 2003.

Wynkoop, Mildred Bangs. *A Theology of Love: The Dynamic of Wesleyanism*. Kansas City, MO: Beacon Hill, 1972.

Yinger, Kent L. *Paul, Judaism, and Judgment According to Deeds.* New York: Cambridge University, 1999.

Ziesler, John. *The Epistle to the Galatians.* London: Epworth, 1992.

Zwiep, Arie W. *Christ, the Spirit and the Community of God: Essays on the Acts of the Apostles.* Tübingen: Mohr Siebeck, 2010.

Subject Index

Scripture Index

Genesis

3	77
6:17	1n1
7:22	1n1
12:2–3	42n24
15:5	42n24
15:6	137
15:14–21	12, 135n6
17:1–13	12, 135n6
17:9–27	148n62
17:10	135n7
22:7–14	148n62
22:19	42n24
45:27	1n1

Exodus

12:43–51	148n62
15:26	137n13
17:6	148n62
19:5–6	137n13
20:7	127n68

Leviticus

12:3	138
19:12	127n68

Numbers

9:12	148n62
20:8–12	148n62

Deuteronomy

5:11	127n68
18:15–22	148n62
21:22–23	148n62
25:1	137
29:18–20	67n111

Joshua

5:2–9	138

Judges

15:19	1n1

1 Samuel

19:20–23	51

1 Kings

8:32	137
8:54	152

2 Kings

1:13	152

1 Chronicles

4:9–10	123

2 Chronicles

6:13	152
15:1–2	67n111

1 Corinthians

Made in the USA
Middletown, DE
04 August 2018